# Criminal Justice Research Sources

## Fourth Edition

**Quint C. Thurman**

Wichita State University

**Lee E. Parker**

Wichita State University

**Robert L. O'Block**

**anderson publishing co.**
2035 Reading Rd.
Cincinnati, OH 45202
1-800-582-7295

*with* **Rebecca Zeleny**

**Criminal Justice Research Sources, Fourth Edition**

Copyright © 1983, 1986, 1992, 2000
Anderson Publishing Co.
2035 Reading Rd.
Cincinnati, OH 45202

Phone 800.582.7295 or 513.421.4142
Web Site www.andersonpublishing.com

**Library of Congress Cataloging-in-Publication Data**

Thurman, Quint.
    Criminal justice research sources / Quint Thurman, Lee Parker. -- 4th ed.
       p.   cm.
    Rev. ed. of: Criminal justice research sources / Robert L. O'Block. 3rd ed. c1992.
    ISBN 0-87084-860-7 (pbk.)
    1. Reference books--Criminal justice, Administration of.   2. Criminal justice, Administration of--Bibliography.   3. Criminal justice, Administration of--Information services.   4. Criminal justice, Administration of--Library resources.   I. Parker, Lee, 1955-  .   II. O'Block, Robert L., 1951-  Criminal justice research sources.   III. Title.
Z5703.4.C73024   1999
[HV7419]
016.364--DC21

99-34074
CIP

# ACKNOWLEDGMENTS

The authors would like to acknowledge the contributions of Rebecca Zeleny in providing resource and Internet research. We also would also like to acknowledge Robert L. O'Block as the author of previous editions of *Criminal Justice Research*.

# INTRODUCTION

*Criminal Justice Research Sources* is a carefully compiled, comprehensive handbook designed to make criminal justice research less frustrating, more efficient, and more complete than it has been in the past. Many students believe that the typical library is very complex, and they may be familiar only with the card catalog, the *Reader's Guide to Periodical Literature*, and a few major criminal justice journals. As a result, term papers and theses may be written without students having the benefit of other major sources of information.

When the needs of students are met through the use of this handbook, professors will also benefit. They will be relieved of the time-consuming responsibility of locating or referring students to appropriate sources, and they can expect more thorough and complete research papers. Students claiming they "cannot find a thing in the library on . . ." will become rare in criminal justice departments that use this resource book. At the same time, students will gain an understanding of, and an appreciation for, the holdings of any particular library. Knowledge of the literature, especially that which is available in one's own library, is something students should begin acquiring during the first year of college. This text can be clearly understood by the first-year student yet is comprehensive enough to assist the junior, senior, or graduate student.

*Criminal Justice Research Sources* provides hundreds of sources, making it a major reference text to accompany any criminal justice course that requires outside assignments—from annotated bibliographies to major research projects. It also addresses the importance of information that can be obtained from private and community service agencies. Many sources have been annotated to further expedite the literature search. Each chapter of the text includes a descriptive introduction that explains the importance and uses of the particular category of information sources being described. The major components of a research paper are also described in an appendix.

*Criminal Justice Research Sources* takes students through the steps of a literature search. It will assist students with their preliminary search and will facilitate the rest of the research process as well as help maintain the student's interest in the project.

# FOR THE PROFESSOR

*Criminal Justice Research Sources* compiles into one easy-to-use source a comprehensive collection of materials that can help criminal justice students as they gather information for reports, term papers, and research projects. Many students are not aware of all the bibliographies, directories, encyclopedias, periodicals, abstracts, indices, computerized literature search services, and other materials and services that are at their disposal in libraries. The larger the library, the more materials a researcher will be able to access. Some of the materials described in this book are very expensive, and smaller libraries do not have the budgets or the room for them. Therefore, sources may not be directly available in every library, but they can usually be obtained through such services as interlibrary loans and electronic databases. Further, many items listed in the chapter on the National Criminal Justice Reference Service (NCJRS) are available free of charge; other items described in the Government Documents chapter can be obtained at a nominal cost. Finally, a chapter on Internet research has been included to aid in searching the World Wide Web.

# FOR THE STUDENT

Students sometimes experience a feeling of helplessness when they first walk into the reference department of the library. Where do you go first? What library materials should you look for first? When should you ask the reference librarian for help and what information can you supply about the material to make the librarian's job easier? What are some sources outside the library that might supply the needed information? This book will help you answer these questions and it will be a guide to thorough research—allowing you to write a high-quality paper.

# Contents

# The Research Process

## CHOOSING THE INVESTIGATIVE TOPIC

Students assigned a topic to study are relieved of the responsibility of the first step in research—selecting the subject. Students who must choose their own research problem gain the experience of the most important step in the research effort.

### Criteria for Selecting a Research Topic

Selecting a research topic has several criteria. And, although no rules guarantee the suitability of the topic chosen, the researcher should follow certain guidelines in order to make a wise choice.

1. Students should select topics which interest them and motivate them to conduct a thorough approach to the research. They must also be careful not to let their biases and prejudices creep into their work. A researcher's convictions should not influence the outcome of his or her research.

2. The topic should be sufficiently original so that the research is not duplicative. This is especially important when the research is the basis of a thesis or dissertation. Since the thesis or doctoral researcher must discover whether similar studies have already been performed, the researcher must avoid the temptation of just summarizing what already has been done by others.

3. The topic should be amenable to study. Many topics are of great interest and can be thoroughly discussed, but cannot be systematically studied to provide objective evidence. For example, the question "Should juvenile offenders work in a community setting rather than go to jail?" is a general and a somewhat philosophical issue—not easily subject to scientific determination with extensive experiments. The research topic would be more answerable if the question were rephrased and the research directed toward determining a specific dimension of the original broad question, such as "What risks do juvenile offenders serving their sentence in community work settings pose to society compared to those offenders sentenced to jail?" Conclusions could then be drawn from this question that might help answer the broader question that was originally asked.

4. The problem should be significant enough so that the results of the research will add knowledge to the field of criminal justice. Many significant problems in the field need solutions, and researchers should try not to waste time on less significant topics that lack the potential to advance scientific knowledge. In fact, documenting the significance of a study is essential to a sound research proposal. Criteria to consider in selecting a research problem of significance include:

✳ (a) Practical problems encountered by practitioners in criminal justice

✳ (b) Criminal justice problems or procedures that are under active inquiry by the media, practitioners, or theorists

✳ (c) Emerging problems that have not yet been studied

5. The research problem must be manageable in scope (or doable in terms of time and available resources). A research topic that proposes to document the whereabouts of every handgun ever manufactured in the United States would add to the knowledge of the field, but it is not feasible. Another example of an unfeasible study would be to describe terrorist attacks in foreign countries. A researcher would be inundated with literature and would still be sitting at the library table going over attacks in just one country while the rest of the class graduated. To avoid this, the subject should be narrowed further, which may take several steps. The initial step in such a process is to perform a preliminary scan of the literature in order to better understand what and how much has been written on the topic.

## PUTTING THE EVIDENCE TOGETHER

Once the problem has been selected, the researcher is ready to begin the literature search. Like a detective, the researcher must investigate all places where information on the topic might be recorded. Some tips and clues to help in this investigation are listed below.

### Tips and Clues

1. Researchers should not be overwhelmed by the number of information sources cited in this book, the number of sources available in the library, or what they might find surfing the Internet. If the topic has been wisely selected and its scope is sufficiently refined or narrowed, the literature search can prove quite manageable.

2. The extent of an information search will depend upon the research project. A student writing an undergraduate term paper, as opposed to a thesis or dissertation, can be more selective of the information sources he or she chooses to evaluate. There will be more than enough material for the backbone of a term paper from the major works published in the field. To learn more about the major works, a student need only search the card catalog or electronic catalog of holdings and a few indexes and abstracting services covering the major journals in the field. Thesis and dissertation candidates, on the other hand, will need to get their picks and shovels ready because they will have a lot more digging to do. Graduate research projects require comprehensive information searches. All forms of publications likely to provide information should be evaluated. In essence, the term-paper student will rarely be expected to evaluate all the pertinent information sources, although as many of the relevant outstanding works as possible should be identified and used as the foundation for the paper. The thesis or dissertation student will be expected to use a wide variety of sources to ensure coverage of the entire field of study on the topic.

3. If the available literature is voluminous, perhaps the topic is not specific enough and needs to be narrowed. If the literature is scant, perhaps the scope of the research topic should be broadened. Some preliminary reading and research is useful before a topic is adequately defined. A search can be considered conclusive when the major and secondary works in the area fail to turn up any new sources not already known to the researcher.

4. A researcher should make some determination as to the period of time represented by the information search. Some topics, such as victim compensation, witness assistance programs, and community-based corrections are fairly new, and literature concerning these topics will have been published within the last few years. Other topics, such as drug smuggling and canine-assisted patrol, are older, and literature addressing these subjects will span many years. The researcher should not automatically rule out the older studies. They will usually have a great deal to offer in terms of historical background and may provide insight into significant developments that influenced the "state of the art" as it is today. If older sources have relevance to the topic, the information search should extend

far enough back to cover these sources. Current relevant sources should not be overlooked.

5. A complete bibliographic record of each literature source that is read, paraphrased, or quoted should be kept. Each source should be recorded separately on a 3" x 5" card. Cards are ideal for this purpose because each source can be alphabetized and rearranged as needed. The author, title of the publication, location and name of the publisher, date of publication, and inclusive page numbers should be recorded. Many word processing packages allow a researcher to record this information electronically.

6. Notes that will contribute to the research paper should be made on larger cards. These cards should note the author, title, and exact page number of the material used. Additional information is not necessary because the 3" x 5" cards should detail the complete bibliographic citation.

7. Brief notes summarizing the main theme or points of the source should be sufficient during the preliminary search of the literature. A brief sentence describing each paragraph of an article, for example, should be enough to remind the researcher of the bulk of information presented in each paragraph. This is a good way to remember the contents of the entire article. If direct quotations are made, the exact page number should be included because this information will be needed when footnoting the source. Failure to include this information is a frequent oversight that causes a lot of trouble later—the researcher either has to return to the library and look up the source again, or turn in the paper without the page number and hope the professor doesn't notice.

8. The first rough draft of the paper should be based on the preliminary research and maintain a consistent thought pattern or theme. This rough draft will probably be the first of many drafts. Once the theme is developed throughout a paper, additional editing can take place to tighten and focus the paper for the sake of presentation. It is more important to maintain a thought pattern than to interrupt for editing.

9. Revisions with added information and documentation will be needed after the rough draft is written. A paper in rough draft form is always a work under construction that can be improved with each additional revision.

10. Long quotes should not be used unless the passage is absolutely necessary to the content of the paper, or its meaning would be distorted if paraphrased.

11. Credit must be given to sources of information cited. Failure to do so could result in charges of plagiarism, which is the misrepresentation of another's work as your own. Paraphrasing another's ideas or patterns of thought without referencing the work is a more common form of plagiarism and should also be avoided.

12. A variety of sources should be used so that the report is not limited to information gathered exclusively from books (particularly textbooks), encyclopedias, or dictionaries.

13. References cited in books, articles, and other publications can be excellent sources of information, although some of these references may be older than desired.

14. Unless it is a proposal for a study to be done in the future, the paper should be written in the past tense.

15. The researcher should thoroughly understand the research topic and strive to become an expert during the research process.

16. Complete sentences should always be used.

17. The writer should be aware of what the reader of the paper might expect from reading the paper's title and opening paragraphs.

18. If a reference to oneself is necessary in the paper, the reference should be "the researcher," "the investigator," or "the writer," rather than "I." Better yet, the researcher should write in third person whenever possible.

19. After an initial draft is completed, the writer should allow some time to pass before making any revisions. Sometimes it is helpful to read the document aloud to expose portions of the work that are choppy, redundant, confusing, or meaningless.

20. A copy of the final paper (complete with a cover page that provides the student's name, telephone number, and the intended reader) should be made before turning it in to the professor. Some departments do not return papers to students. The student should keep an extra copy for his or her own records, in case the paper is lost before it is graded.

21. The researcher should not hesitate to request the services of the librarians. Reference librarians are experts at locating information and can be immensely helpful.

## PRESENTING THE EVIDENCE

As with the detective's report of a crime, the researcher must prepare a clear, written report of the findings. Within a short time after beginning the investigation and search of the literature, the researcher may acquire a large amount of information without knowing how to present it in an organized written form. Studying the notes made in the preliminary review of the literature is the first step. Then determine whether the topic should be restricted or narrowed. Next comes a preliminary but detailed outline of divisions and subdivisions derived from the researcher's notes. There will likely be gaps in this outline that must be filled by additional and more thorough reviews of the literature. After these inadequacies have been compensated for, the first draft can be written. Be sure to maintain a consistent thought pattern when writing this first draft, rather than spending much time perfecting each sentence or paragraph as each is written. Editing for presentational style can come later.

The exact style, format, and content of the paper will depend upon requirements set forth by the professor, department, or university. Many professors, for example, will require the use of a certain style manual, while others will leave the choice of style to the student. In some colleges and universities, the style manual is determined by departmental policy. The writer should be aware of any type of required style manual before beginning the research paper—otherwise he or she could spend a lot of time and effort only to have the project disqualified for noncompliance. The content and purpose of the paper will also vary according to various other requirements and conditions. An undergraduate research paper will generally differ in scope and purpose from a graduate research paper, and the basic elements of a research paper may or may not be pertinent to the undergraduate research project, depending upon the course objectives and the individual instructor's requirements.

## THE RESEARCH PAPER

The parts of any research paper, unless otherwise specified by the intended reader or grader, will follow a similar pattern. In the sections below, we divide the paper format into four major parts. Undergraduate papers which merely summarize available research normally will not include data or statistical analysis. Instead, professors may ask that students use this section to engage in discussion or suggest research that is needed.

## Part One

*Introduction.* The introduction is a broad overview of the problem to be studied. It should acquaint the reader with the nature of the subject matter and briefly point toward the scope and dimensions of the topic to be discussed. It should attract and stimulate the reader's interest in the paper. The first sentence should state the essence of the study: "This study was undertaken to. . . ." Only brief documentation is needed at this point. The introduction should be between one and two pages in length and should conclude with a smooth transition to the statement of the problem.

*Statement of the Problem.* The statement of the problem should be a concise sentence, which identifies the goal of the study and sets the direction for the study. It must be carefully and clearly described so that there can be no misunderstanding concerning the exact subject matter and the question the research hopes to answer. The statement of the problem serves as the basis from which the purpose of the study is drawn.

*Statement of Purpose.* The statement of purpose should tell the reader the reason for the study. A statement of the problem will not suffice for a statement of purpose. The statement of purpose should be concise and tell the reader exactly what is to be achieved. Many studies will have more than one purpose and each purpose should be addressed individually.

*Significance of the Study.* This is a very important section and should clearly present the need for the research as well as describe the expected benefits of the research. The need for the study should be documented by quotes or paraphrased statements of authorities in the field that reflect the need for further research in that particular area. All such statements must be fully footnoted. A concluding paragraph or sentence further explains the significance of the study.

***Theoretical Framework.*** This section should support the statement of the problem through a brief discussion of various theories proposed by others that relate to the research topic. For example, "This study is based on the theoretical frameworks of Doe, who maintained that aggression in humans has a direct effect upon job performance, and Smith, who proposed that empathic ability influenced interaction with other persons, and Jones, who stated that perceived power and authority among law enforcement personnel was always higher than actual or given power and authority." (These theories are fictitious.) Further discussion and elaboration of the supporting theoretical frameworks is now in order.

***Hypothesis.*** Depending upon the type of paper, hypotheses may or may not be appropriate. A hypothesis is a statement of a relationship between two or more variables to be tested. Here, the specific prediction of expected outcome of the study is stated. Hypotheses in the null form are simply statements of no relationship. Generally, rationale or reasons for the particular outcome predicted by the researcher, whether a statement of relationship or a statement of no relationship, will be required. Historical research projects will not have hypotheses but will ask questions that need to be resolved by the results of the study. Descriptive studies may or may not require hypotheses or null hypotheses, but experimental studies will always require a declaration regarding relationship, and it is this declaration that the study is testing. (For more information on the different types of research studies, the researcher should consult the references cited in the "Collecting Original Data" section of this book.) The sample research study of the causative factors of violation of the exclusionary rule by police officers is a descriptive study that seeks to identify relevant data and does not require a hypothesis.

***Definitions and Terms.*** This section is sometimes optional but, if included, should define all unclear, ambiguous, or newly coined terms used in the study because these terms have the potential of being unfamiliar to or misinterpreted by the reader. *Exclusionary rule, police officer,* and *violation* are all examples of terms used so far which should be defined. Persons outside the field of criminal justice who may read the paper cannot be expected to know the meaning of exclusionary rule, and police officer and violation used in this sense are rather vague or broad terms that the writer should clarify. Exactly what is meant by police officer, for example, should be clearly stated to lessen confusion as to whether other law enforcement officers, such as auxiliary police officers, probation and parole officers, and even deputy sheriffs, are included.

***Limitations.*** A limitation is the recognition of a variable that has bearing on the study but which the researcher cannot control. Some limitations will be apparent at the beginning of the study. Others, such as unreturned questionnaires, will not become apparent until after the data have been collected. This section is for the protection of the researcher, and to help ensure the quality of the study. If the investigator has done a good job in recognizing weaknesses of the study, no one can say that "this" or "that" has not been considered, or that the validity of the results of the study and the conclusions that can be drawn are questionable.

***Delimitations.*** Delimitations are variables having a bearing on the study that the researcher does control. Unlike limitations, they are not weaknesses of the study, but they should be recognized because they still might affect the results. Examples of delimitations are the period of time involved in the study, the subjects studied, and even the literature and other information sources available for review. For example, if the researchers wanted to restrict the study of violations of the exclusionary rule to only full-time police officers, or violations of the rule by male police officers only, these are delimitations and should be listed as such. The literature available for review is listed as a delimitation because usually this review is limited to materials available from one or two libraries and possibly a few other outside sources. However, the investigator cannot be expected to review everything ever written on the research topic, and the sources the researcher does choose to use are assumed to be good ones that will not be a weakness to the study.

***Assumptions.*** Assumptions are statements accepted as universal truths that have application to the study. A descriptive study of violations of the exclusionary rule assumes that there have been documented cases that will be available for examination.

## Part Two

*Review of Literature.* The review of literature summarizes pertinent problems, methods, and findings of other investigators. Proper documentation with footnotes, endnotes, or some other approved form must be given. The writer's analysis as to strengths, weaknesses, agreements or disagreements with other findings is applicable here. The literature review is an important component of the study and should not be clouded with improperly conducted, biased, or poorly written studies. The researcher should ask the following questions when critiquing research studies:

What information is valuable in the work?

What method of research was used to carry out the study?

What statistical tool was used to measure the data?

What were the specific procedures for gathering data?

Who conducted the research study?

Were the research results affected by limitations or delimitations?

Is the research report presented in such a way that it could be replicated?

Is the research tool reliable?

Does the researcher present conclusions based on the results of the study?

Has the researcher avoided interjecting his or her opinions and biases into the study, except where permissible, as in the review of literature?

The review of literature would consist of background information on the subject in a synthesized manner. It would include studies relating to the topics. In most cases, this part should be organized into major subdivisions and conclude with a brief summary of the review of literature.

## Part Three

*Research Design.* The research design should begin with an introductory paragraph, briefly restating the goals of the study and briefly describing, in general terms, what was done. Subheadings should be used to identify the elements comprising the research design and each of these elements should be described in detail so that another person could set up and carry out the study in exactly the same manner. Where appropriate, describe each of the following elements:

A. *Sample.* The population on which the study was based should be described, explaining how the sample was derived. For example, if 100 violations of the exclusionary rule were studied, the researcher should explain exactly how these particular violations were chosen out of the total sample population. Was every fourth one on record selected, or was another sampling technique used? From where did the sample come—one large police department or several small departments? For additional information on sampling techniques, the student should consult one of the many research books cited in Chapter 2, "Collecting Original Data."

B. *Controls.* What controls or conditions were constant for one group but were varied for another? How were the control group and experimental group derived? Was the "double blind" technique used?

C. *Tool.* The instrument used to gather the data (questionnaire, interview, test, observation checklist, etc.) should be identified. It should be clear whether the tool was developed by the researcher or was a standardized tool. The method of development and the method used to establish validity and reliability should be described, such as "Standardized tools are fully described in *The Mental Measurement Yearbook*" (see Chapter 2, "Collecting Original Data," under the subheading, "Reference Books").

D. *Procedures for data collection.* The method or methods used to obtain the information must be stated. For instance, was a separate questionnaire mailed to each person in the sample group? Did the researcher go before the sample population in person and explain the questionnaire? Did the researcher follow up on unreturned questionnaires mailed? If the researcher observed, how was that observation made?

E. *Statistical analysis.* The statistical design used to treat the data collected should be indicated.

## Part Four

*Presentation and Analysis of Data.* This section should describe, present, illustrate, and analyze the data obtained. Charts, graphs, and tables, in addition to the written description of the data, are appropriate to help illustrate the results. Data should be examined and presented according to any subgroups identified within the sample population so that differences, if any, in the responses of subgroups can be identified and compared. Any significant differences should be examined singularly, with a step-by-step analysis of treatment of the data. This part should conclude with a summary of significant values.

## Bibliography

The bibliography should list all of the sources of information used during the preparation of the paper. This includes references used but not cited as footnotes or endnotes in the body of the paper. For arrangement of the bibliography, the researcher should consult the required form and style manual of the professor or department. If there is no required manual, one of the following style manuals will provide additional information on manuscript and footnote format and preparation:

*American National Standards for Writing Abstracts.* (New York: American National Standards Institute, 1979).

*The Chicago Manual of Style.* 14th edition, revised and expanded. (Chicago: University of Chicago Press, 1993).

*The Complete Guide to Citing Government Information Resources: A Manual for Writers and Librarians.* Revised by Diane L. Garner and Diane H. Smith, with additional chapters by Debora Cheney and Helen Sheehy. (Bethesda, MD: Congressional Information Service, Inc., 1993).

*Form and Style in Thesis Writing.* Campbell and Ballou. (Boston: Houghton-Mifflin, 1978).

*Form and Style: Theses, Reports, Term Papers*, Eighth Edition. (Boston: Houghton-Mifflin, 1990).

*A Handbook for Scholars*, Revised Edition. Mary-Claire van Leunen. (New York: Oxford University Press, 1992).

*A Manual for Writers of Term Papers, Theses, and Dissertations*, Sixth Edition. Kate L. Turabian. Revised by John Grossman and Alice Bennett. (Chicago: University of Chicago Press, 1996).

*Mastering APA Style: Instructors Resource Guide. Mastering APA Style* is designed to test students' weaknesses on APA's points of style in their writing before they begin that research paper, allowing the professor to concentrate on course material. "The Instructor's Resource Guide" contains eight multiple-choice mastery tests, correction keys, and answer sheets, along with informative instructions. An essential resource, *Mastering APA Style: Instructor's Resource Guide*, enables students to polish their writing skills as they gain a thorough knowledge of the *Publication Manual of the APA*, Third Edition, revised. (Washington, DC: American Psychological Association, 1994).

*Mastering APA Style: Student's Workbook and Training Guide.* This is the source students need to improve their writing skills. Designed and student-tested for self-study, this book begins with a writing evaluation test followed by exercises with identifiable errors. As they work through the exercises, students learn correct applications of the *Publication Manual of the APA, Third Edition*. This valuable educational workbook will help students reduce style errors in future research and term papers, improve their grades, and allow them to master APA style (Washington, DC: American Psychological Association, 1994).

*MLA Handbook: For Writers of Research Papers, Theses, and Dissertation*, Fifth Edition. (New York: Modern Language Association of America, 1999).

*NEA Style Manual for Writers and Editors*. (Washington, DC: National Education Association, 1974).

*Prentice-Hall Handbook for Writers*. Glenn H. Leggett, et al. (Englewood Cliffs, NJ: Prentice-Hall, 1991).

*Publication Manual of the American Psychological Association*, Third Edition. Key information on the preparation of manuscripts for publication. The third edition introduces new and reorganized material, clearly defines the requirements of APA style for the preparation of manuscripts submitted for publication, and includes a sample single-experiment paper. You will find information on the process of publication from organizing, writing, and typing the manuscript to submitting the manuscript and handling the accepted article. The *Publication Manual* describes the APA journal program and publication policies and provides checklists to help authors assess their manuscripts. (1994)

*The Random House Handbook*, Sixth Edition. Frederick Crews. (New York: McGraw-Hill, 1992).

*Style Manual: Guide for the Preparation of Reports & Dissertations*. Martha L. Manheimer. (New York: Dekker, 1973).

*Words Into Type*. Marjorie Skillen and Robert Gay (eds.). (Englewood Cliffs, NJ: Prentice-Hall, 1986).

*Writing for Social Scientists. How to Start and Finish Your Thesis, Book, or Article*. Howard S. Becker with a Chapter by Pamela Richards. (Chicago: University of Chicago Press, 1986).

When no particular style is specified, the student is advised to follow the style of the major journal in the field such as *Justice Quarterly* or *Criminology*. Whatever style is chosen, consistency is important, so that the same style is used from start to finish.

# 2

# Collecting Original Data

## DESCRIPTIVE AND HISTORICAL RESEARCH

The two most common types of research done by students are descriptive and historical. Historical research is done by reviewing archival data. The examination of historical data is relatively easy for students who have access to collections of existing records. However, there are methodological dangers to accepting historical information as fact. The researcher may not know how the information was collected, and so the reliability of aggregate data could be suspect. Likewise, historical information, such as personal diaries, may reflect the biases of that individual's perspective and therefore not portray actual events accurately.

Descriptive research usually involves looking at the characteristics of a group or subgroup of a specific category, such as the attitudes of Hispanic police officers on a certain subject. This delineation is a depiction, portrait, or illustration and quantification of the subject's quality or qualities.

Because experimental research can have methodological problems, cost challenges, and the need for random sampling of representational groups, students usually opt for descriptive or historical research projects. Following are some basic guidelines for the collection and examination of data by students.

Many students, particularly those working on a thesis or dissertation, will have the opportunity to collect original data for their research project. Several data collection techniques are available, such as direct observation, personal interviews, mail questionnaires, and focus group interviews. But before data collection begins, the researcher should be very familiar with the collection method in order to avoid the many types of sampling errors, and to make certain that the collection process unfolds smoothly. For example, if interviews are used, avoid questions that could be answered by searching other easily accessible sources. Failing to adhere to the correct procedures for data collection could make the data invalid and unreliable.

In addition to following the correct procedures, permission forms may be needed before the research can begin. Colleges and universities usually have written guidelines and requirements by which students must abide, in addition to a committee that approves research proposals. Academic advisors should be consulted regarding any existing regulations, and clearance or permission should be obtained well in advance of when the actual data collection process begins. In most cases, human subjects' permission must also be obtained from cooperating agencies that will directly contribute to the research project, such as correctional institutions, police departments, halfway houses, state hospitals, and schools. These agencies generally have standardized regulations regarding their participation in research projects, and students must sometimes make changes in their original research proposal in order to stay within the guidelines. This is why it is extremely important to obtain permission early. In case a proposal is not acceptable, there will be time to revise it according to the agency's or university's specifications. Students should not expect to present their proposal one day and collect the data the next day, as usually there will be "red tape" in obtaining the needed permission. If a student intends to collect data by interviewing inmates of a correctional institution, for example, the proposal must first be approved by the criminal justice department and a university-wide, human-subjects review committee. Then the proposal must be discussed with the administrator of the correctional institution. This discussion will provide the student with an idea of the institution's requirements and expectations. Permission should be obtained in writing.

Generally students will be asked to furnish information about the basic nature of their research, the significance of their study, the exact method of data collection (observation, interviewing, etc.), the approximate amount of time required to complete the data collection, and possible complications or adverse effects to subjects as a result of participating in the study. The agency will generally request a copy of the results of the research.

## REFERENCE BOOKS

A number of sources detail scientific procedure in the collection, presentation, and analysis of data. Among many useful references are the following:

*Adult Learning: Psychological Research and Applications.* Michael J.A. Howe (ed.). (London, New York: Wiley, 1977).

*Basics of Qualitative Research.* Anselm Strauss and Juliet Corbin. (Newbury Park, CA: Sage Publications, 1990).

*The Basics of Social Research.* Earl R. Babbie. (Belmont, CA: Wadsworth Publishing, 1999).

*Case Study Research: Design and Methods*, Second Edition. Robert Y. Yin. (Newbury Park, CA: Sage Publications, 1994).

*Categorical Longitudinal Data.* Jacques A. Hagenaars. (Newbury Park, CA: Sage Publications, 1990).

*Computer Simulation Applications: An Introduction.* Marcia Lynn Whicker and Lee Sigelman. (Newbury Park, CA: Sage Publications, 1991).

*Criminal Justice Research in Libraries: Strategies and Resources.* Marilyn Lutzker and Eleanor Ferrall; foreword by Edward Sagarin. (Westport, CT: Greenwood Press, 1986).

*Decision Research: A Field Guide.* John S. Carroll and Eric J. Johnson. (Newbury Park, CA: Sage Publications, 1990).

*Doing Field Research.* John M. Johnson. (New York: The Free Press, 1978).

*The Essence of Social Research.* Charles Lachenmeyer. (New York: The Free Press, 1973).

*Ethics and Values in Applied Social Research.* Allan J. Kimmel. (Newbury Park, CA: Sage Publications, 1988).

*Experiencing Fieldwork.* William B. Shaffir and Robert A. Stebbins. (Newbury Park, CA: Sage Publications, 1990).

*Foundations of Behavioral Research*, Third Edition. F.N. Kerlinger. (New York: Holt, Rinehart, and Winston, 1992).

*Fundamental Research Statistics*, Second Edition. John T. Roscoe. (New York: Holt, Rinehart, and Winston, 1975).

*Fundamentals of Criminal Justice Research.* John Curtis and Steve Brown. (Lexington, MA: Anderson Publishing, Co., 1987).

*Heuristic Research.* Clarke Moustekas. (Newbury Park, CA: Sage Publications, 1990).

*Integrating Research: A Guide for Literature Reviews.* Harris M. Cooper. (Newbury Park, CA: Sage Publications, 1989).

*Interviewer's Manual,* Revised Edition. (Ann Arbor, MI: Survey Research Center, Institute for Social Research, 1976).

*Introduction to Criminal Justice Research and Statistics.* Larry S. Miller and John T. Whitehead. (Cincinnati, OH: Anderson Publishing Co., 1996).

*An Introduction to Social Research: Quantitative and Qualitative Approaches.* Keith F. Punch. (Thousand Oaks, CA: Sage Publications, 1998).

*Introduction to Social Research*, Third Edition. Sanford Labovitz and Robert Hagedorn. (New York: McGraw-Hill, 1981).

*Investigative Methods.* James D. Scott. (Reston, VA: Reston Publishing, 1978).

*Investigative Methods.* Art Buckwalter. (Boston: Butterworth, 1984).

*Investigative Methods in Library and Information Science: An Introduction.* John Martyn and F. Wilfred Lancaster. (Arlington, VA: Information Resources Press, 1981).

*Investigative Social Research.* Jack D. Douglas. (Beverly Hills, CA: Sage Publications, 1976).

*Linking, Auditing and Meta-Evaluation: Enhancing Quality In Applied Research.* Thomas A. Schwandt and Edward S. Halpern. (Newbury Park, CA: Sage Publications, 1988).

*The Mental Measurements Yearbook*, Thirteenth Edition. The Buros Institute. (Lincoln, NE: The Buros Institute, 1988). Indices, describes and evaluates thousands of tests used in research projects.

*Methods for Policy Research.* Ann Majchrzak; forward by Amitai Etzion. (Newbury Park, CA: Sage Publications, 1990).

*The Modern Researcher,* Fifth Edition. Jacques Barzun and Henry F. Graff. (Orlando, FL: Harcourt, 1992).

*Observing the Law: Field Methods in the Study of Crime and the Criminal Justice System.* George McCall. (New York: The Free Press, 1978).

*Obtaining Citizen Feedback: The Application of Citizen Surveys to Local Governments.* Kenneth Webb and Harvey Hatry. (Washington, DC: Urban Institute Press, 1973).

*The Paradigm Dialog.* Egon G. Gruba. (Newbury Park, CA: Sage Publications, 1990).

*Participatory Action Research.* William Foote Whyte. (Newbury Park, CA: Sage Publications, 1990).

*Photographing the Self.* Robert C. Ziller. (Newbury Park, CA: Sage Publications, 1990).

*Practical Sampling.* Gary T. Henry. (Newbury Park, CA: Sage Publications, 1990).

*The Practice of Social Research.* Eighth Edition. Earl R. Babbie. (Belmont, CA: Wadsworth Publishing, 1998).

*Psychological Research,* Fourth Edition. Arthur B. Bachrach. (New York: McGraw, 1981).

*Psychological Research: Innovative Methods and Strategies.* (New York, NY: Routledge, 1996).

*Qualitative Evaluation and Research Methods.* Michael Quinn Patton. (Newbury Park, CA: Sage Publications, 1990).

*The Research Almanac,* Second Edition. Nancy Polette. (O'Fallon, MO: Book Lures, 1986).

*The Research Craft: An Introduction to Social Science Methods,* Second Edition. John B. Williamson, et al. (Boston: Little, Brown and Company, 1982).

*Research in Education,* Sixth Edition. John W. Best and James V. Kahn. (Englewood Cliffs, NJ: Prentice-Hall, 1989).

*Research with Hispanic Populations.* Gerardo Marin and Barbara Vanoss Marin. (Newbury Park, CA: Sage Publications, 1991).

*Research Methods in Criminal Justice: An Introduction,* Second Edition. Jack D. Fitzgerald and Steven M. Cox. (Chicago, IL: Nelson-Hall, 1994).

*Research Methods in Criminal Justice and Criminology,* Fourth Edition. Frank E. Hagan. (Needham Heights, MA: Allyn and Bacon, Inc., 1997).

*Research Methods in Criminology and Criminal Justice.* Edwin S. Johnson. (Englewood Cliffs, NJ: Prentice-Hall, 1981).

*The Sampling Survey: Theory and Practice.* Donald Warwick and Charles A. Lininger. (New York: McGraw-Hill, 1975).

*Secondary Research: Information Sources and Methods,* Second Edition. David W. Stewart and Michael A. Kamins. (Newbury Park, CA: Sage Publications, 1993).

*Social Statistics Without Tears.* Allan G. Johnson. (New York: McGraw-Hill, 1977).

*Standardized Survey Interviewing: Minimizing Interviewer-Related Error.* Floyd J. Fowler, Jr. and Thomas W. Mangione. (Newbury Park, CA: Sage Publications, 1989).

*Survey and Opinion Research: Procedures for Processing and Analysis.* John A. Sonquist and William C. Dinkelberg. (Englewood Cliffs, NJ: Prentice-Hall, 1977).

*Survey Research.* Charles Backstrom and Gerald Hursh. (New York: Macmillan, 1981).

*Survey Research by Telephone,* Second Edition. James H. Frey. (Newbury Park, CA: Sage Publications, 1989).

*The Survey Research Handbook.* Pamela L. Alreck, Robert E. Settle. (Homewood, IL: Richard D. Irwin, 1985).

*Survey Research Methods.* Earl R. Babbie. (Belmont, CA: Wadsworth Publishing, 1990).

*Survey Research Methods,* Revised Edition. Floyd J. Fowler. (Newbury Park, CA: Sage Publications, 1988).

*Survey Sampling.* Leslie Kish. (New York: J. Wiley and Sons, Inc., 1995).

*Telephone Survey Methods: Sampling, Selection and Supervision,* Second Edition. Paul J. Lavrakas. (Newbury Park, CA: Sage Publications, 1993).

*Understanding Research in the Social Sciences: A Practical Guide to Understanding Social and Behavioral Research.* Curtis Hardyck and Lewis Petrinovidh. (Philadelphia: Saunders, 1975).

*Writing Research Papers,* Eighth Edition. James D. Lester. (Glenview, IL: Scott, Foresman, 1998).

## DISSERTATION AND THESIS ABSTRACTS

Theses and dissertations can provide a significant contribution to a research project because they are assumed to provide original knowledge of research that is of value to a particular field of study. Master's theses and doctoral dissertations are listed in special bibliographies, so they cannot be located unless one of these bibliographies is consulted.

*The Analysis of Public Policy: A Bibliography of Dissertations, 1977-1982.* Compiled by John S. Robey. (Westport, CT: Greenwood Press, 1984). *The Analysis of Public Policy* is a current annotated bibliography covering the doctoral work done primarily in the United States, and to a lesser extent in Canada and Great Britain, in a number of specific areas of academic concern. It offers a systematic and thorough guide to the recent research findings of more than 1,000 English-language dissertations selected from those reported in *Dissertation Abstracts International.* Public policy-making in 16 fields of concentration is represented, including state and local administration, agricultural policy, civil and women's rights, taxation, education, housing, energy, judicial, military, welfare, foreign policy, and international trade.

*Comprehensive Dissertation Index.* This publication is published annually and consists of five volumes. The first two volumes abstract selected dissertations pertaining to the sciences (biology, chemistry, agriculture, health, physics, engineering, mathematics, earth sciences, environmental sciences). Volumes three and four contain selected abstracted dissertations relating to the social sciences and humanities (education, fine arts, library science, communications, music, psychology, anthropology, business and economics, geography, history, language, law and political science, philosophy, religion, sociology). Volume five consists of an author index. (Keywords appear in bold-faced type in the title of dissertations.) (Ann Arbor, MI: University Microfilms International).

*Criminal Justice and Law Related Titles: A Dissertation Bibliography.* This bibliography contains a selected listing of more 1,300 doctoral dissertations and 145 master's theses relating to the field of criminal justice, and related law titles. (Ann Arbor, MI: University Microfilms International).

*Dissertation Abstracts International.* This is the most comprehensive source for doctoral dissertation abstracts written in the United States. It is divided into two sections: Section A—the Humanities, and Section B—the Sciences. Abstracts of doctoral dissertations submitted by more than 400 cooperating institutions in the United States, Canada, and Europe are included. Keyword title and author indexes are published each month and cumulated annually. Bibliographic entries are classified and arranged alphabetically by important keywords in the title, which make up the keyword title index. (Ann Arbor, MI: University Microfilms International). Section A includes five broad subject categories of communication and the arts, education, language, literature, and linguistics, philosophy, religion and theology, and social sciences. The criminal justice student should seek Section A and look in the table of contents under social sciences. The word "criminal," for example, will most likely prove to be a very productive keyword in the search for abstracts pertaining to criminal courts, criminal procedure, criminals, etc. Section B includes five broad subject categories of biological sciences, earth sciences, health and environment sciences, physical sciences, and psychology.

*Guide to Lists of Masters Theses.* Dorothy Black. (Chicago: American Library Association, 1965.) This guide lists masters theses written through 1964 at institutions in the United States and Canada. Subject and institutional lists provide access.

*Harvard Graduate School of Education: A Bibliography of Doctoral Dissertations, 1918-1987.* John W. Collins III and Leslie DiBona. (Westport, CT: Meckler Corporation, 1989).

*Higher Education in American Life, 1636-1986: A Bibliography of Dissertations and Theses.* Arthur P. Young. (Westport, CT: Greenwood Press, 1988).

*Index to Theses Accepted for Higher Degrees in the Universities of Great Britain and Ireland.* This is an annual publication arranged by subject classification. (London: Association of Special Libraries and Information Bureau, 1953-present).

*Law and Criminology, A Dissertation Catalog.* This catalog lists doctoral dissertations pertaining to law and criminology published by University Microfilms International. Each entry supplies the author, full title, degree earned, school name, date of degree, number of text pages, citation to DAI or Master's Abstracts, and order number for purchase. Approximately 450 citations are included. (Ann Arbor, MI: University Microfilms International, 1980).

*Master's Abstracts.* Published quarterly, this publication provides a selective annotated list of master's theses by students from numerous United States colleges and universities. (Ann Arbor, MI: University Microfilms International).

*Masters Theses in the Pure and Applied Sciences, Vol. 32: Accepted by Colleges and Universities of the United States and Canada.* W.H. Shafer. (New York: Plenum Publications, 1989).

*Microfilm Abstracts: A Collection of Abstracts of Doctoral Dissertations and Monographs Which Are Available in Complete Form on Microfilm.* This publication abstracts dissertations which are available in their entirety on microfilm. (Ann Arbor, MI: University Microfilms, 1938-present).

*Research in Institutional Advancement: A Selected, Annotated Compendium of Doctoral Dissertations.* Westley A. Rowland and Robert Carbone. (Washington, DC: Council for Advancement and Support of Education, 1986.)

*Social Service Review.* "*Doctoral Dissertations in Social Work.*" Published annually since 1954, this bibliograph provides abstracts of completed dissertations by students of schools of social work with doctoral programs. Dissertations in progress are also listed. (Chicago: University of Chicago Press).

## GRANTS

Students of any major may be particularly interested in sources of grants. There is always the possibility of having a research project or other academic activity funded, and in some cases, specific funds may be set aside for such projects. Several sources exist that can help researchers obtain grants.

### Computerized Database for Funding Sources

IRIS is an online computerized file containing descriptions of over 3,000 funding opportunities from federal agencies, private and corporate foundations, and other not-for-profit organizations. More specifically, the IRIS database contains information on continuing programs for institutions, faculty, and graduate and undergraduate students. These programs support activities such as research, travel, teaching, and advanced study. Several restrictions have been placed on the type of funding opportunities included in IRIS. Programs that disburse funds in a limited geographic area are not included, as IRIS is used nationwide. One-time solicitations or requests for proposals (RFPs) are not included because of their short turnaround, making them inappropriate to the design and intended function of IRIS. Also excluded are opportunities that require the recipient to enroll for credit at specific institutions and have permanent employment opportunities.

The results of a search of the database will provide sufficient information for the user to identify programs that warrant further consideration. When conducted in cooperation with, or under the auspices of an office of sponsored programs, the search can provide a firm foundation for further inquiry.

Information for the IRIS database is obtained directly from funding sources rather than from resource books or newsletters, which can often contain out-of-date or misinterpreted data. In addition, whenever notification of program changes are received outside of the usual funding cycle, these changes are immediately incorporated into the database.

### Foundation Directory

Current year's data
5,148 records
Semiannual revision
The Foundation Center, New York, NY
http://fdncenter.org/

The Foundation Directory provides descriptions of over 3,500 foundations that have assets of $1 million or more or that make grants of $100,000 or more annually.

## Foundation Grants Index

1973 to the present
355,314 records
Bimonthly
The Foundation Center, New York, NY
http://fdncenter.org/

The Foundation Grants Index contains information on grants awarded by 400 major American philanthropic foundations, representing all records from the Foundation Grants Index section of the bimonthly *Foundation News*. Information on grants given by foundations is useful in determining types and amounts of grants awarded since foundations seldom announce the availability of funds for specific purposes. Approximately 20,000 new grants are added to the file each year.

### *Foundation Center Offices*

**New York:** 79 Fifth Avenue, New York, NY 10003-3076, Tel: (212) 620-4230

**Field Offices:**

**Washington, DC:** 1001 Connecticut Avenue, NW (entrance at K Street), Suite 938, Washington, DC 20036, Tel: (202) 331-1400

**Cleveland:** 1422 Euclid Avenue, Suite 1356, Cleveland, OH 44115-2001, Tel: (216) 861-1933

**Atlanta:** 50 Hurt Plaza, Suite 150, Atlanta, GA 30303-2914, Tel: (404) 880-0095

**San Francisco:** 312 Sutter Street, Room 312, San Francisco, CA 94108-4314, Tel: (415) 397-0902

## Grants

Grants is the source of thousands of grants offered by federal, state, and local governments, commercial organizations, associations, and private foundations. All grants included in the database carry application deadlines up to six months ahead. Each entry includes full description, qualifications, money available, and renewability. Full name, address, and telephone number for each sponsoring organization are included when available.

## National Foundations

National Foundations provides records of all United States foundations that award grants, regardless of the assets of the foundations or the total amounts of grants they award annually. Each foundation conforms to the general description of a "nongovernmental, nonprofit organization, with funds and program managed by its own trustees or directors, and established to maintain or aid social, educational, charitable, religious, or other activities serving the common welfare, primarily through the making of grants."

## Funding Sources

*Annual Register of Grant Support.* This is a subject guide to public and private sources of grant support, with organization, geographic, and personnel indexes. Annual. (Chicago: Marquis Academic Media).

*The Complete Grants Sourcebook for Higher Education,* Second Edition. David G. Bauer. Profiles of private, corporate, and governmental funding sources with a subject index. Includes helpful tips on writing a successful proposal. (New York: Macmillan, 1985).

*Catalog of Federal Domestic Assistance.* This catalog contains indexes, including agency, subject, applicant eligibility. Entries for programs give funding agency, authorization, objectives of program, types of assistance, uses and use restrictions. (Washington, DC: U.S. Government Printing Office, annual).

*Grants in the Humanities: A Scholar's Guide to Funding Sources.* William E. Coleman. Especially useful are sections showing a sample proposal and budget. (New York: Neal-Schuman, 1980).

*Directory of Research Grants, 1979.* William K. Wilson and Betty J. Wilson (eds.). This annual publication describes more than 2,000 private and public research grants in 90 different categories. The "where, when, and how" of securing federal, state, and local governmental grants are described as well as those awarded by foundations, educational institutions, private donors, corporations, etc. Grants available to graduate as well as undergraduate students are included. The arrangement is by subject areas and each entry includes information on qualifications of the recipients, when and where to apply, the sponsoring agency, amount of money available, and the application deadline. (Phoenix: Oryx Press, 1979).

*Directory of Research Grants.* This guide contains more than 4,000 sources in all areas, with subject and sponsoring agency indexes. May also be searched by computer through the MARS service. (Phoenix: Oryx Press, annual).

*The Federal Register.* This daily publication provides much information on grant sources, as well as other governmental news. (Washington, DC: U.S. Government Printing Office). (See Chapter 10, "Government Documents," for additional information on this source.)

*Foundation Center National Data Book,* Third Edition. Two volumes. This publication provides information about more than 21,000 nonprofit organizations. Arranged by name and state, information given includes total dollar amount of grants awarded for the year, assets, principal officer, etc. Currency of information varies. (New York: Columbia University Press, 1981).

*Foundation Directory.* This is an annual publication arranged by state, with indexes of field of interest, name of foundation, etc. It is a brief summary of purpose, financial data, address, and officers. Grant application information is also included. It may also be searched by computer through the MARS service. (New York: Foundation Center, annual).

*Foundation Grants Index,* 19th Edition. This is a comprehensive list of grants of $5,000 or more awarded by private foundations. It may also be searched by computer through the MARS service. (New York: Columbia University Press, 1990).

*Getting Grants.* Craig W. Smith and Eric W. Skjei. This publication takes the guesswork out of getting grants. It portrays how the grant system works and how it can work for you. (New York: Harper and Row, 1980).

*A Guide to Scholarships, Fellowships and Grants: A Selected Bibliography.* (Printed by the Institute of International Education, 809 United Nations Plaza, New York, New York 10017).

*The International Foundation Directory,* Fourth Edition. H.V. Hodson (ed.), (Detroit: Gale Research, 1986).

*National Data Book,* Seventh Edition. This document provides information about more than 21,000 non-profit organizations. It is arranged by name and state. Information given includes total dollar amount of grants awarded for the year, assets, principal officer, etc. Currency of information varies. It may also be searched by computer through the MARS service. (New York Foundation Center, 1983).

*Challenge Grants: Guidelines, Application Instructions, and Administrative Requirements.* (Washington, DC: National Endowment for the Humanities, 1999).

*National Institute on Alcohol Abuse and Alcoholism Research Programs.* National Institute on Alcohol Abuse and Alcoholism. (www.niaaa.nih.gov/)

*Directory of Financial Aids for Minorities, 1995-1997.* Gail Ann Schlachter. (Delray Beach, FL: B. Klein Publications, 1997). This directory is a list of scholarships, fellowships, loans, grants, etc., awarded primarily to minorities.

*Directory of Financial Aids for Women, 1997-99.* Gail Ann Schlachter. (Santa Barbara, CA: Reference Service Press, 1997). This publication is a guide to scholarships, grants, and awards "designed primarily or exclusively for women."

*Grantseeking in North Carolina: A Guide to Foundation and Corporate-Giving.* Anita Gunn Shirley. (Raleigh, NC: N.C. Center for Public Policy Research, 1985). Funding sources are arranged by size with indexes by funding interest and name. It also includes tips on writing the proposal.

## Writing the Proposal

*The "How To" Grants Manual: Successful Grantseeking Techniques for Obtaining Public and Private Grants*, Second Edition. David G. Bauer. (New York: Published for the American Council on Education by Macmillan, 1988).

*Grant Money and How to Get It: A Handbook for Librarians*. Richard W. Boss. (New York: R.R. Bowker, 1980).

*Fund Raising; The Guide to Raising Money From Private Sources*, Second Edition. Revised and enlarged. Thomas E. Broce. (Norman, OK: University of Oklahoma Press, 1987).

*The CISP International Studies Funding Book*, Fourth Edition. Walter T. Brown, et al. (eds.). (New York: Council on International and Public Affairs. 1986).

*How to Get Federal Grants*, Third Edition. Daniel Lynn Conrad. (San Francisco: Public Management Institute, 1980).

*Grants for Libraries: A Guide to Public and Private Funding Programs and Proposal Writing Techniques*, Second Edition. Emmett Corry. (Littleton, CO: Libraries Unlimited, 1986).

*How to Write Successful Foundation Presentations*. Joseph Dermer (ed.). (Rockville, Md: The Taft Group, 1984).

*Fundraising For Nonprofit Institutions*. Sandy F. Dolnick (ed.). (Greenwich, CT: JAI Press, 1987).

*Plain Talk About Grants: A Basic Handbook*. Robert E. Geller. (Sacramento, CA: California State Library Foundation, 1986).

*Grants for Arts, Culture and the Humanities*. Rebecca MacLean (ed.). (New York, NY: The Foundation Center, 1997).

*Grants for Research and Demonstrations*. (Baltimore: Health Care Financing Administration, Office of Research, Demonstrations, and Statistics, 1981).

*Grants Magazine: The Journal of Sponsored Research and Other Programs*. Quarterly. (New York: Plenum, 1978-present). Tips in writing and presenting proposals, where to find grant funding. Each issue has an example of a "winning proposal."

*The Grant System*. John W. Kalas. (Albany, NY: State University of New York Press, 1987).

**3**

# Sources of Books

Most libraries are now computerized to some extent. Many libraries have taken out the old catalog filing cabinets altogether, some have a mix of sources on both manual cards and computers, and a few still use only the card catalog. Students should be aware that in most libraries, only books, monographs, and government documents are in the general catalog. There are many other sources of information in a typical library, including commercial computer data bases, indexes, abstracts, periodicals, newspapers, microfilm, and others.

This chapter on sources of books will start by describing the card catalog. If your library is fully online, this information still applies, but think of your computer terminal as an electronic card catalog.

## CARD CATALOG

The card catalog contains most of the books in the library's collection, and is a good starting point for a researcher. However, extensive research for books is unnecessary. A scan of the catalog will acquaint the researcher with the books that are available. Books can provide a great deal of detailed information on a topic, and a review of a few may generally educate the researcher about the topic. But books may not be as valuable as some of the more current sources, such as journals. The researcher can always return to the card catalog if it is necessary to broaden the literature search with additional books.

The card catalog is an A-through-Z file of cards, indicating the catalog entries of author (last name first), title (excluding A, An, and The), and subject of most of the books in the library. All cards are tagged with a classification or call number, generally in the upper left-hand corner of the card. This number indicates the location of the book on the shelf. Fiction books may be arranged alphabetically by author on a shelf, instead of having a call number. Authors can be an individual, a society, an institution, or a government department or bureau. A librarian can also direct the researcher to specific locations of call numbers within the library. A researcher who is not sure of an author and title should consult a reference librarian.

If a researcher needs books about a particular subject but has no specific titles in mind, a look under that subject will help. Some libraries distinguish the subjects by red headings or capitalized black headings and some have divided catalogs for author-title cards and subject cards. A list of subject headings contained within a library's card catalog is generally available from the reference librarian. Such a list will provide an overview and general idea of the library's holdings, along with what term or subject headings one should look under. More comprehensive lists of subject headings relating to criminal justice can be found in the following sources:

> *Library of Congress Subject Headings*, Volume I, 13th Edition. (Washington, DC: Library of Congress, 1990.)

> *Sears List of Subject Headings*. Barbara M. Westby (ed.). (New York: H.W. Wilson Company, 1982.)

*National Criminal Justice Thesaurus.* (Washington,
DC: National Institute of Justice/National Criminal
Justice Reference Service, June 1982.)

## Call Numbers

One of two different classification systems will be used by every library. These systems are the Dewey Decimal Classification System and the Library of Congress Classification System. The two systems have different call numbers. Major categories of the Dewey Decimal Card Catalog System are as follows:

| | |
|---|---|
| 000 – 099 – | General Works |
| 100 – 199 – | Philosophy |
| 200 – 299 – | Religion |
| 300 – 399 – | Social Sciences |
| 400 – 499 – | Language |
| 500 – 599 – | Pure Science |
| 600 – 699 – | Technology |
| 700 – 799 – | The Arts |
| 800 – 899 – | Literature |
| 900 – 999 – | History |

Categories in the Library of Congress Classification System are as follows:

| | | | | | |
|---|---|---|---|---|---|
| A | — | General Works/Polygraphy | M | — | Music |
| B | — | Philosophy/Religion | N | — | Fine Arts |
| C | — | History/Auxiliary Sciences | P | — | Language and Literature |
| D | — | History and Topography (except America) | Q | — | Science |
| E/F | — | America | R | — | Medicine |
| G | — | Geography/Anthropology | S | — | Agriculture/Plant and Animal Husbandry |
| H | — | Social Sciences | T | — | Technology |
| J | — | Political Science | U | — | Military Science |
| K | — | Law | V | — | Naval Science |
| L | — | Education | Z | — | Bibliography and Library Science |

Books pertaining to criminal justice are classified under the social sciences, are designated by the prefix letters of HV, and will have call numbers ranging from 340 to 360. To find a specific book, the researcher should consult the card catalog to determine the book's call numbers and proceed to the correct location.

Most academic libraries have, or are in the process of, converting from the Dewey Decimal Classification System to the Library of Congress Classification System. Therefore, there is a good possibility that a researcher will be confronted with the two systems at once, which may be confusing. If the desired book is not at the location indicated by the card catalog classification number, a check of the sorting shelves located in a designated area in the library may be helpful. If the book still cannot be located, the circulation desk can determine whether the book has been checked out. If it has not, the library will usually initiate a search for the book. If the book has already been checked out to someone else, it can be reserved, and the library will notify the researcher when it is returned.

## BOOKS IN PRINT

*Books in Print* (New York: R.R. Bowker) is an annual publication that lists most available books in any given area of knowledge. It should be used as a supplement to the card catalog of any library because the card catalog contains only the holdings of the library. There will be many more books written on criminal justice than the average library will possess. The 1998-99 edition of *Books in Print* listed approximately 1,450,000 titles from 62,400 publishers. The current edition consists of nine volumes, the first four of which are arranged alphabetically by author. Volumes five through eight are alphabetically arranged by title. Volume nine also includes a list of publishers whose books are listed.

Information provided for books listed includes author, title, edition, publisher, and year of publication. *Books in Print* does not include information on out-of-print books, periodicals, government literature, or unpublished research such as dissertations. However, it is an excellent source because it provides information on the vast majority of books published in criminal justice. *Books in Print* also publishes a seven-volume subject guide. Subject headings contained in *Books in Print* that relate to criminal justice include:

| | | |
|---|---|---|
| crime and criminals | criminal investigation | criminologists |
| crime in literature | criminal jurisdiction | gangs |
| crime prevention | criminal justice-administration of criminal law | offenses against the person |
| criminal anthropology | criminal liability | organized crime |
| criminal courts | criminal procedure | rehabilitation of criminals |
| criminal and dangerous | criminal psychology | reparation |
| criminal intent | criminal statistics | victims of crime |

It also includes headings of specific crimes such as gambling, murder, and robbery.

Another good source of books is the *Cumulative Book Index* (New York: H.W. Wilson, 1898-present). This is a monthly index, listing all new books published in various areas of interest, many of which may not yet be available to academic libraries. Also included are selected government documents. Books are listed by author, title, and subject.

## INTERLIBRARY LOAN

Books which are unavailable in a researcher's library might be located through the library's interlibrary loan service. This service makes material not owned by the library available for research. In addition to books, articles and government documents may be obtained through interlibrary loan. It is difficult, however, to borrow theses, dissertations, complete issues of journals or newspapers, rare or fragile materials, reserve books, and reference materials.

When using interlibrary loan, the researcher will be required to fill out an interlibrary loan request form, which may be obtained at the reference desk. Undergraduate students are sometimes required to have their request form approved by their faculty advisor. Information needed for the form includes the title, author's full name, publisher, place of publication, date, and the source of this bibliographical information. If the material is part of a series, the series title will also be required. The completed form should be given to a member of the interlibrary loan or reference staff. After receiving the request, the library will locate the nearest establishment possessing the material requested. Interlibrary loan material should be requested well in advance of when it will actually be needed, because it takes an average of two weeks, and in some cases up to six weeks, for the order to be filled. Most libraries will notify the requester by mail when the requested item arrives. Some materials, such as journal articles and newspaper clippings, will be photocopied and can be kept by the student. Loans, however, are usually not renewable and can be kept a maximum of one to two weeks, depending upon the lending library. There may be a small service charge to cover photocopying, postage, or insurance. Most libraries charge ten cents per photocopied page, but this amount may vary. There should be a space on the request form to indicate the researcher's price limit for photocopying charges.

Libraries participating in the interlibrary loan program have the opportunity to offer their users virtually every book, article, or other material that has ever been written.

Many documents no longer in print (including books, journal articles and dissertations) can be purchased by writing University Microfilms International (UMI), 300 North Zeeb Road, Dept. P.R., Ann Arbor, MI 48106, http://www.umi.com/. And of course, books can be ordered and purchased through a bookstore or publisher.

**Figure 3.1**
**Typical Interlibrary Loan Request Form**

---

**INTERLIBRARY LOAN *BORROWING* REQUEST**

_____book _____dissertation _____thesis _____document _____newspaper

PLEASE:          1. USE A SEPARATE FORM FOR EACH ITEM YOU REQUEST.
                 2. PRINT NEATLY AND LEGIBLY IN INK.
                 3. USE FULL NAMES FOR AUTHOR, TITLE, SERIAL, ETC. DO NOT ABBREVIATE.

Borrower's name_____ Department_____ Phone # _____

Mailing address _____ City _____ State _____ Zip Code _____

Check one:    ☐ faculty     ☐ staff    ☐ graduate student     ☐ undergraduate

Faculty signature (required for undergraduates): _____

Today's date _____ Need by _____ Not needed after _____

NOTE: INCOMPLETE OR INCORRECT INFORMATION CAUSES CONSIDERABLE DELAY IN PROCESSING OF REQUESTS.

Author: _____

Title: _____

_____

Publisher _____ Place _____ Date _____

This edition only_____ ISBN, ISSN, OCLC, or CODEN if known _____

VERIFICATION: PLEASE INDICATE THE SOURCE IN WHICH THE ABOVE REFERENCE WAS FOUND. VERIFICATION IN A STANDARD REFERENCE
WORK IS PREFERRED. A LIST OF STANDARD VERIFICATION SOURCES IS AVAILABLE AT THE REFERENCE DESK.

Title _____

Volume _____ Date _____ Page _____ Item # _____

NOTE: I agree to pay charges that may be incurred to obtain this material. Maximum amount _____.

Signature_____ Date_____

**Figure 3.2**

# The NCJRS Criminal Justice
# Document Loan Program

### An Interlibrary Loan Service

## Document Loan Program

The National Institute of Justice/NCJRS (National Criminal Justice Reference Service), an information clearinghouse serving practitioners, researchers, students, and the general public, maintains a collection of nearly 100,000 documents related to criminal justice. It also has an interlibrary loan program.

The collection grows by about 6,000 documents annually and includes such subjects as child abuse, corrections, courts, crime prevention, dispute resolution, domestic violence, drugs and crime, juvenile justice, law enforcement, sexual assault, and victims.

To facilitate research and to improve access to research results, NCJRS makes most items in this collection accessible for a nominal fee to people in the United States and Canada through interlibrary loan.

## Borrowing Procedures

• NCJRS lends documents only to other libraries. Contact your local public, academic, agency, or corporate library to borrow documents.
• You must request each document on a separate interlibrary loan form—the standard four-part American Library Association (ALA) form. NCJRS cannot give you the ALA forms but can tell you where to get them. Call NCJRS at the number listed on this page.
• You may borrow documents for up to 6 weeks. Libraries in the Washington, D.C., area may allow you to hand carry loan requests and pick up materials in person from the NCJRS Reading Room; in this case the borrowing period is 4 weeks.
• Renewals must be arranged through the borrowing library.
• NCJRS assesses a $12 charge for each lost or damaged document in addition to the cost of replacing the document.
• NCJRS does not routinely photocopy materials in lieu of lending.

## Identifying Documents in the Collection

Each document in the NCJRS collection is identified by a unique accession number—the NCJ number. Be sure to cite this number on the ALA form.

If you are searching for a specific title, the following NCJRS products and services are excellent sources for identifying criminal justice documents and their NCJ numbers:
• *Document Retrieval Index (DRI)*—an annually updated microfiche catalog of the entire NCJRS collection.
• *NIJ Reports*—a bimonthly journal that includes abstracts of the most significant additions to the NCJRS collection.
• *Topical Searches, Topical Bibliographies, and Custom Searches*—listings of abstracts from the 100,000-item data base representing published and unpublished documents in the collection. The accession number shown on these products is the NCJ number. On records retrieved through DIALOG on File 21, the NCJ number is displayed as the DIALOG number before each citation.
• *Index to the NCJRS Microfiche Collection*—access by author, subject, and title to more than 25,000 documents in the collection that are also available on microfiche from NCJRS.

For more information, call NCJRS.

**The National Institute of Justice/NCJRS**
**toll-free number is 800-851-3420;**
**301-251-5500 from Metropolitan**
**Washington, D.C., or Maryland.**

## RESERVE BOOKS

Books for use in specific courses will generally be placed on "reserve" in the library by the professor because they will be in heavy demand by students. Some libraries will designate reserve books by placing a red card in the card catalog. Others will maintain notebooks containing lists of reserve books. These notebooks may be arranged alphabetically by the professor's name, or alphabetically by title of the book. Books on reserve must be obtained from the reserve reading room within the library and are usually circulated for a period of two hours during the day.

## BOOK REVIEWS

Book reviews are another writer's interpretation and opinion of the original work, and should not be used as a substitute for the researcher reading the entire book. Upon comparing a review with the actual book, a researcher might find that his or her opinions differ from those of the reviewer. The researcher should formulate independent opinions of the book, particularly if the work will be cited as a reference source. Following are sources of book reviews.

*Book Review Digest.* (New York: H.W. Wilson, annual.) This is a monthly publication, with the exception of February and July, that indexes selected book reviews appearing in approximately 75 English and American periodicals. The orientation is toward popular, rather than scholarly, journals. Approximately 350 book titles with brief descriptions are presented each month. Title and subject indexes are provided.

*Book Review Index.* (Detroit: Gale Research, annual.) This bimonthly publication lists current book reviews in the social sciences, indexed by author.

*A Guide to Book Review Citations: A Bibliography of Sources.* Richard A. Gray (Columbus: The Ohio State University Press, 1968.) This publication provides an annotated list of sources of book review citations.

*Index to Book Reviews in the Humanities.* (Williamston, MI: Phillip Thomson, 1963-present.) This annual publication includes book reviews in the social sciences as well as the humanities. Several thousand titles are indexed in each issue.

*Technical Book Review Index.* (Pittsburgh: JAAD, 1987.) This is a monthly publication, with the exception of July and August, which indexes reviews appearing in scientific, technical, and trade journals.

## MICROFORMS

Most libraries want to acquire as much material as possible in order to maintain an up-to-date collection of data, but they also have limited space that must be utilized as efficiently as possible. Microforms come in a variety of forms: microfilm, microcards, microprint, microfiche, and ultra microfiche. As an example of the space-saving advantage of microforms, a 4" x 6" microfiche can hold up to 98 book pages. The ultra microfiche method can contain as many as 1,200 pages on a 2" x 2" card.

Some materials available in microform cannot be found in print, such as rare books, periodicals, manuscripts, government documents, and newspapers. But despite these advantages, students sometimes become intimidated by the special readers and the rows of filing cabinets filled with drawer after drawer of cards. And unless the researcher's library lends microfiche and microfiche readers, the material cannot be taken home. Nonetheless, microforms are here to stay and will undoubtedly increase in usage during the years ahead.

Books on microform will be listed as such in the card catalog. Government documents, serials, periodicals, and other publications on microform are identified through corresponding indexes. If the researcher is uncertain about which materials are on microform and which are not, the researcher should check the library's guide to its microform collection. This should be available at the reference desk and the microform service desk.

# 4

# Indexing Services

## INDICES

Indices are bibliographic tools specializing in periodicals for a variety of subjects or academic disciplines. They provide a quick method for locating literature on a specified topic in an organized fashion. Library materials covered by indexing services are important contributors to the content of reports, term papers, and other research projects. Journal literature, for example, is current, is reflective of trends in the field, presents results of recent research, and provides different points of view on a given topic. It is difficult to acquire these same advantages from books.

Bibliographical information in an index includes the author's name, the title of the publication, the name of the publishing journal or periodical, the date of publication, and the length of the publication.

The two most common kinds of indices are subject and author. In these, all articles concerning a particular subject area or topic will be categorized and alphabetized. Pertinent information about the periodical will be given. The researcher should next look up the titles of the periodicals in the library's checklist, and if the library has them, request that they be retrieved.

Following the subject index, most indices will include an alphabetized author index that provides a listing of publications by author, rather than by subject. Other kinds of indices include geographical, abbreviation, reference, and keyword-title in which the initial word of a heading or subheading is indexed.

Current indices are generally published on a monthly, bi-weekly, or quarterly basis and include publications of the preceding months or weeks. Cumulative indices list publications on a particular subject that have been published within the last three months to one year. These indices are then compiled quarterly or annually. There also are retrospective indices that include articles on a particular subject published during previous decades. Most libraries will locate their indices near the card catalog in the reference department.

One of the most popularly used indices is the *Reader's Guide to Periodical Literature*. This is a cumulative, alphabetized author/subject index to periodicals of general interest published in the United States. The *Reader's Guide* covers publications such as *Time, U.S. News and World Report, Consumer Reports,* and *Newsweek,* among many others. Topic headings relating to criminal justice included in the *Reader's Guide* vary from month to month, depending upon the subjects of the articles cited. Typical citations may include the following subject headings:

| | |
|---|---|
| capital punishment | juvenile delinquency |
| commercial crimes | narcotics |
| crime and criminals | prisons |
| crime prevention | self-defense |
| detectives | trials |
| escapes | victims of crime |
| fugitives | women and crime |
| gangs | |

Students are also advised to look under specific crimes such as arson, bribery, burglary, fraud, murder, robbery, and so forth.

The majority of students are probably more familiar with this periodical index than with any other. The use of general interest publications as sources for research papers is discouraged by many professors, however, so it is wise to check for any such restrictions before consulting the *Reader's Guide* for information. In addition, all other available avenues of information, such as abstracts and indices of professional journals, should first be exhausted. A researcher familiar with the *Reader's Guide* should have little trouble using the more specialized indices, as they all list articles by subject.

## ABSTRACTING INDICES

An abstracting index will include all of the bibliographical information presented in a regular index, but it will also include a brief synopsis or summary of the publication. The summary includes the main theme of the article and generally includes the results of any research conducted. After reading an abstract, the reader should have a better idea of the total content of the original publication so that he or she can judge whether there is a need to consult the entire text.

The effective use of index and abstract services is the key to a thorough review of the literature for any subject whether current or retrospective. Such a vast amount of literature exists for any given field of study that even avid readers cannot keep pace with it. Thus, the indexing services first assist the researcher by organizing the printed matter by topic, author, etc. Then, once the researcher has gained an insight into the literature available, he or she can read the condensed summaries of the publications to find the articles that will be most applicable to the research needs. An example of an abstract is provided below:

Webster, Stephen H., and Kenneth E. Matthews, Jr. "Survey of Arson and Arson Response Capabilities in Selected Jurisdictions." (Washington, DC: United States Department of Justice, Law Enforcement Assistance Administration Item 968H-1, February, 1979), p. 41.

Report on arson incidence and the resources and activities of arson control units in 174 cities with 50,000 or more population. Data are based on 1978 mail survey of fire chiefs and cover fiscal years ending 1977 or 1978.

Contents:

A. Narrative analysis, with text, statistics, four charts, and eleven tables on relationship between total fire and arson rates, and 1970-75 change in city size; arson motives and dollar losses; legal restrictions on sharing information with insurance companies; and arson investigation and prevention activities and equipment (pp. 1-27).

B. Appendices with facsimile questionnaire and one table showing for each survey city 1975 population; fire department budget; number and types of fire; arson investigations, arrests, and fatalities; and arson unit characteristics and training (pp. 18-41).

Source:    *American Statistics Index 1979*, Abstracts Volume, Supplement No. 5 (Washington, DC: Congressional Information Service) p. 76.

A student researching financial implications of arson, for example, would probably want to consult the entire text of the article because the abstract specifically indicated that dollar loss due to arson was a part of the subject matter addressed.

There are many specialized abstracts and indices relating to criminal justice and any library is bound to have some of them. Several of the most pertinent abstracts and indices to criminal justice are briefly described below, followed by a listing of many others that may also be of service to the criminal justice student.

*Abstracts of Supreme Court Decisions Interpreting the Interstate Commerce Act.* (Association of Transportation Practitioners, 1211 Connecticut Ave. N.W. Ste. 310, Washington DC 20036).

*Abstracts on Adult Corrections, 1983-1990.* This publication includes more than 1,600 abstracts on community-based and institutional adult corrections. (Monsey, NY: Criminal Justice Press).

*Abstracts on Juvenile Justice and Delinquency, 1983-1990.*This publication includes more than 1,600 abstracts on juvenile justice systems, corrections, courts, policing and delinquency causes, patterns, and prevention. (Monsey, NY: Criminal Justice Press).

*Abstracts on Police, 1983-1990.* More than 1,500 abstracts on police management, community policing, personnel, and other topics are included. (Monsey, NY: Criminal Justice Press).

*Applied Science and Technology Index.* This cumulative index to English language periodicals contains subject and author indices. Subject fields indexed include aeronautics and space science, chemistry, computer technology and applications, construction industry, energy resources and research, fire and fire prevention, food and food industry, geology, machinery, mathematics, minerology, metallurgy, oceanography, petroleum and gas, physics, plastics, textile industry and fabrics, transportation, engineering, and other industrial and mechanical arts. Of particular interest to criminal justice students would be the topic headings: crime and criminals, criminal investigation, crime prevention, crimes aboard aircraft, criminal statistics, security, burglar alarms, and other specific technological security items. (New York: H.W. Wilson Company).

*Criminal Justice Abstracts.* (Formerly *Crime and Delinquency Literature.*) Sponsored by the National Council on Crime and Delinquency, Hackensack, NJ, this source is published quarterly (March, June, September, December) and cumulated annually. It contains in-depth abstracts of current literature, international in scope, on criminal justice policies, theories, programs, and administration. Headings include: Crime and the Offender, Juvenile Delinquency and the Delinquent, Law and the Courts, Law Enforcement and the Police, Corrections, Drug Abuse, and Related Social Issues. Also included are Letters to the Editor and a subject index. Each issue contains approximately 150 abstracts of the latest books, articles, reports, and studies published worldwide.

*Criminal Justice Periodical Index.* This is a comprehensive criminal justice periodical reference source published three times annually (May, September, January). The final issue in January is cumulative. The reference source contains thousands of specialized entries from over 90 significant criminal justice journals. Entries are listed under various subject headings such as family disturbance/intervention, hostages, pre-trial diversion, terrorism, etc. (University Microfilms International, 1990).

*Criminology & Penology Abstracts.* Indexed: Excerp. Criminol. Former titles: Abstracts on Criminology and Penology; Excerpt Criminologica. (Amsteveen, Netherlands: Kugler Publications, 1961).

*Current Law Index.* 1980-present. This index covers the same subject matter as the *Index to Legal Periodicals*, but the range of journals indexed is much broader and the indexing more thorough.

*Human Resources Abstracts.* This complements *Public Administration Abstracts*. It is international in coverage and abstracts material not found elsewhere. Covering such subject areas as public policy and planning, and public health, it is an excellent resource in public administration. (Newbury Park, CA: Sage Publications).

*Index to Canadian Legal Periodical Literature.* (Text in English and French) q. P.O. Box 386, N.D.G. Station, Montreal, Que. H4A 3P7, Canada (1960).

*Index to Chinese Legal Periodicals.* Chung Wen Fa Lu Lun Wen So Yin. a. University, Library—Tung Wu Ta Hsueh Tu Shing Kuan, Wai Shuang Hsi, Taipei, Taiwan, Republic of China. (reprint service avail.) Key Title: Zhongwen Falu Lauwen Suoyin. (1970).

*Index to Foreign Legal Periodicals.* (Subject headings in English with translation into French, German and Spanish included in a. cumulation) 1960. q. (a. cumulations) American Association of Law Libraries, School of Law Library. Description: Index of legal and business periodicals from 59 countries. Includes legal essays. (Berkeley, CA:University of California Press, 1960).

*Index to Indian Legal Periodicals.* (New Delhi, India: Indian Law Institute, 1963).

*Index to International Public Opinion.* Prepared by Survey Research Consultants International, Inc. Annual. (see Chapter 14, "Sources of International Data" for a complete description).

*Index to Legal Books.* M.C. Susan DeMaio (ed.). This index merges and cites index entries from leading law books, national in scope and importance, and cross-references under major legal subject categories. (New York: R.R. Bowker, Legal Reference Publishing).

*Index to Legal Periodicals*, published in two series. [1] Vol. 1 (1908)—Vol. 18 (1925) and [2] Vol. 1 (1926)—to date. This is a subject index without abstracts, covering English language law journals. There is a useful "Table of Cases Referred to in Articles" in each issue starting with 1917.

*Index to Periodical Articles Related to Law.* This index covers law-related articles in general social science periodicals which are not indexed in *Index to Legal Periodicals.* (Dobbs Ferry, NY: Glanville Publishers, Inc., 1974).

*International Federation for Documentation.* P-Notes. 1931. Federation Internationale d'Information et de Documentation—International Federation for Information and Documentation, Box 90402, 2509 LK The Hague, Netherlands. (Subscr. to: Distribution Centre, Blackhorse Rd., Letchworth, Herts. SG6 1HN, United Kingdom).

*Police Science Abstracts.* This international abstracting service provides more than 1,500 abstracts concerning police science, the forensic sciences, and forensic medicine. *Police Science Abstracts* is published six times a year (January, March, May, July, September, and November) and the last issue includes cumulative subject and author indices. (Amsterdam, Netherlands: Kugler Publications).

*Psychological Abstracts.* The leading abstracting index for the field of psychology. It is published monthly and cumulated annually. It provides synopses on an international basis of literature in psychology and related disciplines. Subject and author indices are provided. Subject headings of related criminal justice articles that have been abstracted include: adjudication, correctional institutions, crime, criminals, conviction, criminal law, criminology, prisons, as well as specific crimes, i.e., homicide, rape, etc. (This is also available as a computerized database—see Chapter 9, "Computerized Literature Searches.") (Arlington, VA: Psychological Abstracts Information Service, American Psychological Association.)

*Public Affairs Information Service* (*PAIS*). Robert S. Wilson (ed.). This abstracting index is published monthly and cumulated annually. It covers many sources of literature of the social sciences. Broad categories include economics, business, finance, banking, government, public administration, public policy, political science, and statistics. Subject headings relating to criminal justice include black criminals, capital punishment, crime, crime and criminals, computers and crime, correction, crime news, crime prevention, crime records, criminal investigation, criminal jurisdiction, criminal justice, criminal law, criminal liability, criminal procedure, criminal research, criminal syndicalism, criminals-insane, female offenders, juvenile delinquents, parole, political crimes, victims of crime, and white collar crimes, as well as specific crimes. (PAIS is also available in a computerized database—see Chapter 9, "Computerized Literature Searches.") (New York: Public Affairs Information Service, Inc.)

*Sage Public Administration Abstracts.* This is the only indexing service devoted exclusively to public administration. International in coverage, the material abstracted includes books, pamphlets, government publications, speeches, legislative research studies, and ephemera, in addition to journal articles. (Newbury Park, CA: Sage Publications).

*Social Science Citation Index.* An international index of articles appearing in more than 1,000 social science journals. An index of previously published articles that are being cited in current literature is included. This enables one to follow the development of ideas and hypotheses and reactions to them over a period of time. Keyword-title and author indices are also included in this annual publication.

*Social Sciences Index.* A cumulative index to English language periodicals in the fields of anthropology, area studies, economics, environmental sciences, geography, law and criminology, medical sciences, political science, psychology, public administration, and sociology. Access is by author and subject entries. Annual cumulations. (New York: H.W. Wilson Company.)

*Social Work Research and Abstracts.* Articles and books are abstracted with subject and author access, in addition to an original research paper in each issue.

*Sociological Abstracts.* Published five times yearly (April, June, August, October, and December). These issues are cumulated annually. Subject headings pertaining to criminal justice include crime, criminal, criminality, criminally, criminogenic, criminogenesis, criminology, delinquency, delinquent, and courts, as well as specific crimes. (San Diego: Sociological Abstracts, Inc.) (This is also available in a computerized database—see Chapter 9, "Computerized Literature Searches.")

The following is a list of other pertinent or related abstracts and indices.

*ABC Political Science*
*Abstracts on Police Science*
*Advance Bibliography of Law and Related Fields*
*Alcoholism Digest Annual*
*Applied Science and Technology Index*
*Bibliography on Foreign and Comparative Law*
*Biography Index*
*Book Review Digest*
*British Technology Index*
*Bulletin Signaletique 390: Psychology et Psychopathology, Psychistrig*
*Bulletin Signaletique 524: Sociology*
*Business Periodicals Index*
*Canadian Book Review Annual*
*Canadian Business Periodicals Index*
*Computer Abstracts*
*Crime and Delinquency Literature*
*Cumulative Book Index*
*Current Contents, Social and Behavioral Sciences*
*Current Index to Journals in Education*
*Current Index to Statistics*
*Current Publications in Legal and Related Fields*

*Dissertation Abstracts*
*Drug Abuse Bibliography*
*Education Index*
*Federal Index*
*Gallup Opinion Index*
*Government Reports*
*Highway Safety Literature*
*Humanities Index*
*Index Medicus*
*Index to Book Reviews in the Humanities*
*Index to Current Urban Documents*
*Index to Post-1944 Periodical Articles on Political, Economic, and Social Problems*
*Index to U.S. Government Periodicals*
*International Bibliography of the Social Sciences—Economics*
*International Bibliography of the Social Sciences—Political*

*International Bibliography of the Social Sciences—Sociology*
*International Political Science Abstracts*
*Key to Economic Science and Managerial Sciences*
*London Bibliography of the Social Sciences*
*Magazine Index*
*The National Newspaper Index*
*Peace Research Abstracts Journal*
*Personal Management Abstracts*
*Population Index*
*Poverty and Human Resources Abstract*
*Sage Public Administration Abstracts*
*Sage Race Relations Abstracts*
*Sage Urban Studies Abstracts*
*Ulrich's International Periodicals Directory*
*Urban Affairs Abstracts*

# 5

# Journals

All too often, undergraduate students return from an excursion to the library only to report to their professor that they could find nothing written on their research topic. These students are usually overlooking at least one major source of research: journals. The majority of research and current information published at any point in time is found in scholarly, refereed journals rather than in books. Unfortunately, most students are not exposed to these journals until they reach graduate school.

There are two systematic ways to study a research topic found in journals—either by consulting one of the abstracts or indices to the journals (see Chapter 4) or performing a computer search of the topic by accessing one of the computerized databases (see Chapter 9).

While investigating a topic, the student must distinguish between refereed publications and trade magazines. Refereed journals usually accept an article only after it has been reviewed by two or more accomplished reviewers (called "referees") and a majority of the referees believe the article is methodologically sound and contributes knowledge to the field. An article accepted for publication in a major refereed journal is considered meritorious and an honor by the academic community. Trade publications, while useful, do not carry the same scholarly weight as refereed publications. Articles in trade publications are usually not subjected to the same rigorous academic scrutiny as are the articles in refereed journals. Indeed, articles for trade publications may be selected merely on the basis of their appeal to the subscriber.

The following is a list, by category, of many of the major (and minor) scholarly journals published in the criminal justice field. The first list generally applies to the major journals in criminal justice and criminology while the sections that follow include subfields of study in criminal justice and other related disciplines.

## CORRECTIONS

*Apalachee Diary*, Apalachee Correctional Institution, P.O. Box 699, Seads, FL 32460. [ceased publication]

*California Correctional News*, 211 Lathrop Way, Suite M, Sacramento, CA 95815-4242.

*Canadian Journal of Criminology*, 383 Parkdale Ave. Suite 304, Ottawa, Ontario K1Y 4R4, Canada.

*Contact Newsletter*, P.O. Box 81826, Lincoln, NE 68501. [ceased publication]

*Correctional Industries Association Newsletter*. Correctional Industries Assoc., Inc., 235 N. Brackenburg Lane, Charlotte, NC 28270-0979.

*Corrections Compendium*, 3900 Industrial Ave. North, 2nd Floor, Box 81826, Lincoln, NE 68501-1826.

*Corrections Digest*, 3918 Prosperity Ave. Ste. 318 Fairfax, VA 22031-3334.

*Corrections Today*, American Correctional Association, 4380 Fobes Blvd., Lanham, MD 20706-4322.

*Corrective and Social Psychiatry and Journal of Behavioral Technology Methods and Therapy*, Martin Psychiatric Research Found., Box 3365, Fairfield, CA 94533-0587.

*Federal Probation*, U.S. Adm. Office of the U.S. Courts, Federal Corrections & Supervision Division, Washington, DC 20402-9371.

*Fortune News*, Fortune Society, 39 W. 19th St., New York, NY 10011.

*Grapevine*, Box 49122, Chicago, IL 60649-0122.

*Howard Law Journal*, Howard University School of Law, 2900 Vanness St. NW, Washington, DC 20008.

*Jail & Prisoner Law Bulletin*, Americans for the Effective Law Enforcement Inc., 5519 N. Cumberland Ave., Ste. 1008, Chicago, IL 60656-1471.

*Journal of Correctional Education*, Kancz, McGing & Assoc. Inc. Box 75502, St. Paul, MN 55175.

*Journal of Offender Counseling Services and Rehabilitation*, The Haworth Press, Inc., 12 West 32nd St., New York, N.Y. 10001.

*National Prison Project Journal*, American Civil Liberties Union Foundation, Inc., National Prison Project, 1875 Connecticut Ave. NW, Ste. 410, Washington, DC, 20009.

*National Review of Criminal Sciences*, Nat. Center for Social & Criminological Research, Zamebek, P.O. Cairo, Egypt.

*New England Journal on Prison Law*, 154 Stuart Street, Boston, MA 02116-5687.

*Prison Action Group Newsletter*, 121 N. Fitzhugh Street, Rochester, NY 14614.

*The Prison Journal*, Sage Publications Inc., 2455 Teller Rd., Thousand Oaks, CA 91320.

*Probation Journal*, Nat. Assoc. of Probation Officers, 3-4 Chivalry Rd., Battersea, London, SW11 1HT England.

*Probation and Parole*, Dept. of Justice, Bureau of Justice Statistics, 633 Indiana Ave. NW, 11th Fl, Washington, DC 20531.

*Probation & Parole in the U.S.*, U.S. Dept. of Justice, Bureau of Justice Statistics, 633 Indian Ave. NW, Washington, DC 20531.

*Question Mark*, Norfolk Inmate Council Publishing, Box 43, Norfolk, MA 02056-0043.

*Rocketeer*, Missouri Training Center For Men, Box 7, Moberly, MO 65270.

*Southern Coalition Report on Jails and Prisons*, Box 120044, Nashville, TN 37212.

# COURTS AND THE LAW

*American Criminal Law Review*, Georgetown University Law Center, 600 New Jersey Avenue NW, Washington, DC 20009.

*American Journal of Comparative Law*, American Society of Comparative Law, University of California, 394 Boalt Hall, Berkeley, CA 94720.

*American Journal of Criminal Law*, University of Texas Austin, School of Law Publ., Box 149084, Austin, TX 78714-9084.

*California Youth Authority Status of Female Employees Report*, 4241 Williamsburgh Drive, Sacramento, CA 95823.

*Case Western Reserve Law Review*, Case Western Reserve University, School of Law, 11075 East Blvd., Cleveland, OH 44106-7148.

*Center Court*, National Center for State Courts, 300 Newport Ave., Williamsburg, VA 23187-8798.

*Chicago Kent Law Review*, Chicago Kent College of Law, 565 W. Adams St., Chicago, IL 60661-3691.

*Civil Disorder Digest*, P.O. Box 185, Harvard Square Station, Cambridge, MA 02138.

*Columbia Human Rights Law Review*, Columbia University School of Law, 435 West 116th Street, New York, NY 10027.

*Columbia Journal of Transnational Law*. Columbia Journal of Transitional Law Association, Columbia University, 435 West 116th Street, New York, NY 10027.

*Cornell International Law Journal*, Cornell Law School, Myron Taylor Hall, Ithaca, NY 14853.

*Court Review*, National Center for State Courts, 300 Newport Ave., Williamsburg, VA 23187-8798.

*Criminal Defense*, Newsletter State Apellate Defender, Office Legal Resources Project, 3rd floor North Tower, 1500 6th Ave., Detroit, MI 48226.

*Criminal Justice*, Howard League, 708 Holloway Rd., London N119 3NL, England.

*Criminal Law Bulletin*, Warren, Gorham, & Lamont, 395 Hudson St., New York, NY 10014.

*Criminal Law Quarterly*, Canada Law Book Inc., 240 Edward St., Aurora, Ontario L4G 3S9 Canada.

*Criminal Law Review*, Clark-Boardman-Callaghan, 375 Hudson St., New York, NY 10014.

*Denver University Law Review*, University of Denver, College of Law, Porter Adm. Bldg., 7039 E. 18th Ave., Denver, CO 80220-1826.

*Duke Law Journal*, Duke University, School of Law, Box 90364, Durham, NC 27708-0364.

*Emory Law Journal*, Emory University, School of Law, Gambrell Hall, Atlanta, GA 30322.

*Federal Bar News-Journal*, Federal Bar Association, 2215 M Street NW, Washington, DC 20037.

*Federal Probation*, U.S. Adm. Office of the U.S. Courts, Federal Corrections & Supervision Division, Washington, DC 20402-9371.

*Federal Trial News*, American Bar Association, National Conference of Fed. Trial Judges, 750 N. Lake Shore Dr., Chicago, IL 60611.

*Georgetown Law Journal*, Georgetown University Law Center, 600 New Jersey Avenue NW, Washington, DC 20009.

*Harvard Civil Rights-Civil Liberties Law Review*, Harvard University, Harvard Law School, Publications Center, Hastings Hall, Cambridge, MA 02138.

*Harvard Law Review*, Harvard Law Review Association, Gannett House, Cambridge, MA 02138.

*Hastings Law Journal*, 200 McAllister Street, San Francisco, CA 94102-4978.

*Insurance Law Journal*, Butterworths Division of Reed International Books Australia Pty. Ltd., 271-273 Lane Cove Rd., North Ryde N.S.W. 2113, Australia.

*International Journal of Offender Therapy and Comparative Criminology*, Sage Publications, Inc., 2455 Teller Rd, Thousand Oaks, CA 91320.

*International Review of Criminal Policy*. United Nations Publications, Sales & Marketing Section, Rm. DC2-0853, New York, NY 10017.

*Journal of Crime and Justice*, Anderson Publishing Co., 2035 Reading Rd., Cincinnati, OH 45202.

*Journal of Criminal Justice*, Elsevier Science Ltd., Pergamon, P.O. Box 800, Kidlington, Oxford, OX5 1DX England.

*Journal of Criminal Law and Criminology*, Northwestern University, School of Law, 357 E. Chicago Ave., Chicago IL 60611.

*Journal of Divorce*, The Haworth Press Inc., 12 W. 32nd St., New York, NY 10001.

*The Journal of Law & Economics*, The University of Chicago Press, Journals Division, P.O. Box 37005, Chicago, IL 60637.

*Journal of Legal Education*, Assn. of American Law Schools, 1201 Connecticut Avenue NW, Ste. 800, Washington, DC 20036-2605.

*Journal of Legal Studies*, University of Chicago Press, Journals Division, Box 37005, Chicago, IL 60637.

*Journal of Psychiatry and Law*, Federal Legal Publications, Inc., 157 Chambers St., New York, NY 10007.

*Journal of Quantitative Criminology*, Plenum Publishers, 233 Spring Street, New York, NY 10013-1578.

*Journal of Research in Crime and Delinquency*, Sage Publications, Inc., 2455 Teller Rd., Thousand Oaks, CA 91320.

*Journal of Security Administration*, London House Press, BLSS Inc., Box 164509, Miami, FL 33116-4509.

*Judicature*, American Judicature Society, 180 N. Michigan Ave, Ste. 600, Chicago, IL 60601-7401.

*Jurimetrics Journal*, American Bar Association, Science & Technology Section, 750 N. Lake Shore Dr., Chicago, IL 60611.

*Law & Social Inquiry*, The University of Chicago Press, Journals Division, 750 N. Lake Shore Dr., Chicago, IL 60611.

*Law Technology*, 1000 Connecticut Ave. Suite 202, Washington, DC 20036.

*Law and Contemporary Problems*, Duke University School of Law, Room 006, Durham, NC 27706.

*Law and Human Behavior*, Plenum Publishers, 233 Spring St., New York, NY 10013.

*Law and Society Review*, Law & Society Assoc. Hampshire House, University of Massachusetts, Amherst, MA 01003.

*Legal Reference Services Quarterly*, The Haworth Press, 12 W. 32nd St., New York, NY 10001.

*The National Bar Bulletin*, The National Bar Association, 1900 L Street NW, Ste. 203, Washington, DC 20036.

*The National Journal of Criminal Defense*, National College of Criminal Defense, Bates College of Law, Houston, TX 77004.

*New England Journal on Criminal & Civil Confinement*, New England School of Law, 154 Stuart St., Boston, MA 02116-5687.

*New York University Law Review*, 110 W. 3rd St., New York, NY 10012.

*Notre Dame Law Review*, University of Notre Dame, School of Law, Box 988, Notre Dame, IN 46556.

*Pennsylvania Board of Probation and Parole*, Box 1661, Harrisburg, PA 17110.

*Probation and Parole*, U.S. Dept. Of Justice Statistics, 633 Indiana Avenue NW, 11th Fl., Washington D.C. 20531.

*Probation and Parole Law Reports*, Knehans-Miller Pub., Box 88, Warrensburg, MO 64093-0088.

*The Prosecutor*, National District Attorneys Assoc., 99 Canal Center Plaza, Ste. 510, Alexandra, VA 22314.

*Rutgers Computer and Technology Law Journal*, Rutgers University, School of Law-Newark, 15 Washington St., Newark, NJ 07102.

*Search and Seizure Law Report*, Clark-Boardman-Callaghan, 375 Hudson St., New York, NY 10014.

*Searchlight*, Rt. 8, Cormel, NY 10512.

*Soviet Law and Government*, 80 Business Park Dr., Armonk, NY 10504.

*Stanford Law Review*, School of Law, Crown Quadrangle, Stanford University, Stanford CA 94305-8610.

*Statutes & Decisions: The Laws of the USSR & Its Successor States*, M.E. Sharpe, Inc., 80 Business Park Dr., Armonk, NY 10504.

*Temple Law Review*, Temple University School of Law, Philadelphia, PA 19122.

*Trial*, Association of Trial Lawyers, 1050 31st St., NW, Washington, DC 20007.

*Uniform Commercial Code Law Journal*, Warren, Gorham & Lamont, One Penn Plaza, New York, NY 10119.

*University of Illinois Law Review*, University of Illinois at Urbana–Champaign, College of Law, Champaign, IL 61820.

*Wisconsin Law Review*, University of Wisconsin at Madison Law School, 975 Bascom Hall, Madison WI 53706-1399.

*Yale Law Journal*, Yale Journal Co., Inc., Box 208215, New Haven, CT 06520-8215.

# CRIMINOLOGY AND CRIMINAL JUSTICE

*ACJS Today Newsletter*, Academy of Criminal Justice Sciences, Suite 101, Beauregard St., Alexandria, VA 22311.

*American Journal of Criminal Justice*, The Southern Criminal Justice Assoc., School of Justice Administration, College of Urban & Public Affairs, University of Louisville, Louisville, KY 40292.

*Australian and New Zealand Journal of Criminology*, 271 273 Lane Cove Rd., North Ryde, N.S.W. 2113, Australia.

*British Journal of Criminology*, Oxford University Press, Academic Division, Great Clarendon St., Oxford OX2 6DP England.

*Canadian Journal of Criminology*, Canadian Criminal Justice Association, 383 Parkdale Avenue, Ste. 304, Ottawa, Ontario K1Y 4R4, Canada.

*Cjain*, Criminal Justice Archive & Information Network, The University of Michigan, P.O. Box 1248, Ann Arbor, Michigan 48106.

*CJ International*, CJ International, 1333 S. Wabash, Box 53, Chicago, IL 60605.

*Contemporary Crises*, Kluwer Academic Publishers, P.O. Box 17, 3300 AA Dordrecht, Amsterdam, Netherlands.

*Crime and Delinquency*, Sage Publications, Inc., 2455 Teller Rd., Thousand Oaks, CA 91320.

*Crime & Justice*, The University of Chicago Press, Journal Division, 5720 S. Woodlawn Ave., Chicago, IL 60637.

*Crime, Law & Social Change*, Kluwer Academic Publishers, P.O. Box 17, 3300 AA Dordrecht, Amsterdam, Netherlands.

*Crime and Social Justice*, P.O. Box 40601, San Francisco, CA 94140.

*Criminal Justice and Behavior*, Sage Publications, Inc., 2455 Teller Rd., Thousand Oaks, CA 91320.

*Criminal Justice Ethics*, Institute for Criminal Justice Ethics, John Jay College of Criminal Justice, 444 W. 56th St., New York, NY 10019.

*Criminal Justice Newsletter*, Pace Pub. Inc. 443 Park Avenue S., New York, NY 10016.

*Criminal Justice Policy Review*, Center for Criminal Justice, University of Massachusetts Boston, Boston MA 02125-3393.

*Criminal Justice Review*, Georgetown State University, Box 4018, University Plaza, Atlanta, GA 30303-4018.

*Criminologist*, Countrywise Press Ltd. Little London, Chichester West Sussex, P.O. 19 IPG England.

*The Criminologist*, American Society of Criminology, 1314 Kinnear Rd., Ste. 212, Columbus, OH 43212.

*Criminology*, American Society of Criminology, 1314 Kinnear Rd., Ste. 212, Columbus, OH 43212.

*Criminology: An Interdisciplinary Journal*, American Society of Criminology, 1314 Kinnear Rd., Ste. 212, Columbus OH 43212.

*The International Criminal Justice Review*, College of Public & Urban Affairs, Georgia State University, University Plaza, Atlanta, GA 30303-3091.

*International Journal of the Sociology of Law*, Academic Press Ltd., 24-28 Oval Rd., London NW1-7DX England.

*International Journal of Comparative and Applied Criminal Justice*, Dept. of Criminal Justice, Box 135, Wichita, KS 67260.

*International Journal of Offender Therapy and Comparative Criminology*, Sage Publications, Inc., 2455 Teller Rd, Thousand Oaks, CA 91320.

*International Review of Criminal Policy*, United Nations, Sales & Marketing Section, Rm DC2-0853, New York, NY 10017.

*Journal of Contemporary Criminal Justice*, Sage Publications, Inc., 2455 Teller Rd, Thousand Oaks, CA 91320.

*Journal of Crime and Justice*, Anderson Publishing Co., 2035 Reading Rd., Cincinnati, OH 45202.

*Journal of Criminal Justice*, Pergamon & Maxwell House, Fairview Park, Elmsford, NY 10523.

*Journal of Criminal Justice Education*, Academy of Criminal Justice Sciences, Suite 101, Beauregard St., Alexandria, VA 22311.

*Journal of Criminal Law and Criminology*, Northwestern University, School of Law, 357 E. Chicago Ave., Chicago IL 60611.

*Journal of Interpersonal Violence*, Sage Publications, Inc. 2111 Hillcrest Dr., Newbury Park, CA 91320.

*Journal of Research in Crime and Delinquency*, Sage Publications, Inc., 2455 Teller Rd., Thousand Oaks, CA 91320.

*Judicature: The Journal of the American Judicature Society*, AJS, 25 East Washington St., Chicago IL 60602.

*The Justice Professional*, Criminal Justice Institute, Long Island University, C.W. Post Campus, Roth Hall, Brookville NY 11548.

*The Justice Professional*, Dept. of Sociology & Social Work, Pembroke State University, Pembroke, NE 28372.

*Justice Quarterly*, Academy of Criminal Justice Sciences, Suite 101, Beauregard St., Alexandria, VA 22311.

*Sociology & Social Research Journal*, Dept. of Sociology, University of Southern California, University Park, Los Angeles, CA 90089-0032.

*Victimology: An International Journal*, Victimology Inc., 2333 N. Vernon St., Arlington, VA 22207.

*Women in Criminal Justice*, 10 Alice St., Binghamton, NY 13904-1580.

# FORENSICS

*American Journal of Forensic Medicine and Pathology*, Lippincoh-Reven Pub., 227 E. Washington Sq., Philadelphia, PA 19106.

*American Journal of Law and Medicine*, American Society of Law, Medicine & Ethics, 765 Commonwealth Ave., Ste. 1634, Boston, MA 02215.

*The Expert and the Law*, National Forensic Center, 17 Temple Terr., Lawrenceville, NJ 08648.

*Forensic Accounting Review*, Computer Protection Systems, Inc., 12275 Appletree Dr., Plymouth, MI 48170-3739.

*Forensic Science Gazette*, Box 35728, Dallas, TX 75235.

*Identification News*, International Assoc. for Identification, Box 6054 Kinston, NC 28501-0054.

*Inform Quarterly Newsletter*, Int. Reference Org. in Forensic Medicine & Sciences, c/o Dr. William G. Eckert Ed., 3114 State St. Dr, New Orleans, LA 70125-4241.

*Journal of Forensic Sciences*, 1916 Race Street, Philadelphia, PA 19103.

*Medico Legal Bulletin*, Department of Health, Medical Examiner Division, 9 North 14th Street, Richmond, VA 23219.

*News & Views in Forensic Pathology*, American Academy of Forensic Sciences & The Forensic Sciences Foundation, Inc., 11400 Rockville Pike, Ste. 515, Rockville MD 20852.

*News & Views in Forensic Toxicology*, American Academy of Forensic Sciences & The Forensic Sciences Foundation, Inc., 11400 Rockville Pike Ste. 515, Rockville MD 20852.

# JUVENILE DELINQUENCY

*Juvenile and Family Court Journal*, National Council of Juvenile and Family Court Judges, P.O. Box 8970, Reno, NV 89507.

*Juvenile Justice*, National Council of Juvenile Court Judges. Judicial College Bld., University of Nevada, Reno, NV 89507.

*Juvenile Justice Digest*, Washington Crime News Services, 3918 Prosperity Ave., Ste. 318, Fairfax, VA 22031-3334.

*Juvenile Law Digest*, National Council of Juvenile & Family Court Judges, P.O. Box 8978, Reno NV 89507.

# NARCOTICS AND DRUG ABUSE

*Advance in Alcohol and Substance Abuse*, The Haworth Press, Inc., 12 W. 32nd St., New York, NY 10001.

*Alcoholism Treatment Quarterly*, The Haworth Press, Inc., 10 Alice St., Binghamton, NY 13904.

*Bulletin on Narcotics*, United Nations Publications, Rm DC2-0853, New York, NY 10017.

*Contemporary Drug Problems*, Federal Legal Publications, Inc., 157 Chambers St., New York, NY 10007.

*Drug Abuse & Alcoholism Newsletter*, Vista Hill Foundation, 3420 Camino del Rio North, Ste. 100, San Diego, CA 92108.

*Drug Enforcement*, (BNDD Bulletin) Drug Enforcement Administration/U.S. Dept. Justice, 1405 I St. NW, Washington, DC 20537.

*Drugs and Society*, The Haworth Press, Inc., 12 W. 32nd St., New York, NY 10001.

*Drugs in the Work Place*, Business Research Publications, Inc. 817 Broadway, New York NY 10003.

*International Drug Report*, International Narcotic Enforcement Officers Association, 112 State St., Ste. 1200, Albany, NY 12207.

*Journal of Adolescent Chemical Dependency*, The Haworth Press, Inc., 12 W. 32nd St., New York, NY10001.

*Journal of Chemical Dependency Treatment*, The Haworth Press, Inc., 10 Alice St., New York, NY 13904.

*Journal of Drug Issues*, Box 4201, Tallahassee, FL 32303.

*Narcotics Control Digest*, Washington Crime News Services, 3918 Prosperity Ave., Ste. 318, Fairfax, VA 22031.

*Substance Abuse Issues*, Movish & McLennan Comp., 1166 Avenue of the Americas, New York, NY 10036.

*Washington Drug Letter*, Washington Bus. Information Inc.,1117 N. 19th St., Arlington, VA 22209.

# POLICE

*Accident Analysis and Prevention*, Elsevier Science Ltd., Pergamon, P.O. Box 800, Kidlington, Oxford OX5 1DX, England.

*American Journal of Police*, Anderson Publishing Co., 2035 Reading Rd., Cincinnati, OH 45202. Now see: *Policing: An International Journal of Police Strategies and Management.*

*Australian Police Journal*, New S. Wales Police Dept., Co. G.P.O. Box 45 Sydney N.S.W. 2001, Australia.

*California Highway Patrolman*, Box 161209, Sacramento, CA 95816.

*Campus Law Enforcement Journal*, Int. Association of Campus Law Enforcement Administration, 638 Prospect Ave., Hartford, CT 06105.

*Canadian Police Chief Newsletter*, Canadian Association of Chiefs of Police, 130 Albert St., Ste. 1710, Ottawa, Ontario, K1P 5G4, Canada.

*Canadian Police College Journal*, P.O. Box 8900 Ottawa, Ontario, K1G 3J2, Canada.

*FBI Law Enforcement Bulletin*, U.S. Federal Bureau of Investigation, FBI Academy, Madison Bldg, Rm 209, Quantico, VA 22135.

*From the State Capitals*, Public Safety, 300 N. Washington St., Alexandria, VA 22314.

*Georgia FOP News*, 2684 Industrial Row, Troy, MI 40804.

*Illinois Police Association Official Journal*, Illinois Police Association, 220 Yosemite Cir. N., Minneapolis, MN 55422-5032.

*Illinois Sheriff's News*, 413 West Monroe, Springfield, IL 62705.

*International Criminal Police Review*, International Criminal Police Organization, Secretariat General-Organization Internationale de Police Criminelle, 200 quai Charles de Gaulle, 69006 Lyon, France.

*International Drug Report*, Suite 1200, 112 State Street, Albany, NY 12207.

*Iowa Police Journal*, Iowa State Policeman's Association, Box 1768, Fort Dodge, IA 50501.

*Journal of Drug Education*, Baywood Publ. Inc., 26 Austin Ave., Box 337, Amityville, NY 11701.

*Journal of Police Science and Administration*, International Association of Chiefs of Police, Inc., Ste. 200, 1110 N. Glebe Rd., Arlington, VA 22201.

*The Justice System Journal*, Institute for Court Management, Denver, CO 80202.

*Kansas Peace Officer*, Box 2592, Wichita, Kansas 67201.

*Law Enforcement Journal*, Box 21, Bethel Island, CA 94511.

*Law Enforcement News*, John Jay College of Criminal Justice, 899 Tenth Ave., New York, NY 10019.

*Law Enforcement Technology*, PTN Publishing Corp., 445 Broad Hollow Rd., Ste 21, Melville, NY 11747-4722.

*Law Officer's Bulletin*, The Bureau of National Affairs, Inc., 1231 25th Street NW, Washington, DC 20037.

*Law and Order*, Hendon Inc., 1000 Skokie Blvd., Wilmette, IL 60091.

*Long Island Police News*, Box 36, Copiague, NY 11726.

*Maryland Crime Control Directory*, Box 3208, Baltimore, Maryland 21228.

*Michigan Peace Officer*, State Lodge of Michigan, G 3094 Bertha, Flint, Michigan 48504.

*Michigan Police Chief's Newsletter*, Michigan Association of Chiefs of Police, No. 200,Okemos, MI 48864.

*Military Police*, U.S. Army M.P. School, Ft. McClellan, Alabama 36205.

*Minnesota Police Journal*, Minnesota Police and Peace Officers Association, 375 Shelby Ave., St. Paul, MN 55102.

*Minnesota Sheriff*, 287 E. Sixth Street, St. Paul, MN 55101.

*Missouri Police Chiefs Journal*, Central Missouri State University, Suite 400 A. Hunphrey's Blds, Warrensburg, MO 64093.

*Narcotics Control Digest*, Washington Crime News Services, 3918 Prosperity Ave., Ste. 318, Fairfax, VA 22031-3334.

*National Police Review*, National Police Association, 7811 Old Tree Run, Louisville, KY 40222-4694.

*Newsletter for Dispatchers*, PSCS Ltd., 1807 24th Ave., Longmont, CO 80501.

*Oklahoma Law Enforcement Bulletin*, State Bureau of Investigation, 2132 N.E. 36th, Oklahoma City, OK 73107.

*On The Beat*, 299 Broadway, New York, NY 10007.

*Pennsylvania Chiefs of Police Association Bulletin*, Pennsylvania Chiefs of Police Association, Public Relations Committee, 2941 N. Front St., Harrisburg, PA 17110.

*Pennsylvania Police Criminal Law Bulletin*, Stanley Cohen, Ed & Pub., 2579 Warren Rd., Indiana, PA 15701.

*Police*, Police Federation of England & Wales, 15 17 Langley Rd., Surbiton, Surrey, KT6 6LP England.

*Police*, Bobit Publishing Co., 2512 Artesia Blvd., Redondo Beach, CA 92278.

*Police and Law Enforcement*, AMS Press Inc., 56 E. 13th Street, New York, NY 10003.

*Police Chief*, International Assoc. of Chiefs of Police Inc., 515 N. Washington St., Ste. 400, Alexandria, VA 22314-2340.

*Police Journal*, Barry Rose Law Periodicals, Little London, Chichester, W. Sussex, P019 IPG England.

*Police Law Journal*, Appalachian State University, Boone, NC 28608.

*Police: The Law Officer Magazine*, Hare Publications, 6200 Yarrow Dr., Carlsbad, CA 92008.

*The Police Plaintiff*, North Publishing, Box 3132, Glen Ellyn, IL 60138-3132.

*Police Review*, Police Review Pub. Co., Celcon House, 5th Fl., 289-293 High Holborn, London WC1V 7HU, England.

*Police Studies*, Anderson Publishing Co., 2035 Reading Rd., Cincinnati, OH 45202. Now see: *Policing: An International Journal of Police Strategies and Management.*

*Police Times*, American Federation of Police, 3801 Biscayne Blvd., Miami, FL 33137.

*Policing: An International Journal of Police Strategies and Management*, MCB University Press Ltd., 60-62 Toller Ln., Bradford, West Yorkshire BD8 9BY, England.

*Policing & Society: An International Journal of Research & Policy*, International Publishers Distributor, Box 32160, Newark, NJ 07102.

*Royal Canadian Mounted Police Quarterly*, Royal Canadian Mounted Police, Ottawa, Ontario, K1A OR2 Canada.

*Sheriff Magazine*, Nat. Sheriff's Assoc. 1450 Duke St., Alexandria, VA 22314-3490.

*Sheriff and Police Reporter*, 1506 Brigman Ave., No. A, Jefferson, IN 47130-4710.

# SECURITY AND CRIME PREVENTION

*Access Control & Security Investigation*, Intertec Publishing Corp., 6151 Powers Ferry Rd. NW, Atlanta, GA 30339-2491.

*Alert Bulletin*, Aviation Crime Prevention Institute, P.O. Box 3443, Frederick, MD 21701.

*Assets Protection*, Assets Protections Pub., P.O. Box 5323, Madison, WI 53705-0323.

*Bank Fraud*, Bank Administration Foundation, 1 N. Franklin St., Chicago, IL 60606.

*Burning Issues*, ANSUL Fire Protection, 1 Stanton St., Marinette, WI 54143-2542.

*Canadian Security*, Security Publishing Ltd., 46 Crockford Blvd., Scarborough, ON M1R 3C3 Canada.

*Cerberus Security*, Cerberus Ltd., Maennedorf, Switzerland, C 4 8798.

*College Security Report*, Rusting Publications, P.O. Box 190, Port Washington, NY 11050.

*Computer Security*, Computer Security Institute, 360 Church St., Northborough, MA 01532.

*Computer Security Digest*, Computer Protection Systems, Inc., 12275 Appletree Dr., Plymouth, MI 48170-3739.

*Corporate Security Digest*, Washington Crime News Services, 3918 Prosperity Ave., Ste. 318, Fairfax, VA 22031-3334.

*Corporate Security International*, Lloyd's of London Press, 611 Broadway, New York, NY 10003.

*Counter-Terrorism & Security Intelligence*, Interests, Ltd., 8512 Cedar St., Silver Spring, MD 20910-4322.

*Credit Card Merchant*, Fraud & Theft Information Bureau, 217 N. Seacrest Blvd., P.O. Box 400, Boynton Beach, FL 33425.

*Crime Control Digest*, Washington Crime News Services, 3918 Prosperity Ave., Ste. 318, Fairfax, VA 22031-3334.

*Crime Prevention Review*, Attorney General's Office Crime Prevention Unit, 3580 Wilshire Blvd., Suite 938, Los Angeles, CA 90010.

*Cryptologia*, Rose-Hulman Institute of Technology, Terre Haute, IN 47803.

*Data Processing & Communications Security*, Assets Protection Pub., P.O. Box 5323, Madison, WI 53705.

*EDPACS, The EDP Audit Control and Security Newsletter*, One Penn Plaza, New York, NY 101119.

*Employment Screening & Testing Report*, Strafford Pub., Inc., 1375 Peachtree Street NE, Ste. 235, Atlanta, GA 30367.

*The Expert Witness Journal*, Expertise Institute, Inc., Box 38-1494, Miami, FL 33138.

*Hospital Security & Safety Management*, Rusting Publications, P.O. Box 190, Port Washington, NY11050.

*IFAR Reports*, International Foundation for Art Research Inc., 500 Fifth Ave, Ste. 1234, New York, NY 10110.

*The Investigative Journal*, PI Pub. Inc., P.O. Box 11628, Jacksonville, FL 32239-1628.

*Investigative News*, Marathon Press, 13575 Martinique Dr., Chino Hills, CA 91709.

*The Investigator*, John E. Reid & Associates, Inc., 250 S. Wacker Dr., Ste. 1100, Chicago, IL 60606.

*The Journal of Polygraph Science*, National Training Center of Lie Detection, Inc., 200 W. 57th St., Ste. 1400, New York, NY 10019.

*Library Security Newsletter*, The Haworth Press, Library and Archival Security, 149 5th Ave., New York, NY 10010.

*The Lipman Report*, Gaurusmark, Inc., P.O. Box 444, Memphis, TN 38101.

*Military Police Journal*, U.S. Army MP School, Ft. McClellan, AL 36205-5030.

*On The Line Newsletter*, American Correctional Assn., 4321 Hartwick Rd., Ste. L-208, College Park, MD 20740.

*Parking Security Report*, Rusting Pub., P.O. Box 190, Port Washington, NY 11050.

*Police & Security Bulletin*, Lomond Pub., P.O. Box 88, Mt. Airy, MD 21771.

*Police & Security News*, Days Communications, Inc., 1690 Quarry Rd., Kulpsville, PA 19443.

*Privacy Journal*, P.O. Box 15300, Washington, DC 20003.

*Private Security Case Law Reporter*, Strafford Pub., Inc., Specialized Info. Services, 590 Dutch Valley Rd. NE, Drawer 13729, Atlanta, GA 30324-0729.

*Protection of Assets Bulletin*, The Merritt Company, P.O. Box 955, Santa Monica, CA 90406.

*Protection News*, International Foundation for Protection Officers, Bellingham Business Park, 4200 Meridian, Ste. 200, Bellingham, WA 98226.

*Risk Assessment*, Business Risks Int., 3100 West End Ave., Ste. 550, Nashville, TN 37203.

*Risk Report*, Int. Risk Management Inst., Inc., 12222 Merit Dr., Ste. 1660, Dallas, TX 75251-2217.

*Risk Retention Reporter*, Insurance Communications, P.O. Box 50147, Pasadena, CA 91115.

*Security*, Cahners Pub. Co., Division of Reed Elsevier Inc., Box 5080, E. Touhy Ave., Des Plaines, IL 60018-5080.

*Security Distribution and Marketing*, 1350 E. Touhy Ave., Box 5080, Des Plaines IL 60018-5080.

*Security Gazette*, AGB Business Pub. Ltd., Maclaven House, 19 Scarbrook Rd., Croydon, CR9 1QH, England.

*Security Journal*, Elsevier Science Ireland Ltd., P.O. Box 85, Limerick, Ireland.

*Security Law Newsletter*, 2125 Bancroft Place NW, Washington, DC 20008-4019.

*Security Letter*, Robert D. McCrie, Ed & Pub., 166 E. 96th St., New York, NY 10128.

*Security Management*, ASIS, 1655 North Fort Myer Dr., Ste. 1200, Arlington, VA 22209-3198.

*Security Management Bulletin*, Bureau of Business Practice, 24 Rope Ferry Rd., Waterford, CT 06386.

*Security Personnel Newsletter*, Security Seminars Press, P.O. Box 70162, Ocala, FL 32670.

*Security Police Digest*, U.S. Air Force Chief of Security Police, Washington, DC 20314.

*Signal*, Suite 1150, 170 Pennsylvania Blvd. NW, Washington, DC 20004.

*Social Defense*, Government of India, Dept. Of Publications, Civil Lines, Delhi 110 054, India.

*Terrorism*, J.L. Scherer, 4900 18th Ave., South Minneapolis, MN 55417.

*TVI Report (Terrorism, Violence, Insurgency Journal)*, TVI Inc., Box 849, Klamath Falls, OR 97601.

*Wrongful Termination Litigation Reporter*, Andrews Publication, Inc., P.O. Box 200, Edgemont, PA 19028.

## SELECTED POLITICAL SCIENCE JOURNALS

*American Journal of Political Science*, University of Wisconsin Press, Journal Division, 114 N. Murray St., Madison, WI 53715.

*American Political Science Review*, American Political Science Assoc., 1527 New Hampshire Avenue NW, Washington, DC 20036.

*American Politics Quarterly*, Sage Publications, Inc., 2455 Teller Rd., Thousand Oaks, CA 91320.

*Journal of Politics*, Southern Political Sciences Association, University of Texas Press, Journal Division, Box 7819, Austin, TX 78713.

*New American*, American Opinion Pub. Inc., Box 8040, Applerton, WI 54913.

*Policy Review*, The Heritage Foundation, 214 Massachussetts Avenue NE, Washington, DC 20002.

*Political Research Quarterly*, University of Utah, 252 Orson Spencer Hall, Salt Lake City, UT 84112.

*Political Science Quarterly*, The Academy of Political Science, 475 Riverside Dr., Ste. 1274, New York, NY 10115-1274.

## SELECTED PSYCHOLOGY JOURNALS

*American Academy of Psychiatry and the Law Journal*, American Academy of Psychiatry & the Law, Box 30, Bloomfield, CT 06002-0030.

*Archives of General Psychiatry*, American Medical Association, 515 N. State St., Chicago, IL 60610.

*Criminal Justice and Behavior*, Sage Publications, Inc., 2455 Teller Rd., Thousand Oaks, CA 91320.

*Journal of the American Psychoanalytic Association*, International University Press, 59 Boston Post Rd., Madison, CT 06443.

*Journal of Applied Behavior Analysis*, Society for the Experimental Analysis of Behavior, Inc., c/o Dept. of Human Development, University of Kansas, Lawrence, KS 66045.

*Journal of Applied Social Psychology*, V.H. Winston & Sons, Inc., c/o Bellwether Pub., Ltd., 8640 Guilford Rd, Ste. 200, Columbia, MD 21046.

*Journal of Personality*, Duke University Press, Box 90660, Durham, NC 27708-0660.

*Journal of Psychiatry & Law*, Federal Legal Publications, Inc., 157 Chambers St., New York, NY 10007.

*Journal of Research in Personality*, Academic Press Inc., 525 B St., Ste. 1900, San Diego, CA 92101-4495.

*Journal of Social Psychology*, Heldref Pub., 1319 Eighteenth Street NW, Washington, DC 20036-1802.

*Law and Human Behavior*, Plenum Publishers, 233 Spring St., New York, NY 10013.

The following journals are published by the American Psychological Association, 1200 17th Street NW, Washington, DC 20036:

*Behavioral Neuroscience*

*Clinician's Research Digest*

*Contemporary Psychology*

*Developmental Psychology*

*Journal of Abnormal Psychology*

*Journal of Applied Psychology*

*Journal of Comparative Psychology*

*Journal of Consulting and Clinical Psychology*

*Journal of Counseling Research and Practice*

*Journal of Educational Psychology*

*Journal of Experimental Psychology: Animal Behavior Processes*

*Journal of Experimental Psychology: General*

*Journal of Experimental Psychology: Human Perception and Performance*

*Journal of Experimental Psychology: Learning, Memory, and Cognition*

*Journal of Personality and Social Psychology*

*Psychological Abstracts*

*Psychological Assessment*

*Psychology, Public Policy and Law*

Also consult the book titled *Journals in Psychology: A Resource Listing Authors*, current edition. The *Journals in Psychology* is a reference source and can answer many of your questions about where to submit your papers for publication. *Journals in Psychology*, APA's directory written exclusively for psychology authors, gives you complete information on over 280 U.S. periodicals in the behavioral and social sciences. All this information in one guidebook helps save time, money, and effort. It contains editor's name/address, editorial policy, circulation, index terms, publisher, select notes on submissions, and more.

## SELECTED SOCIOLOGY JOURNALS

*Adolescence*, Libra Pub., 3089 Clairmont Dr., Ste. 383, San Diego, CA 92117.

*American Behavioral Scientist*, Sage Publications, Inc., 2455 Teller Rd., Thousand Oaks, CA 91320.

*American Journal of Sociology*, University of Chicago Press, Journals Division, Box 37005, Chicago, IL60637.

*American Sociological Review*, American Sociological Assoc., 1722 N. Street NW, Washington, DC 20036.

*Child Welfare*, Transaction Pub., Transaction Periodicals Consortium, Dept., 3092, Rutgers University, New Brunswick, NJ 08903.

*Environment and Behavior*, Sage Publications, Inc., 2455 Teller Rd.,Thousand Oaks, CA 91320.

*Family Process*, Family Process Inc., Box 460, Vernon, NJ 07462- 0460.

*Journal of Applied Behavioral Science*, Sage Publications, Inc., 2455 Teller Rd, Thousand Oaks, CA 91320.

*Social Justice Review*, Catholic Central Union of America, 3835 Westminster Place, St. Louis, MO 63108-3409.

## MISCELLANEOUS

*American Journal of Orthopsychiatry*, 19 W. 44th St., New York, NY 40036.

*American Polygraph Association Newsletter*, American Polygraph Association, Box 8037, Chatanooga, TN 37414-0037.

*California Office of Criminal Justice Planning Bulletin*, 3149 Clairidge Way, Sacramento, CA 95823.

*Community Home Schools Gazette*, 85 Exeter Road, Dawlish EX7 OA6 England.

*Economic Crime Digest*, National District Attorneys Association, 1033 N. Fairfax St., Ste. 200, Alexandria, VA 22314-1503.

*Family and Conciliation Courts Review*, Sage Publications, Inc., 2455 Teller Rd.,Thousand Oaks, CA 91320.

*Fire and Arson Investigator*, V.G. Reed & Sons, Inc., 300 S. Broadway, Ste. 100, St. Louis, MO 63102-2808.

*Full Disclosure*, Box 1533, Oil City, PA 16301-5533.

*IACP News*, IACP Publications, Dept. 1110, N. Glebe Rd., Ste. 200, Arlington, VA 22201.

*Insurance Industry Newsletter*, Box 18630, 4325 Old Shepherdsville Rd., Louisville, KY 40218.

*Interface*, Search Group. Inc., 7311 Green Haven Dr., Ste. 145, Sacramento, CA 31036.

*International Journal of Comparative and Applied Criminal Justice*, Department of Criminal Justice, Box 135, Wichita State University, Wichita, KA 67260-0135.

*International Risk Management*, Inst. Inc., 12222 Ment Dr., Ste. 1660, Dallas, TX 75251-2217.

*Journal of Family Violence*, Plenum Publishers, 233 Spring St., New York, NY 10013-1578.

*The Journal of Polygraph Science*, The Nat. Training Center of Lie Detection, Inc., 200 W. 57th St., Ste. 1400, New York, NY 10019.

*Organized Crime Digest*, Washington Crime News Services, 3918 Prosperity Ave., Ste. 318, Fairfax, VA 22031-3334.

*Polygraph*, APA, P.O. Box 8037, Chattanooga, TN 37414-0037

*RAND Checklist*, Published Monthly, The RAND Corporation, 1700 Main St., P.O. Box 2138, Santa Monica, CA 90406-2138.

*The Sentinel Industrial Risk Insurers*, 85 Woodlands St., Hartford, CT 06120.

*Victimology*, Victimology Inc., 2333 N. Vernon St., Arlington, VA 22207.

*Violence & Victims*, Springer Publ. Company, 536 Broadway, New York, NY 10012-3955.

*Violence Update*, Sage Publications, Inc., 2455 Teller Rd., Thousands Oaks, CA.

## AUTHORS' NOTE

The following works were consulted in the original compilation of this chapter.

*The Serials Directory*, An International Reference Book, EBSCO Publishing Division of EBSCO Industries.

*The Standard Periodical Directory*, 14th Edition, Oxbridge Community, Inc. 1991.

*Ulrich's International Periodicals Directory*, 29th Edition, R.R. Bowker, Division of Reed Pub. (USA) Inc., New York.

# General Reference Sources

Reference materials are guides to information about particular subjects. They may be general, such as an encyclopedia that encompasses a wide variety of subjects, or they may be specific, such as a dictionary of legal terms. Students new to the research process may be overwhelmed by the number of reference sources to be found in most libraries. Sometimes there is overlapping and repetition among the sources, so certain information may be found in several different places. Generally, however, reference materials are designed to fill a specific need, and each will have some new information to contribute to the field.

Dictionaries, encyclopedias, bibliographies, biographical indices, directories, almanacs, and atlases are all examples of reference materials. They are designed to be consulted for specific information, rather than read from cover to cover. These references are not circulated outside the library but can be checked out for use within the library, usually for a set period of time.

Among the major reference sources listed in this section are:

*Biographies:* Written histories of an individual's life which gives an account of their achievements.

*Dictionaries:* Reference books that list alphabetically names or terms that are of importance to the discipline.

*Encyclopedias:* Collections of general information and knowledge that give a comprehensive treatment to the particular subject arranged in alphabetical order.

*Almanacs:* Publications usually published annually that contain information in statistical or tabular form.

*Newspapers:* One of the fastest sources of information available to the general public. Although they may not be the most accurate, most major newspapers are archived on microfilm and provide a source for the retrieval of contemporary journalism.

*Annuals and Yearbooks:* Annuals are publications that are published each year. Yearbooks are compilations of statistics or facts.

*Information Guides:* Collections and classifications concerning the storage and retrieval of recorded knowledge.

## THE FLOOD OF INFORMATION

As can be seen by the vast number of listings in this book, the student/scholar is faced with a tremendous amount of information. There are several types of information sources. The researchers should be aware of the distinctions between them.

*Primary Source:* The original data or information.

*Secondary Source:* Information of data that has been edited, analyzed, evaluated, or manipulated. Secondary sources are usually books or articles.

*Scholarly Literature:* Journals such as *Criminology* or *Justice Quarterly* are written by scholars for other scholars.

*Professional Literature:* Magazines such as *Police Chief* that are written for the practitioner in the field.

*Popular Literature:* Magazines that are indexed in the *Reader's Guide to Periodical Literature*. This would include magazines such as *Time, Newsweek,* and *U.S. News and World Report*.

*Guide to Reference Books*, Tenth Edition. Eugene P. Sheelty (ed.). Often refered to as the "granddaddy" of all guides to reference books, this is the most extensive work available on reference sources. Of special interest to the criminal justice researcher is the section on social and behavioral sciences which contains more than 300 pages. (Chicago: American Library Association, 1986).

*American Reference Books Annual*, Wynar, Bohdan S. (ed.). Annual. This is a comprehensive listing of reference books published in the United States during the preceding year with brief descriptive reviews. It is arranged by subject, then by type of reference work. Index. (Littleton, CO: Libraries Unlimited, 1970 to date).

*Editorial Research Reports*. This is an excellent source for an overview of a topic. Extensive articles are presented on newsworthy topics, such as "Capital Punishment" (March, 1995), "Teenage Crime" (March, 1996), "Hate Crimes" (January, 1993), "Drugs" (March 1993), "Prison Overcrowding" (February, 1994), and "Gun Control" (June, 1994). Bibliographies at the end of each chapter lead to further materials. Weekly updates. (Washington, DC: Congressional Quarterly Inc., 1991 to present).

*How and Where to Find the Facts: Researching Criminology*. Jack E. Whitehorse. (Saratoga, CA: R & E Publishers, 1983).

*How and Where to Find the Facts: Researching Corrections Including Probation and Pardon*. (Saratoga, CA: R & E Publishers, 1983).

## BIOGRAPHY

*Webster's Biographical Dictionary*. The purpose of this Merriam-Webster Dictionary is to provide in a single volume a work of biographical reference not restricted in its selection of names by considerations of historical period, nationality, race, religion, or occupation, and to supply the reader with full information on the syllabic division and the pronunciation of the names included. Since the Dictionary is intended primarily for English-speaking users, American and British names have been included on a generous scale and often accorded fuller treatment.

The number of names included (upwards of 40,000) will be found adequate for the usual purposes of most consultants. Only in certain classes of contemporaries may some consultants feel an inadequacy. The names of persons prominent (sometimes only briefly) in sports, in motion pictures, in the contemporary theater, and in radio are so numerous that the editors were compelled, however reluctantly, to curtail their representation to the minimum, relying on the many specialized works of reference and the great volume of current periodical literature in these fields to supply the wants of consultants particularly interested in such names. As for the treatment given each entry, every effort has been made to provide information most likely to be sought by the consultants of this Dictionary. Names of persons included because of a single incident, a single writing, a single discovery, are accorded the briefest treatment, with emphasis duly laid on this single item. In this way, additional space has been obtained to provide longer entries for persons whose lives or works contain many details likely to be sought by the consultant.

# REFERENCE BOOKS

*Guide to Microforms in Print,* James A. Dias (ed.). This is an annual, cumulative, alphabetized guide to books, journals, and other materials with the exception of theses and dissertations that are available in microform from United States publishers. (Washington, DC: Microcard Editions, 1990).

*Introduction to Reference Work.* Volume I: Basic Information Sources. Volume II: Reference Services and Reference Processes. The first volume concerns basic reference sources: bibliographies, abstracts, indexes, etc. The second volume explores channels of communication, reference searches, automation, and other reference services and processes. (New York: McGraw-Hill, 1987).

*National Directory of Addresses and Telephone Numbers.* This directory has information for more than 75,000 corporations, all SEC registered companies, major law and accounting firms, banks and financial institutions, zip and area code guide, toll-free numbers, hotels and vacation resorts, consumer/government information, airlines, and car rental agencies. It has information regarding the federal government, executive, legislative and judicial branches, independent agencies, federal information centers, embassies, county and state government offices, colleges and universities, 2- and 4-year colleges, graduate schools and programs. It also has information on associations and organizations, national associations, foundations, political parties, unions, UN agencies and missions, computer hardware/software services, hospitals, media and information sources, newspapers, magazines, radio, TV stations and cable, business newsletters, research services, business service firms, advertising agencies, brokerage firms, messengers and couriers, business finance sources, venture capital firms, SBA offices, and state and local lending institutions. (Hillside, IL: Concord Reference Books).

*The Reference Shelf. The Reference Shelf* has been a dependable source of objective and thorough coverage of vital and often controversial social issues and trends, providing timely information for research papers and oral reports, classroom discussion and debate, and independent study. Consisting of excerpts from a wide range of influential publications, each of the six *Reference Shelf* compila-

tions published each year is devoted to a single issue of contemporary concern, and covers historical background, current concerns, and future implications. The 1985 volume of *The Reference Shelf* will give the same balanced coverage to these important topics: immigration, the federal deficit, sports in America, drugs and alcohol, capital punishment, representative American speeches, 1984-1985. (Bronx, NY: H.W. Wilson Co., 1990).

*A Research Guide for Law Enforcement and the Criminal Justice System.* Jack E. Whitehouse. This publication is a comprehensive bibliography of bibliographies, journals, research and reference materials published prior to 1983. This 162-page (in very small print) source book lists references for a full range of criminal justice topics including research methodology, general reference, demography and social indicators, field operations, investigations, police methods and tactics, auxiliary and staff functions, police community relations, comparative police administration, forensic sciences, industrial security, police management, police personnel administration, courts, corrections, probation and parole, crime and criminology, specific crimes (i.e., arson, burglary, kidnaping, etc.), juvenile delinquency, crime prevention, terrorism, extremist groups, violence, civil disorder, criminal law, social problems and criminal justice related journals. This is an excellent bibliography although some of the material is somewhat dated. (Saratoga, CA: R & E Publishers, 1983).

*State Court Organization.* This publication presents an overview of the structure, administration, and jurisdiction of court systems in all 50 states and United States territories. It contains information regarding aspects of the states' judicial systems. Comparisons of the existing court system and the American Bar Association Standards relating to court organization is included. (Williamsburg, VA: American Bar Association Committee on Implementation of Judicial Administration, National Center for State Courts Publications Department).

*Use of Criminology Literature.* Martin Wright (ed.). This publication provides a guide to major literature sources and reference tools through the collection of short chapters on specific topics relating to criminology. A variety of topics is included. (Hamden, CT: Archon Books, 1974).

Reference materials that provide assistance to the criminal justice student include those concerned with political and social science, as well as psychology. Selected references in these areas are described below.

## POLITICAL SCIENCE

*The Book of States*. This biennial publication presents information on the structure, operations, financial, and functional activities of state governments. It also provides a complete listing of elected state officials and members of the legislature. Up-to-date supplements are provided. (Lexington, KY: Council of State Governments).

## GENERAL REFERENCES

*American Reformers*. Alden Whitman (ed.). Offering concise biographies of 508 men and women who were the principal architects of reform in America from the seventeenth century to modern times, this authoritative reference work is designed for students and the general reader. The book considers a broad range of reformers from all political and ideological persuasions, including the movements for religious tolerance, abolition, freedom of speech, Native American rights, racial and sexual equality, universal suffrage, labor rights, prison reform, and temperance. The list of subjects includes such well known reformers as Anne Hutchinson, Thomas Paine, Henry David Thoreau, Harriet Tubman, Harriet Beecher Stowe, "Mother" Bloor, Eugene V. Debs, Herbert Croly, Margaret Sanger, Clarence Darrow, Louis Brandies, and Malcolm X. However, *American Reformers* is especially notable for its coverage of those men and women active in numerous causes who are not so widely known or written about. (Bronx, NY: H.W. Wilson Co., 1985).

*The Standard Periodical Directory*. This directory includes information on approximately 20,000 periodicals published in the United States and Canada. (New York: Oxbridge Communications, 1997).

*Subject Directory of Special Libraries and Information Centers*. Margaret Young, et al. (eds.). This is an excellent source containing names and addresses of law and other special libraries. (Detroit: Gale Research, 1990).

*Ulrich's International Periodicals Directory*. Lists by subject approximately 28,000 periodicals published in more than 100 countries, and provides information on frequency of publication, subscription price, address of publisher, and which, if any, periodical indexes cover the journal. (New York: R.R. Bowker, 1998).

## DICTIONARIES

Dictionaries pertaining to criminal justice may prove to be a valuable source for bits and pieces of information. Several pertinent dictionaries are listed below.

*The Alcohol/Drug Abuse Dictionary and Encyclopedia*. John J. Fay. Professionals and lay persons alike will find this extensive dictionary and encyclopedia essential to the understanding of the basic terms and concepts of alcohol and drug abuse. More than 1,400 entries are defined and cross-referenced, from the street jargon of the illicit drug subculture to the complex dialect of pharmacology. Insights into the special worlds of addicts, traffickers, police officers, jurists, and others are also examined. (Springfield, IL: Charles C Thomas, 1988).

*The American Political Dictionary*, Tenth Edition. Jack C. Plano & Milton Greenberg. (New York: Harcourt Brace College Pub., 1996).

*Ballentine's Law Dictionary*. James A. Ballentine. Defines English and Latin legal terms and phrases and lists abbreviations of legal literature. (Rochester, NY: Lawyers Cooperative Publishing Company, 1969).

*Black's Law Dictionary*, Sixth Edition. Henry C. Black & Joseph R. Nolan. No doubt the best known and widely used legal dictionary. Defines words, terms, phrases, ranging from early to modern usage and covers all forms of law. A table of abbreviations is included.(St. Paul, MN: West Publishing, 1990).

*Butterworth's Security Dictionary: Terms and Concepts*. John Fay. More than a listing of definitions, *Butterworth's Security Dictionary* explains and describes the context for terms and concepts that have become a part of the multidisciplinary world of today's security profession. Containing over 5,000 definitions and abbreviations, it also gives ready access to the basic principles behind procedures in security as well as legal and organizational concepts. (Boston: Butterworth, 1987).

*Crime Dictionary*. Ralph De Sola. This dictionary combines the terms used by both criminals and law enforcement professionals. In preparation for 12 years, it is an exhaustive compilation containing definitions of over 10,000 terms relating to every aspect of law and law enforcement. From types of weapons, nicknames of prisons, names of terrorist groups, medical and psychiatric terms relating to criminals, to the definitions of slang used by criminals, its scope is immense. Appendices. Bibliography. (New York: Facts on File, 1988).

*The Criminal Justice Dictionary*, Second Edition. Erik Beckman. (Ann Arbor: Pierian, 1983).

*Dictionary of American Penology*. Vergil L. Williams (ed.). Expanded and Revised. Covers a broad range of topics dealing with prisons and prisoners today. Each topic covered includes a bibliography of sources. Includes overall coverage of correctional systems of each state in the U.S. (Westport, CT: Greenwood Pub. Group, Inc., 1996).

*Dictionary of Behavior Science*, Second Edition. Benjamin B. Wolman. (San Diego: Academic Press, 1989).

*A Dictionary of Concepts on American Politics*. James B. Whisker. (New York: John Wiley, 1980).

*Dictionary of Criminal Justice*, An alphabetical compilation of over 4,000 definitions of terms important to the study of criminal justice. The addition of over 700 Supreme Court case summaries provides a valuable new dimension to the volume's utility. (Lanham, MD: American Correction Assoc., 1998).

*The Dictionary of Criminal Justice Data Terminology: Terms & Definitions Proposed for Interstate & National Data Collection & Exchange*. This dictionary defines criminal justice terms used in statistical reports issued by the federal government. It also proposes model definitions so that criminal justice experts can use the terms more consistently. (Washington, DC: U.S. Dept. of Justice, Bureau of Justice Statistics, 1982).

*Dictionary of Criminology*. George Rush & Sam Torres. (Incline Village, NV: Copperhouse Pub. Co., 1997).

*The Dictionary of English Law*. Changes in this edition reflect the exclusion of Scottish legal terms, reorganization of the court system, remodeling of local and central government, etc. A first supplement was published in 1981. (Littleton, CO: Fred B. Rothman & Co., 1991).

*Dictionary of International Law and Diplomacy*. Melquiades J. Gamboa. (Quezon City, Philippines: Central Lawbook Publishing Company, 1974).

*A Dictionary of Politics*. Walter Laquer (ed.). (New York: Free Press, 1974).

*Dictionary of Street Alcohol and Drug Terms*. Dr. Peter Johnson (ed.). Fourth Edition. Catalogs and defines over 3,500 words, names and expressions. Includes more than 750 Hispanic terms, fast becoming the dominant lingo across North, South, and Central America. Marijuana, for example, has more than 700 other names. Also explained is drug and alcohol sign language. (Upland, PA: DIANE Publishing Co., 1993).

*Elsevier's Dictionary of Criminal Science in Eight Languages*. Johann A. Adler. (Amsterdam: Elsevier, 1960).

*Encyclopedic Dictionary of American Government*, Fifth Edition. Alex Wellek. (Guilford, CT: Dushkin Publishing Group, 1991).

*Encyclopedic Dictionary of American History*, Fourth Edition. John Faragher (ed.) (Guilford, CT: Dushkin Publishing Group, 1991).

*The Law Dictionary*, Seventh Edition. This pronouncing law dictionary contains more than 6,000 legal words, phrases and maxims. Newly revised, and containing a table of abbreviations, it is ideal for the criminal justice student and practitioner. (Cincinnati, OH: Anderson Publishing Co., 1997).

*Law Dictionary*, Fourth Edition. Steven H. Gifis. Intended as a ready reference source in paperback for the student. More than 3,000 terms are defined, many with relevant legal citations. Pronunciation indicated for Latin and French terms. Appendixes provide American Bar Association Code (1969) and Rules (1983). (Hauppauge, NY: Barron's Educational Series, Inc., 1986).

*Law Dictionary for Non-Lawyers*. Daniel Oran. (St. Paul, MN: West Pub. Co, College & School Division, 1991).

*Legal Terms and Concepts in Criminal Justice*. Michael M. D'Auria, Gary D. Helfand, and Herbert F. Ryan. Divided into three parts, this book both defines and explains the most important and widely used words and concepts in the American system of law. Part I focuses in on the words, terms, and phrases directly related to criminal justice. Part II is a comprehensive listing of criminal justice abbreviations and acronyms. The last section defines the latest and most common drug terms related to substance abuse. (Wayne, NJ: Avery Publishing Group Inc., 1983).

*Modern Legal Glossary*. Kenneth R. Redden and Enid L. Veron. A dictionary "devoted exclusively to a definition of legal terms and related concepts, both old and new" (Pref.), as well as professional associations, government agencies, international organizations, foreign expressions, popular names of cases and statutes, trials, ancient codes, and biographies. (Charlottesville, VA: Michie Co., 1980).

*A New Dictionary of Political Analysis*, Second Edition. Jack C. Plano. (New York: E. Arnold, 1991).

*The New Dictionary of Statistics: A Complement to the Fourth Edition of Mulhall's "Dictionary of Statistics."* August D. Webb. (London, UK: George Routledge and Sons, Ltd., 1974).

*Oran's Dictionary of the Law.* Second Edition. Daniel Oran. A basic dictionary, with standard pronunciation indicated for foreign terms. Appendix provides a brief guide to legal research. (St. Paul, MN: West Publishing Co., 1991).

*The Police Dictionary and Encyclopedia.* John J. Fay. More than 4,900 law enforcement terms and phrases are defined and explained in this comprehensive work. Examples are provided where necessary and applications of important practices have been delineated. The entry-level officer, as well as the seasoned veteran, will find the text to be a valuable guide in updating his or her working vocabulary. (Springfield, IL: Charles C Thomas, 1988).

*Public Administration Dictionary,* Second Edition. William Fox & Ivan Meyers. (Portland, OR: International Specialized Book Series, 1995).

*Security Dictionary.* Richard Hofmeister. (Indianapolis: Howard W. Sams & Co., 1983).

*Thesaurus of Psychological Index Terms,* Eighth Edition. Alvin Walker. The *Thesaurus* contains all the terms used to index the PsycINFO database. PsycLIT on CD-ROM, PsycBOOKS, and Psychological Abstracts. In this edition, over 230 new terms have been added and integrated. Additional cross references and scope notes help the user locate the right terms, and all terms have been updated to indicate the current number of postings. A "down arrow" feature has been included in this edition as well. (Washington, DC: American Psychological Association, 1997).

*Words and Phrases 1958 to Date: All Judicial Constructions and Definitions of Words and Phrases by the State and Federal Courts from the Earliest Times.* A comprehensive dictionary with frequently revised editions. (St. Paul, MN: West Publishing).

## Dictionaries of Slang Terms

*Dictionary of American Slang.* Third Edition. Harold Wentworth and Barbara Kipfer. (New York: Harper Collins, 1995).

*Slang Today and Yesterday.* Eric Partridge. (New York: Bonanza Books, 1961).

## ENCYCLOPEDIAS

There are various specialized encyclopedias, but few pertain specifically to criminal justice, and some of these are quite dated. Nevertheless, a brief listing of encyclopedias oriented toward criminal justice and related subjects is given below. Many of these provide good references for terminology and concepts for fundamental course work and review material for senior and graduate students.

*American Jurisprudence,* 2d. Updated with pocket parts and replacement volumes. (Rochester, NY: Lawyer's Cooperative Publishing Co., 1997).

*Best Encyclopedias: A Guide to General and Specialized Encyclopedias.* Kenneth K. Kister. The reference lists and describes all major encyclopedias published around the world. (Phoenix: ORYX Press, 1994).

*The Concise Encyclopedia of Crime and Criminals.* Harold Scott. This is a useful volume despite its age and lack of index. Some articles are quite extensive; most important movements and ideas are covered. The large number of biographies, unusual for their inclusion of lawyers, judges, and detectives, as well as criminals and criminologists, are particularly helpful. (New York: Hawthorn Books, 1961).

*Corpus Juris Secundum.* This encyclopedia is updated with pocket parts and replacement volumes. It can be used to provide a broad overview of a topic. Articles also cite cases illustrating the points under discussion. In addition to subject indexes, this encyclopedia includes detailed analytical tables of contents for each article. (St. Paul, MN: West Publishing Co.).

*Encyclopedia of Business Information Sources.* Paul Lasserman (ed.). This publication is not intended to provide answers to particular questions, but rather to list sources which are likely to be the "right place to begin" in seeking those answers.

The subject headings used in EBIS are primarily of three types:
1. Line-of-business designations
2. Product and process designations
3. Function and service designations
Subject headings are arranged alphabetically.

Under each subject will be found citations of sources of all kinds which the editors believe would be helpful to a user needing information on that particular subject. The sources gathered together in EBIS subject entries include the following types, each represented by a subheading within the entry (although not all types of sources are found in all entries), arranged in this sequence:

> encyclopedias and dictionaries
> handbooks and manuals
> bibliographies
> abstract services and indexes
> trade associations and professional societies
> periodicals
> directories
> biographical sources
> statistics sources
> price sources
> almanacs and yearbooks
> financial ratios
> other sources
> general works
> research centers and institutes
> on-line databases

For the researcher interested in white-collar crime, this source may prove valuable. (Detroit: Gale Research, 1983).

*The Encyclopedia of American Crime.* Carl Sifakis. With more than 1,500 readable entries, this thoroughly illustrated volume describes the lives and deeds of 700 of the most villainous characters in our history. (New York: Facts on File, 1982).

*The Encyclopedia of American Government.* This encyclopedia contains up-to-date information about every major area of American government and politics: the presidency, congress, the supreme court, lobbies and lobbyists, the federal bureaucracy, state and local government, citizenship and civil rights, the constitution, political parties, the electoral process, public opinion and pressure groups, domestic policy, national defense, government regulation, the federal court system, the administration of justice, state court system, the federal budget and taxation, foreign policy, and much more. (Englewood Cliffs, NJ: Salem Press, 1998).

*Encyclopedia of American Scandal.* George Kohn. (New York: Facts on File, 1990).

*Encyclopedia of Associations*, Fourteenth Edition. This is a guide to national and international non-profit organizations in all fields. It includes description of programs, addresses, phone numbers, and names of chief officials. (Detroit: Gale Research, 1998).

*Encyclopedia of Bioethics.* Second Edition. (Old Tappen, N.J.: MacMillan Pub. Co., Inc., 1995).

*Encyclopedia of Clinical Assessment.* (New York: The Free Press, 1980).

*Encyclopedia of Crime and Justice.* Sanford H. Kadish (ed.). This is an excellent source for background information on a variety of topics dealing with the study of crime and criminal justice. It provides extensive articles on topics such as "Alcohol and Crime," "Aged and Crime," "Capital Punishment," "Drinking and Driving," etc. Articles are accompanied by bibliographies of books, journal articles, and other materials useful for further research. (New York: Macmillan, 1983).

*The Encyclopedia of Drug Abuse.* Robert O'Brien and Sidney Cohen, M.D. (New York: Facts on File, 1984).

*Encyclopedia of Espionage: From the Age of Jericho to the Age of James Bond.* Ronald Seth. Text bibliography. (Garden City, NY: Doubleday, 1974).

*Encyclopedia of Governmental Advisory Organizations.* This document contains basic information on presidential and public advisory committees, boards, panels, task forces and commissions serving in a consultative or investigative capacity. (Detroit: Gale Research, 1981).

*The Encyclopedia of Management*, Third Edition. This encyclopedia contains concise articles on a wide variety of topics, with bibliographies and suggestions for additional relevant topics to check. (New York: Carl Heyel, 1982).

*Encyclopedia of Murder.* Colin Wilson and Patricia Pitman. Text with bibliography. (New York: Putnam, 1962).

*The Encyclopedia of Police Science.* William G. Bailey (ed.). (New York: Garland, 1989).

*Civil Rights for State & Federal Prisoners*, Vol. III. Jack L. Kunsman. (Easton, PA: J.L. Kunsman, 1982).

*Drugs & Crime.* Dorothy Hoobler and Thomas Hoobler. Encyclopedia of Psychoactive Drugs Series: No. 2. (New York: Chelsea House, 1988).

*The Encyclopedia of Words and Phrases, Legal Maxims (Canada 1825 to 1978)*, Third Edition. Gerald D. Sanagan. This dictionary attempts "to extract from Canadian judicial decisions . . . all materials shedding light on the meaning of words and phrases, both legal and otherwise." References to cases and decisions are provided, with notation indicating national or provincial courts. (Toronto: R. De Boo, 1979).

*Open Files: A Narrative Encyclopedia of the World's Greatest Unsolved Crimes.* Jay Robert Nash. (New York: McGraw-Hill, 1983).

*Spy/Counterspy: An Encyclopedia of Espionage.* Vincent Buranelli and Nan Buranelli. The 400 articles in the encyclopedia cover the highlights of espionage, the people, events, organizations, and techniques in its history. The emphasis is on America and Europe. Historical figures, the CIA, KGB, M15, SMERSH, MOSSAD, and their historical counterparts are included. Primary and secondary sources are used. (New York: McGraw-Hill, 1982).

*World Encyclopedia of Police Forces and Penal Systems.* George Thomas Kurian. (New York: Facts on File, 1989).

## Encyclopedias of Education

*American Peoples Encyclopedia.* (New York: Grolier, annual).

*Collier's Encyclopedia.* (New York: Collier, annual).

*Columbia Encyclopedia.* (New York: Columbia University Press, 1963).

*Encyclopedia Americana.* (New York: Americana Corporation, annual).

*Encyclopedia Britannica.* (Chicago: Encyclopedia Britannica, 1974).

*Encyclopedia of Educational Research.* Robert L. Ebel. (New York: Macmillan, 1969).

*The Encyclopedia of Education.* (New York: Macmillan Publishing Company and the Free Press, 1971).

*Encyclopedia International.* (New York: Grolier, annual).

## Popular Crime Encyclopedias

*Almanac of World Crime.* Jay Robert Nash. This almanac contains narrative descriptions of some of the world's most famous or bizarre crimes and criminals. (Garden City, NY: Anchor Press/Doubleday, 1981).

*Bloodletters and Badmen: A Narrative Encyclopedia of American Criminals from the Pilgrims to the Present.* Jay Robert Nash. (New York: M. Evans, 1973).

*Look for the Woman: A Narrative Encyclopedia of Female Poisoners, Swindlers, and Spies from Elizabethan Times to the Present.* Jay Robert Nash. (New York: M. Evans, 1981).

*The Murderers' Who's Who: Outstanding International Cases from the Literature of Murder in the Last 150 Years.* J.H.H. Gaute and Robin Odel. This document gives a brief account

of almost every famous murder case for the period covered. It includes bibliographies for each case. The classified index includes type of weapon, type of crime, and a list of unsolved crimes. (New York: Methuen, 1979).

## FACT BOOKS AND ALMANACS

*The World Factbook.* This publication is produced annually by the Central Intelligence Agency for the use of United States Government officials, and the style, format, coverage, and content are designed to meet their specific requirements. Comments and queries are welcome.

This book of world facts, leaders, and governments is an outstanding publication produced by the CIA and is available to the general public and is carried in many libraries.

There have been some significant changes in the current edition. In the Government section, the former Branches entry has been replaced by three entries—Executive branch, Legislative branch, and Judicial branch. The Leaders entry now has subentries for Chief of State, Head of Government, and their deputies. The Elections entry has been completely redone with information for each branch of the national government, including the date for the last election, the date for the next election, results (percent of vote by candidate or party), and current distribution of seats by party. In the Economy section there is a new entry on Illicit Drugs, which has a vast amount of information. (Washington, DC: Central Intelligence Agency, Public Affairs Division).

*Whitaker's Almanac.* Established in 1868, this annual British publication is interesting and gives information on a large amount of information with nearly 10,000 references. Among the major subject headings are: Government and Public Offices, Law Courts and Offices (England and Wales, Scotland, Northern Ireland), Tribunals, Police Forces, The Armed Forces (The Royal Navy, The Army, The Royal Air Force). (London, UK: J. Whitaker & Sons).

*The World Almanac and Book of Facts.* Published annually since 1868. It contains many topics of interest to criminologists. (Washington, DC: Scripps-Howard).

## HANDBOOKS AND MANUALS

*Drug Testing Legal Manual.* Kevin B. Zeese. The Manual examines the three primary areas of testing: private employment, government employment, and pre-employment testing. Updated annually, this manual provides expert analysis of the applicable statutory and common law issues, with particular attention to matters concerning wrongful discharge . . . privacy and defamation actions . . . negligence claims . . . and Fourth Amendment issues. In addition, the volume covers questions of consent, probable cause, and employer searches. The *Manual* contains coverage and analysis of recent major Supreme Court decisions. (New York: Clark Boardman Company, Ltd.).

*Fraud Examiners Manual.* This manual is a complete course for fraud examiners. After passage of the national examination, successful candidates are certified as fraud examiners. (Austin, TX: National Association of Certified Fraud Examiners, 1989).

*The Guide to Background Investigations*, Fourth Edition. In its 696 pages, the *Guide* shows large and small companies how to use public records to aid their background checks. Included are more than 7,500 sources for public records. Easy-to-read entries detail the procedures each office follows in releasing its records.

The *Guide* enables the user to verify or discover criminal conviction data, college attendance and degrees, worker's compensation claims, driving records, medical licenses and more by phone, mail or fax. Major sections include: criminal records, workers compensation records, driving records, educational records, federal court records, departments of education, medical licensing boards, and corporations. (Tulsa, OK: National Employment Screening Services, 1991).

*Handbook of Loss Prevention and Crime Prevention*, Second Edition. Lawrence J. Fennelly. This is a one-volume encyclopedia on the entire security field. *The Handbook of Loss Prevention and Crime Prevention* brings together the expertise of more than 40 security and crime prevention professionals on the latest technology and trends. Topics include legal aspects of security, executive protection, access controls, internal theft, applicant screening, investigations, and much more.

The text is divided into four major parts. "Methods" includes environmental design, security surveys, fire and safety protection, and emergency planning. "Operations and Equipment" deals with locks, lighting, alarms, CCTV, guard forces and physical barriers. "Applications" zeroes in on security in modern society. "Management" analyzes such important functions as planning, data analysis, budgeting, and public relations. (Stoneham, MA: Butterworth Publishers, 1989).

*Handbook of State Police, Highway Patrols, and Investigative Agencies.* Donald A. Torres. (Westport, CT: Greenwood Press, 1987).

*International Handbook of Contemporary Developments in Criminology.* Elmer H. Johnson (ed.). Contents: v.1, General issues and the Americas; v.2, Europe, Africa, the Middle East, and Asia. Presents state-of-the-art reviews of criminology in specific countries; surveys are written by specialists. Bibliographic references and bibliographies; indexed. (Westport, CT: Greenwood Press, 1983).

*Practical Risk Management.* This handbook covers all aspects of risk management and insurance related problems. Format and contents: Two loose-leaf binders containing in-depth information on: Administration, Risk Financing and Self-insurance, Insurers, Loss Control/Claims Management, Legal and Political Aspects, Property Risk and Insurance, Liability Risk and Insurance, Risk Managers Resources, Special Industry Index and Glossary. Annual. (San Francisco: Warren, McVeigh & Griffin).

*Pre-Law Handbook.* The official guide of ABA-approved law schools. Includes LSAT profiles of recently admitted classes and up-to-date admission standards. (Washington, DC: Association of American Law Schools).

*Protection of Assets Manual.* In five loose-leaf volumes and updated continually, this work provides complete coverage of all major loss prevention and private security topics. Annual. (Santa Monica, CA: The Merritt Company).

*Risk Management and Insurance Audit Techniques.* Dwight E. Levick. In the field of private security and loss prevention, one of the higher paying positions and the least understood by persons working in criminal justice is risk management. This reference work has semi-annual updates and will keep the book current on a broad spectrum of topics including updated coverage information, new risk management strategies, the latest developments in self-insurance, plus discussions of risk management techniques and coverages for "special situations"—banks, hospitals, municipalities, construction industries, and many more. Key chapters give a thorough practical discussion on the value of periodic audits, their objectives, how to choose an auditor, and the important role top management plays in the audit process. An in-depth discussion of the administrative responsibilities of managing the insurance program provides a good review for all insurance and risk management professionals.

The basic principles of risk management, plus insights on the major concerns of risk management professionals and their consultants, are included. A sample audit report identifies the general approach commonly taken by the author in conducting an audit and writing a report. The researcher will learn what he or she can expect and ask for in audits.

Finally, this publication includes a set of practical, ready-to-use specimen forms and checklists specially designed as tools for conducting a risk management and insurance audit. Most of these forms are also useful in day-to-day risk management activities. Annual. (Boston: The John Liner Organization).

*SCSC Security Controls and Systems Catalog.* Published annually, *Security Controls and Systems Catalog* is a reference work for specifiers and buyers of security/facility controls and systems. Contents include manufacturers listing, product index of manufacturers literature, industry-wide manufacturers address listing, industry-wide product directory, local sales and service offices. (Indianapolis: MBC Data Distribution Publications).

*Security Industry Buyer Guide.* This 900-page directory, updated annually, lists publishers, manufacturers and distributors of security-related products. (Bethesda, MD: C & P Telephone of Virginia).

*Security Letter Source Book 1990-1991.* Robert D. McCrie (ed.). This established guide to the industry's leading services, suppliers, and manufacturers provides a gold mine of data on the whos, whats, and wheres in the security field. 100% revised and updated, the new edition gives instant access to sources ranging from alarm, guard, patrol, and screening services to specialized products, individual consultants, and investigators. (Stoneham, MA: Butterworth Publishers, 1990).

*Security Managers Desk Reference.* Richard S. Post and David A. Schachtsiek. A mini-encyclopedia, this quick-access reference provides reliable, up-to-date data on an extremely broad range of security and safety issues. Managers consult it when they need information quickly on any security topic, from general management principles and basic security philosophy to specifics such as bomb threats, personnel selection, and CCTV camera placement. (Stoneham, MA: Butterworth Publishers, 1986).

*A Sourcebook on Child Sexual Abuse.* David Finkelhor et al. (Beverly Hills, CA: Sage Publications, 1986).

*U.S. Identification Manual.* This manual contains 700 pages of information with 200 identification formats and is continuously updated. It is arranged in five sections to verify the identification of documents. Every document is shown in full size and full color where appropriate.

### SECTION I
### State Identification
This is the most comprehensive coverage of state identification documents—shown in full color and actual size for fast visual match up. Every adult, regular driver's license from the U.S. and Canada is included. It includes complete details on commercial/chauffeur's cards, cycle and moped permits, minor's licenses and State ID cards for non-drivers' liquor control cards. Supporting information on military extensions, restricted driver's coding, duplicate licenses, and laminations permitted is included.

### SECTION II
### Vehicle Registration
All U.S. and Canadian license plates are shown in large color reproduction for easy validation. Passenger cars, trucks of all kinds, trailers, and motorcycle license plates are included. Term and expiration for all license plates are identified. All registration stickers in color with detailed explanation are included. This section contains a special registration information section covering—for each U.S. state and Canadian province—alpha-numeric licensing system for all types of vehicles, validation requirements, and personalized plate policies.

### SECTION III
### Federal Identification
This is a complete reference for dependable verification of U.S. military, immigration, and federal employee documents. It contains color reproductions of all ID cards issued by the various armed forces, including active personnel, reservists, retirees, and dependents. Telephone numbers to confirm the validity of federal credentials are also included. Immigration and alien identity documents, including immigration and alien registration cards and permits, arrival-departure records, and crewman's landing permit are included. It also contains a Social Security card coding chart.

### SECTION IV
### Commercial Documents
This is an accurate reference for credit cards, including information for immediate verification at any time. Bank cards, travel, and entertainment cards are shown in full color. Detailed backup on travel and entertainment cards, bank cards, airline, auto rental, gasoline, department stores, hotels, and more are included. Also included are 24-hour telephone numbers and security contacts for emergency assistance and verification. There is an explanation of the numbering system for each card listed.

### SECTION V
### Directory
This is a specialized directory of federal and state agencies and departments most often contacted in matters of identification and law enforcement. It lists national, regional, and local offices with addresses and telephone numbers, as well as names of persons in charge at offices listed for most effective contact. It is arranged alphabetically by agency or department for fast, efficient use. Annual. (Redwood City, CA: U.S. Identification Manual).

## NEWSPAPERS

Newspapers are a valuable source of information because they report conditions and events taking place worldwide. Newspapers also report facts that cannot be found in textbooks or other publications. The importance of newspapers as a source of information should not be underestimated.

When using newspapers, however, the researcher should be aware that facts are often intertwined with opinion. The paper should be critiqued for objectivity, and coverage in an article should be compared with that of other newspapers. It is important to distinguish fact from opinion and recognize the properties of a fact. First, a fact is something such as a person, place, thing, or situation that is experienced through the senses and therefore is known to exist. A fact can be verified by other people through the stimulation of their senses. A fact can also be something which has not been experienced by the senses but is thought to have existed if it is believed that evidence of the fact could be found if looked for. A good clue for distinguishing fact from opinion is to learn to identify the "whos, whats, wheres, hows, and whys" (if they exist) of an article. This information will usually provide the researcher with clearly stated facts, although "why" statements often border on being opinions.

The majority of newspaper literature is stored as microform. The assistance of the librarian may be required in order to view this material, but it can be set up in a matter of minutes. Several sources of newspaper information are described below:

*Newsbank* is an index to news articles in 190 newspapers from 103 cities, representing all 50 states. Printed subject indexes are issued quarterly and cumulated annually, providing subject access to newspaper articles on microfiche. The indexes are divided into 12 categories: Business and Economic Development, Consumer Affairs, Education, Employment, Environment, Government Structure, Housing and Urban Renewal, Law and Order, Political Development, Social Relations, Transportation, and Welfare and Poverty. Business and industrial crime listings are cataloged in the "Business and Economic Development Index."

In addition to *Newsbank*, there are other sources contained in most libraries that provide access to newspaper articles related to criminal justice. Some of these sources are:

> *Alternative Press Index*
> *N.W. Ayer and Sons Directory of Newspapers and Periodicals*
> *Chicago Tribune Index*
> *Index to the Christian Science Monitor*
> *London Times Index*
> *Los Angeles Times Index*
> *National Observer Index*
> *New Orleans Times-Picayune Index*
> *Newspaper Index* (covers the *Chicago Tribune, Los Angeles Times, New Orleans Times-Picayune,* and *Washington Post*)
> *Newspaper Press Directory*
> *New York Times Index*
> *Wall Street Journal Index*
> *Washington Post Index*

These are among the major newspaper indexes. The library may have additional ones to local newspapers which may also be helpful. By noting the date an event was reported in one of the above indices, such as the *New York Times Index*, the researcher can locate similar articles in other newspapers which may be more accessible. (See also Chapter 9, "Computerized Literature Searches," for several computerized newspaper databases, and Chapter 15, "Historical Research Sources," for access to early newspapers.)

## RELATED SOURCES

*Basic Books in the Mass Media: An Annotated Selected Booklist Covering General Communications, Book Publishing, Broadcasting, Film, Magazines, Newspapers, Advertising, Indices, and Scholarly and Professional Periodicals.* Eleanor Blum. The title is self-explanatory and would be helpful in locating a variety of information sources due to its broad scope. (Urbana, IL: University of Illinois Press, 1972).

*Crime: As Reported by the New York Times.* Arleen Keylin and Arto Di-Mirjian, Jr. This is a specialized collection of citations pertaining to crime appearing in the *New York Times.* (New York: Arno Press, 1976).

*Editor and Publisher International Yearbook.* This document contains data on United States, Canadian, and other foreign newspapers covering several aspects of journalism. Annual. (New York: Editor and Publisher, 1920-date).

*Editorial Research Reports.* Hoyt Gimlin (ed.). This document consists of weekly pamphlets containing editorials on issues of current interest to the American public. Outstanding publications on the topic being discussed are cited. Topics on the administration of justice are frequently discussed. It is a good source for views on the pros and cons of an issue, which are useful when preparing for debates and class discussions. Subject and title indices to editorials issued during the previous 18 years are provided in the semiannual cumulated issues. (Washington, DC: Congressional Quarterly, Inc., 1979).

*Editorials on File.* This is a twice monthly selection of editorials from a representative sample of American and Canadian newspapers, with a cumulative subject index. (New York: Facts on File, 1970-date).

*Facts on File, Weekly World News Digest with Cumulative Index.* This weekly publication has quarterly cumulated indices which are rearranged as an annual index at the end of the year. It contains summaries of news printed by various large city newspapers, arranged by subject. (New York: Facts on File, 1900-date).

*Facts on File 5-Year Index.* The *Facts on File 5-Year Index* was developed to meet librarians' and news researchers' requirements. It is based on their suggestions for a fast-working method of multi-annual news indexing. The set of seven indices gives quick access to the facts of 35 years of national and foreign affairs. The seven indices are now available: 1976-80, 1971-75, 1966-70, 1961-65, 1956-60, 1951-55, and 1946-50. (New York: Facts on File).

*Newspaper Indexes: A Location and Subject Guide for Researchers.* Anita C. Milner. (Metuchen, NJ: Scarecrow Press, 1977).

*Newspapers on Microfilm.* This lists thousands of American and foreign newspapers available on microfilm and specifies in which libraries they are available. (Washington, DC: Library of Congress, 1967).

## NEWS BROADCASTS

Much news is communicated by broadcast media rather than newsprint. Thus, the sources below are of interest.

*CBS News Television News Broadcasts.* Microfiche. (Glen Rock, NJ: Microfilming Corporation of America, 1975-date).

*CBS News Index: Key to the Television Broadcasts.* (Ann Arbor: Microfilming Corporation of America, 1975-date). This is a set consisting of microfiche copies of television scripts and printed subject indices to the microfiche. Public affairs programs and hard news articles are put on fiche and indexed. This is a rich source of information about current topics in criminal justice. The researcher will have to search a bit to locate stories on specific topics because indexing is broad.

*Television News Index and Abstracts.* Guide to the Videotape Collection of the Network Evening News Programs in the Vanderbilt Television News Archive. The above is a special source. The abstracts are detailed, specifying what was shown as well as what was said, including the names and people who can be heard and seen.

The *Television News Index and Abstracts* is issued monthly with no cumulations. (Nashville, TN: Vanderbilt University Library, 1968-date).

## ANNUALS AND YEARBOOKS

*The Aldine Crime and Justice Annual.* This publication emphasizes developments relating to the criminal justice system. All articles included have been published in other sources during the preceding year. Annual. (Chicago: Aldine, 1973-date).

*The Annals of The American Academy of Political and Social Science.* Founded in 1891, this academic society publishes annuals that often deal with criminal justice issues, including:

*The American Judiciary: Critical Issues.* A. Leo Levin and Russell R. Wheeler (eds.). This publication addresses broad questions of the role and responsibilities of courts in American government and society. Eleven articles discuss what courts should do, how they should do their work, and the parts played by other branches. (Newbury Park, CA: Sage Publications, 1982).

*Crime and Justice: A Review of Research.* Michael Tonry and Norval Morris (eds.). An interdisciplinary forum on criminology, the *Crime and Justice* series exposes professionals and scholars to the full scope of issues concerning crime, its causes, and its prevention. The criminal lawyer, the sociologist, the psychologist, the political scientist—are all among the professionals who contribute to and benefit from *Crime and Justice's* vital forum.

*Crime and Justice* is supported by the National Institute of Justice. Points of view or opinions expressed in this series are those of the editors or authors and do not necessarily represent the official position of policies of the U.S. Department of Justice. (Chicago: University of Chicago Press, Journals Division, 1979 to present).

### Volume 1

Topics include race relations and the prisoner subculture; ecological and areal studies; American youth violence; police function, structure, and control; deinstitutionalization and diversion of juvenile offenders; crime-causation theory; longitudinal research on crime.

### Volume 2

Topics include urban police and crime in 19th-century America; crime and justice in 18th- and 19th-century England; biology and crime; prisoners' rights.

### Volume 3

Topics include surveys of victimization; use of hypnosis in court; eyewitness testimony; modern private security; historical trends in violent crimes; rights, utility, and crime.

### Volume 4

Topics include violence in school; gun availability and violent crime; gender and crime; crime and mental disorder; situational crime prevention.

### Volume 5

Topics include incapacitation; prison labor and industries; prisons for women; sex offenses and offending; plus a special section on criminological research in five nations.

### Volume 6

Topics include predictions of dangerousness; community service orders; prison overcrowding; modeling offenders' decisions; delinquency careers; the turnabout in the insanity defense; criminological research in Scandinavia.

### Volume 7

Topics include family factors and juvenile delinquency; age and crime; victimization surveys; differences in criminal behavior and court responses among young defendants.

### Volume 8

The first thematic volume in the series examines the impact of environmental design on crime; the effects of crime on a community's schools; gentrification and crime rates; and the influence of community context on the recidivism of released offenders. Contributors include Robert J. Bursik, Jr., Leo Schuerman, Soloman Kobrin, Anthony E. Bottoms, Paul Wiles, Scott C. McDonald, Wesley Skogan, Richard M. McGahey, Robert J. Sampson, Douglas Smith, Lawrence W. Sherman, Ralph Taylor, and Stephen Gottfredson.

### Volume 9

Eleven essays discuss the methodology of prediction and classification; the role of these methods in program evaluation research and in application to guidelines for bail, sentencing, and parole; and the legal and ethical considerations that surround the use of these methods. Contributors include Stephen Gottfredson, David Farrington, John Goldkamp, Joan Petersilia, Susan Turner, Richard Berk, Tim Brennan, Daniel Glaser, and Lee Sechrest.

### Volume 10

Topics include community policing, co-offending and criminal careers, drunk driving, prison populations, and sentencing reform.

### Volume 11

Twelve essays in this multi-disciplinary collection review current research on the legal, social, and criminological issues surrounding family violence. Contributors include Elizabeth Pleck, Robert L. Burgess and Patricia Draper, Joseph G. Weis, Irene Hanson Frieze and Angela Browne, James Garbarino, Mildred Daley Pagelow, Gerald T. Hotaling, Murray A. Straus, Alan J. Lincoln, Jeffrey Fagan, Delbert S. Elliott, Daniel G. Saunders, Sandra T. Azar, and Franklin E. Zimring.

Volume 12
Topics include parole, developmental criminology, neuropsychology of juvenile delinquency, police crackdowns, crime displacement, youth games, and criminal fines.

Volume 13
Comprehensive in its scope, *Drugs and Crime* illuminates the complex relations between drug use and crime and the challenges that confront efforts to reduce them. As they evaluate prevention, treatment, and law-enforcement policies, the contributors offer dynamic analyses of the strategies deployed in the "War on Drugs." Drawing on the best available scholarly evidence, the authors examine the relations between drug use and violent crime, aggression, and consensual crime; the technologies and uses of drug testing; and the corrosive effects of drug trafficking on the quality of life in inner-city minority communities.

Volume 14
The following topics are covered in Volume 14: The Technology of Personal Violence, Philip J. Cook; Burglary, Neal Shover; Sociological Perspectives on Punishment, David Garland; Drug-Control Policies in Britain, Geoffrey Pearson; Drugs and Drug Policy in the Netherlands, Ed Leuw; The Motivation of the Persistent Robber, Jack Katz; Women, Crime, and Penal Responses: A Historical Account, Lucia Zedner; The Needs and Rights of Victims of Crime, Mike Maguire.

*Criminal Law Review.* This is an anthology of some of the most significant articles published during the preceding year. Each volume includes selections in the four areas of substantive criminal law, constitutional rights and remedies, trial and sentencing, and professional responsibility. Each year there is a very useful introductory survey of significant court decisions dealing with criminal law. (New York: Clark Boardman, 1979-date).

*Criminal Justice System Review.* The legal aspects of the criminal justice system is highlighted and unlike other annuals, it contains some previously unpublished material. (Buffalo, NY: William S. Hein).

## Annuals

*Annual Editions* are published by Dushkin Publishing Group, Inc., Guildford, Connecticut.

*Annual Editions: Criminal Justice.* This is an organized collection of articles, indexed, and reproduced in a low-cost format which provides easy and permanent access to the most current literature in the criminal justice field. Published annually since 1977.

*Annual Editions: Drugs, Society and Behavior.* This document is used in introductory courses dealing with drugs and society. Published annually since 1985.

*Annual Editions: Social Problems.* This publication is used in social problems courses. It has been published annually since 1972.

*Annual Editions: Violence and Terrorism.* This document is used in political terrorism courses. It has been published annually since 1990.

## Facts On File

Each week since January 1941, Facts on File has summarized, recorded, and indexed the news of the nation and the world. These weekly publications are indexed and preserved in annual binders. Each binder contains all the year's 52 weekly news digests and an annual index that makes it possible to pinpoint information on any major news event or person prominent in the year's news. Additionally, for a number of years, these indexed records were also published in bound volumes, titled *Facts on File Yearbooks* (New York: Facts on File):

        Set 1    America in World War II (1941-45)
        Set 2    The Truman Administration and the Growth of the Cold War (1946-52)
        Set 3    The Eisenhower Decade (1953-60)
        Set 4    The Kennedy/Johnson Years (1961-68)
        Set 5    The Nixon/Ford Years (1969-76)
        Set 6    The Carter Years (1977-80)

## Yearbooks

The following yearbooks are published by Sage Publications.

*Guide to Resources and Services.* This 525-page guide lists and annotates numerous research studies of value to the criminal justice researcher. Of great importance is the criminal justice archive and information network which is housed by the Inter-University Consortium. Annual. (Ann Arbor: Inter-University Consortium for Political and Social Research).

*The Mental Measurements Yearbook.* Oscar K. Buros. This is a bibliography of books on psychological measurement and of psychological tests published in all English-speaking countries. The section entitled "Books and Reviews" consists of a list of recent books, most of which are followed by excerpts from two or more critical reviews whose sources are cited in full.

*Police Yearbook.* Annual. This yearbook reports the proceedings of the IACP's yearly conference. (Gaithersburg, MD: International Association of Chiefs of Police).

*Proceedings of the American Correctional Association.* This is an annual report on the content of presentations given at the ACA's yearly meeting. Major developments and trends during the previous year are usually the topics addressed at this meeting. (College Park, MD: American Correctional Association).

*Sage Research Progress Series in Criminology.* The following annuals are published in cooperation with the American Society of Criminology. (Beverly Hills, CA: Sage Publications).

Volume 1
*Theory in Criminology: Contemporary Views.* Robert F. Meier (ed.). This volume examines the historical bases and current status of major theories, stressing the need to move beyond accepted hypotheses and improve the utility of contemporary criminological frameworks. 1977.

Volume 2
*Juvenile Delinquency: Little Brother Grows Up.* Theodore N. Ferdinand (ed.). This volume addresses such major concerns as the roles played by police and the courts in determining the outcomes of juvenile cases, the relationship between the theory of "naturalization" and "delinquency", and the juvenile institutions. 1977.

Volume 3
*Contemporary Corrections: Social Control and Conflict.* C. Ronald Huff (ed.). This volume focuses on the sociological, legal, psychological, and policy issues posed by formal systems of legal control. 1977.

Volume 4
*Criminal Justice Planning and Development.* Alvin W. Cohn (ed.). This volume approaches the question of what constitutes effective planning and goal setting in the criminal justice area from the vantage points of the major actors in the justice system. 1977.

Volume 5
*Violent Crime: Historical and Contemporary Issues.* James A. Inciardi and Anne E. Pottieger (eds.). This volume explores the nature and historical roots of crimes and violence, discussing such topics as robbery outlawry on the U.S. frontier, the southern culture of violence, prison violence as exemplified in the George Jackson case, and Americans' fascination with handguns. 1978.

Volume 6
*Crime, Law, and Sanctions: Theoretical Perspectives.* Marvin D. Krohn and Ronald L. Akers (eds.). This volume presents cutting edge perspectives on vital areas of criminological theory, including labeling, law, crime, deterrence, and sanctions. 1978.

Volume 7
*The Evolution of Criminal Justice: A Guide for Practical Criminologists.* John P. Conrad (ed.). This volume recommends innovations in the use of empirically tested knowledge to change the justice system, discussing specific issues ranging from white collar crime and prison reform to deterrence and victim compensation. 1978.

Volume 8
*Quantitative Studies in Criminology.* Charles Wellford (ed.). This volume examines criminological problems to which statistical techniques can be usefully applied and demonstrates the value of a rigorous methodology in criminological research. 1978.

Volume 9
*Discretion and Control.* Margaret Evans (ed.). This volume discusses the relationship among legislation, the courts, and corrections in discretionary sentencing . . . and examines ongoing debates about the impact of discretion on the administration of justice. 1978.

Volume 10
*Biology and Crime.* C.R. Jeffery (ed.). This volume throws fresh light upon the controversial linkages among biological factors, human behavior, and crime. 1979.

Volume 11
*Perspectives on Victimology.* William H. Parsonage (ed.). This volume provides a stimulating overview of major issues in victimology, including the characteristics of special types of victims and offenders, and means of dealing with the social and personal effects of crime and victimization. 1979.

Volume 12

*Police Work: Strategies and Outcomes in Law Enforcement.* David M. Petersen (ed.). This volume probes the challenges confronting contemporary police as they serve diverse functions in law enforcement, crime prevention, and the public service sector, outlining innovative strategies to improve their performance. 1979.

Volume 13

*Structure, Law, and Power Essays in the Sociology of Law.* Paul J. Brantingham and Jack M. Kress (eds.) This volume explores the interplay of social structure, legal ideology, and political processes in the creation and enforcement of criminal law. 1979.

Volume 14

*Courts and Diversion Policy and Operations Studies.* Patricia L. Brantingham and Thomas G. Blomberg (eds.). This volume presents cutting edge efforts to link justice data, theory, and policy, stressing such topics as alternatives to processing through the judicial system and the relationship between the availability of court services and crime control. 1979.

Volume 15

*Taboos in Criminology.* Edward Sagarin (ed.). This volume presents an insightful and heated discussion of these issues in criminology labeled "taboo" by the scholarly community. Six eminent contributors offer diverse viewpoints on such controversial issues as the relationship between the women's movement and female crime and the effects of race and I.Q. on delinquency. 1980.

Volume 16

*Criminal Justice Research: New Models and Findings.* Barbara Raffel Price and Phyllis Jo Baunach (eds.). This volume explores major issues in applied criminology, dealing in particular with evaluation and policy analysis. Each chapter highlights new directions in areas where research has been limited to legal objections to experimental design, victimization, prosecutorial discretion, probation diversion, and model development for program evaluation. 1980.

Volume 17

*Improving Management in Criminal Justice.* Alvin W. Cohn and Benjamin Ward (eds.). This volume acknowledges the need for such tools as goal setting, effective management, and planning in all organizations. Contributors examine pressing issues of management and administration in the criminal justice system, evaluate the effectiveness of specific policies and practices, and offer suggestions for improvement. 1980.

Volume 18

*Understanding Crime: Current Theory and Research.* Travis Hirschi and Michael Gottfredson (eds.). Why do people commit crimes? Contributors representing a wide spectrum of opinions provide fresh insights into this controversial issue. The editors' comprehensive introduction puts the current theory and research reported here into the context of ongoing debates. 1980.

Volume 19

*Evaluation and Criminal Justice Police.* Ronald Roesch and Raymond R. Corrado (eds.). This volume addresses fundamental concerns posed by the methodologies, goals, materials, and uses of evaluation research in the criminal justice system. It contains discussions regarding issues involving differing methodologies and approaches, the sensitive nature of many of the programs examined, and the policy applications of evaluation data. 1981.

Volume 20

*Contemporary Issues in Law Enforcement.* James J. Fyfe (ed.). This volume provides an enlightening overview of current issues and research on police conduct, techniques, and interaction with the community. It examines such specific concerns as the need to establish realistic expectations for police performance, public accountability of law enforcement agencies, and controversies regarding police treatment of minorities. 1981.

Volume 21

*Comparing Female and Male Offenders.* Marguerite Q. Warren (ed.). This volume sheds new light on the importance of gender in studying crime and the criminal justice system . . . while challenging many of the myths and sex stereotypes involved in such study. It proposes new hypotheses regarding the gender-related differences that do exist. 1981.

Volume 22

*Sociology of Delinquency: Current Issues.* Gary F. Jensen (ed.). This volume contains original articles representing traditional sociological positions as well as diverse critical and cross-cultural viewpoints creating an exciting overview of contemporary delinquency research and conceptualization. 1981.

Volume 23

*Crime Spillover.* Simon Hakim and George F. Rengert (eds.). Pioneers in the emerging field of criminal mobility draw upon criminological, economic, and geographical insights to explicate questions related to where crimes take place and why certain neighborhoods have higher crime rates than others. 1981.

Volume 24

*Quantitative Criminology Innovations and Applications.* John Jagan (ed.). These stimulating essays examine creative methodologies, test important hypotheses, and cast new light on major concerns in criminology and criminal justice. They exemplify the growing importance of quantitative criminology as a critical context (in which novel ideas are matched with new kinds of data and new modes of analysis). 1982.

### Volume 25

*Law and the Legal Process*. Victoria L. Swigert (ed.). In this provocative volume, original studies illuminate issues central to continuing debates over the relationship between law and society, differential legal treatment, the operation of the criminal justice system, the impacts of legal processes on individuals, and the implications of law for social organizations. 1982.

### Volume 26

*Implementing Criminal Justice Policies*. Merry Morash (ed.). Contributors address disturbing instances of implementation failure in such areas as gun control, juvenile diversion, and parole programs. They clarify the individual, organizational, and group dynamics that account for implementation difficulties, and pinpoint directions for future research. 1982.

### Volume 27

*Rethinking Criminology*. Harold E. Pepinsky (ed.). Pepinsky contends that professionals need to surpass the boundaries of traditional criminological research which has provided few answers for policymakers and move toward a new understanding of the field. These insightful studies, conducted in independent new ways, underline the potential of innovative research premises and directions. 1982.

### Volume 28

*Deterrence Reconsidered: Methodological Innovations*. John Hagan (ed.). Leading figures in quantitative criminology consider deterrence in new and creative ways. They show how advances in research design and statistical techniques, coupled with theoretical innovation, have had a major impact on our understanding of an enduring policy problem. 1982.

### Volume 29

*Evaluating Juvenile Justice*. James R. Kluegel (ed.). Rapid political shifts have alternately favored liberal approaches aimed at "diverting" some juvenile delinquents from the criminal justice system, and conservative, more punitive approaches to dealing with juveniles. Focusing on a range of programs that reflects these political changes, the authors rigorously evaluate how they work. Kluegel's overview illuminates the current state, and prospects, of programs dealing with juvenile delinquents. Together, they offer policymakers, researchers, students, and professionals a useful basis for decisions concerning the treatment of juvenile delinquents. 1983.

### Volume 30

*Career Criminals*. Gordon P. Waldo (ed.). The pick-pocket, the Mafioso, the corporate executive illegally dumping chemicals into a nearby river, the "career criminal" is seldom caught . . . and comparatively unstudied. These original essays, by such researchers as James A. Inciardi, Julian B. Roebuck, and Frank R. Scarpitti, make a major contribution to the scarce literature on career criminals. Through use of a variety of innovative methods and approaches, the authors enhance our understanding of whether or not there is a national crime conspiracy in the United States, the use of "social network analysis" to study organized criminals, the use of serendipitous participant observation and field methods to study organized crime. A record of significant advances in the study of the career criminal, this stimulating book will interest professionals, researchers, and students in criminology and criminal justice. 1983.

### Volume 31

*Comparative Criminology: Theory and Applications*. Israel L. Barak Glantz and Elmer H. Johnson (eds.). Can the study of crimes against the centrally planned economies of Poland and the USSR offer new insights into white collar crime in the United States? Do Dutch crime statistics indicate that "female emancipation" can be linked to rising crime rates for American women? What can comparative research tell us about such practical concerns as police training and alleviating stresses on prison guards? In analyses addressing these and other timely topics, the authors show that comparative criminology can play an important role in understanding criminal behavior and improving criminal justice policies and practices. 1983.

### Volume 32

*Measurement Issues in Criminal Justice*. Gordon P. Waldo (ed.). Waldo and his colleagues address a problem typical of criminological research: attaining reliability and validity in measuring data obtained under imperfectly controlled conditions. They discuss appropriate operational definitions to use in measuring concepts, the selection of samples, items, and the data collection process, and differing forms of analysis. Topics include the development of a perpetually based offense seriousness scale, the use of self reports to measure crime, the roles of substantive and statistical significance in evaluating research results. *Measurement Issues in Criminal Justice* is a copious source of insights into measurement challenges in the social sciences. 1983.

## Sage Annual Reviews of Studies in Deviance

*Deviance and Mass Media.* Charles Winick (ed.). *Deviance and Mass Media* represents a sound if selective collection of theory and research. It may well serve as one of several texts for undergraduate teaching purposes. 1978.

*Deviance and Mental Illness.* Walter R. Gove (ed.). This publication intensively examines this important form of deviance and related issues associated with care givers, patients, and society as a whole. The authors' insightful analyses, many of which challenge the major paradigm presently used to explain mental illness (labelling theory), address such central concerns as the causes of insanity, modern trends in psychiatric research and treatment, and the impact of mental illness on personal relationships. 1982.

*Deviants: Victims or Victimizers?* Donal E.J. MacNamara and Andrew Karmen (eds.). Prisoners, homosexuals, drug addicts, and prostitutes—are they victims of society? Or victimizers? Experts in criminology, victimology, and deviance studies pursue this hotly debated issue, presenting in-depth arguments and conflicting perspectives on the problems surrounding social deviants. Some view deviants as a threat to other citizens; some argue that deviants are mistreated by society. 1983.

*Law and Deviance.* H. Laurence Ross (ed.). This publication contains discussions regarding the relationships among labelling, deviance, and criminal and civil law. Considering the nature of law (as contrasted with custom and morality), contributors place this view of law and deviance in the context of theoretical developments in both social science and legal scholarship. 1981.

*The Yearbook of Drug and Substance Abuse* (series). (New York: Human Sciences Press).

*The Yearbook of Drug Abuse*, Volume 1. Leon Brill and Ernest Harms (eds.). 1973.

*The Yearbook of Substance Use and Abuse*, Volume II. Leon Brill and Charles Winick (eds.). 1980.

*The Yearbook of Substance Use and Abuse*, Volume III. Leon Brill and Charles Winick (eds.). 1984.

## AMERICAN CORRECTIONAL ASSOCIATION PUBLICATIONS

### Adult Standards

*Standards for Adult Local Detention Facilities*, Third Edition. This publication contains 425 standards covering 32 program areas for adult local detention facilities. 1991.

*1990 Correctional Standards Supplement.* This vital supplement updates all adult and juvenile standards with every approved addition, revision, deletion, and/or interpretation. 1990.

*Standards for Adult Community Residential Services*, Second Edition. This publication contains 191 standards covering 15 program areas ensure that community corrections is a viable and cost-effective alternative to confinement. 1981.

*Standards for Adult Correctional Institutions*, Third Edition. This document contains 495 standards covering 27 critical program areas for effective institutional management, including safety and emergency procedures, security and control, inmate rules and discipline, staff development, physical plant, and medical and health care services. 1990.

*Standards for Adult Local Detention Facilities*, Second Edition. This publication contains 392 standards addressing the special needs of local jails. It focuses on 22 program areas including personnel, training, safety, sanitation, security, health care, reception, and inmate supervision. 1981.

*Standards for Adult Parole Authorities*, Second Edition. This publication contains 129 standards covering 13 program areas associated with parole decision making. 1981.

*Standards for Adult Probation and Parole Field Services*, Second Edition. This publication 208 standards concerning 11 important areas for sound and progressive non-institutional services. 1981.

*Standards for the Administration of Correctional Agencies.* This publication contains 159 standards covering 12 vital areas of the operation of the administrative unit in correctional systems. 1979.

*Standards for Correctional Industries.* This document has 74 standards providing a clear set of guidelines on the purpose, day-to-day operation, and long-term planning of correctional industries. 1981.

*Standards for Small Jail Facilities.* Sixty-three percent of the jails in the United States have capacities of 50 inmates or less. This comprehensive book contains 207 standards for safety and emergency procedures, security and control, food service, sanitation, hygiene, health care services, personnel, record keeping, visitation, and more. 1989.

## Certification Standards

*Certification Standards for Food Service Programs*. 57 standards guide agencies to certification of this vital area while working toward eventual accreditation. Includes sanitation, fiscal and personnel procedures, security, and training for food service programs in juvenile training schools, detention facilities, adult correctional institutions, and local detention facilities. 1989.

*Certification Standards for Health Care Programs*. 92 standards spell out requirements for certification in this essential area by institutions working toward accreditation. Applies to juvenile training schools and detention facilities and to adult correctional institutions and local detention facilities. Includes safety and emergency procedures, sanitation, security, and medical standards. 1989.

*Correctional Officer Resource Guide*. This revised manual continues to be an essential reference on all aspects of a correctional officer's job. An excellent training and reference book, covering such topics as officer's legal liabilities, inmate programming, security, AIDS, and other health issues, use of firearms, segregation, methods of restraining inmates, emergency procedures, officer support programs, and contraband. 1989.

## Foundation/Core Standards

*Foundation/Core Standards for Adult Local Detention Facilities*. A new, alternate approach to accreditation allows certain accredited facilities to prove they comply with all mandatory ACA standards—standards that go beyond the life safety area and address every area of correctional operations. Applicants can benefit from paperwork reduction and the expanded time ACA audit teams can devote to these mandatory standards. 1989.

*Foundation/Core Standards for Adult Community Residential Services*. Adult community residential services can realize reduced paperwork and experience more detailed compliance reviews for all mandatory standards by ACA audit teams under this new, alternate approach to accreditation. 1989.

*Foundation/Core Standards for Adult Correctional Institutions*. This new, alternate approach to accreditation allows certain accredited adult correctional facilities to prove compliance with all mandatory ACA standards. These standards

address every correctional operations area. Reduced paperwork and expanded time devoted to these standards by ACA audit teams will be pluses for applicants. 1989.

## Juvenile Standards

*Standards for Juvenile Community Residential Facilities*, Second Edition. This publication contains 216 standards focusing on 13 important areas for operating programs and outlining residents' access to the surrounding community. 1983.

*Standards for Juvenile Probation and Aftercare Services*, Second Edition. 228 standards direct how to choose the juveniles who should be processed through the court and who should be diverted to other organizations. 1983.

*Standards for Juvenile Training Schools*, Third Edition. This publication contains 326 standards covering 31 program areas for long-term juvenile incarceration. It has an easy-to-use numbering system. 1991.

*Standards for Juvenile Detention Facilities*, Second Edition. 422 standards address the special needs of short-term juvenile detention. 1983.

## Guidelines—Adult

*Guidelines for the Development of Policies and Procedures—Adult Community Residential Services*. This publication contains applicable policies and procedures for the effective management and administration of community facilities. 1981.

*Guidelines for the Development of Policies and Procedures—Adult Correctional Institutions and Adult Local Detention Facilities*. This document offers clear examples for formulating day-to-day policies and procedures. Sample policies cover all aspects of facility operation. It includes a guide to developing policies and procedures by tailoring the sample documents to the needs of a facility. 1987.

*Guidelines for the Development of Policies and Procedures—Adult Parole Authorities/Adult Probation and Parole Field Services*. Model policies and procedures relating to both probation and parole field services and parole authorities are outlined. 1981.

*Guidelines for the Development of a Security Program*. W. Hardy Rauch. This publication presents ideas and concepts for designing or updating a comprehensive security program. It includes discussions of security basics, specific duties and responsibilities, and emergency preparedness. 1988.

## Guidelines—Juvenile

ACA's correctional guidelines provide step-by-step instructions for translating standards into effective and practical procedures. Each guidelines book includes sample forms and policies for universal use. All are invaluable aids for institutions working toward accreditation and for those upgrading everyday operations.

*Guidelines for the Development of Policies and Procedures—Juvenile Community Residential Facilities*. These guidelines contain definitions, sample policies and references for the management and administration of juvenile community residential facilities. 1990.

*Guidelines for the Development of Policies and Procedures—Juvenile Training Schools*. This guide is based on the practical experience of many agencies and facilities for the development of consistent and efficient operational policies and procedures. 1987.

## CAREER INFORMATION GUIDES

Career and occupational literature exists to advise students and job seekers at all levels on career selection or job change, addressing such aspects of employment as job requirements, current job availability, work environment, security, and advancement.

*Career Planning in Criminal Justice*, Third Edition. Robert C. DeLucia and Thomas J. Doyle. A practical, easy-to-use reference, this guide explores the variety of occupations available, including specific job responsibilities and qualifications for many criminal justice career areas. It offers information on internships, graduate school, law school, resume writing and interviewing techniques (Cincinnati: Anderson Publishing Co., 1998).

*Careers in the Criminal Justice System*. This guide describes personnel practices, recruiting, educational requirements, and job descriptions of positions in the areas of corrections, police, and courts. (Washington, DC: United States Department of Justice, Law Enforcement Assistance Administration, National Institute of Law Enforcement and Criminal Justice, 1975).

*Careers in Law Enforcement*. Briefly describes several entry-level positions available in police agencies at the state and local level, e.g., criminal investigator, crime prevention officer, training officer, communications officer, jail officer, bailiff, and police agent. (Washington, DC: United States Department of Justice, NCJRS, 1977).

*Careers in Law Enforcement*. Lists of employment opportunities at the federal level is available. Law enforcement employment opportunities are listed for the Department of Defense, Department of the Interior, Department of Justice, Department of the Treasury, General Services Administration, and United States Postal Service. Addresses for each department and the agencies within are provided. (Washington, DC: Office of Criminal Justice Education and Training, Law Enforcement Assistance Administration).

*Careers in Law Enforcement and Security*. Ruth C. Rosen (ed.) (New York, NY: Rosen Publishing Group, Inc., 1994).

*Chronicle Guidance* Publications:

> Correctional Officers. Brief 467.
> Criminologists. Brief 456.
> Psychologists. Brief 144.
> School Counselors. Brief 145.
> School Social Workers. Brief 432.
> Social Workers. Brief 84.
> Sociologists. Brief 316.

*Chronicle Occupational Brief and Reprint List*. Over 500 briefs and over 100 reprints. Free upon request. (Moravia, NY: Chronicle Guidance Publications).

*Concise Handbook of Occupations*. Joan Costello and Rita P. Wolfson. This handbook offers detailed information on most occupations. (Chicago: J.G. Ferguson Publishing Company, 1971).

*Criminal Justice Careers Guidebook*. Providing a background on the development and structure of the criminal justice system in the U.S., this guidebook describes criminal justice jobs, requirements, and employment opportunities at the federal, state, and local levels. This is a cooperative publication of the Departments of Labor and Justice. (Washington, DC: U.S. Department of Labor, 1982-date).

*Current Career and Occupational Literature 1984*. Leonard H. Goodman. Renowned as a bibliographic key to significant material published on vocational opportunities and counseling, the 1984 volume of *Current Career and Occupational Literature* offers a wide selection of inexpensive pamphlets, books, and periodicals published by commercial publishers, professional associations, and government agencies, all providing critical information on jobs in more than 700 contemporary occupations. Teachers, career counselors, librarians, and parents use *Current*. (Bronx, NY: H.W. Wilson Co., 1984).

*The Encyclopedia of Vocational Guidance*. William E. Hopke (ed.). This publication is designed to help individuals make an assessment of occupational opportunities and demands. Virtually all fields and individual vocations are addressed. (Chicago: J.G. Ferguson Publishing Company, 1975).

*Federal Employment Information Directory*. This directory is a national employment listing service for the criminal justice system. It offers information on entrance requirements, application procedures, salary levels, and job descriptions for all federal agencies. (Huntsville, TX: National Employment Listing Service, 1978-date).

*Good Works: A Guide to Social Change*. Ralph Nader. This guide provides details on 275 citizen groups for people interested in voluntary or paid employment. (Washington, DC: Center for Responsive Law, 1980).

*National Employment Listing Service (NELS) Bulletin*. This is a monthly publication which lists currently available job opportunities in law enforcement. Areas represented are academia, courts, corrections, human services, and private security. (Huntsville, TX: Texas Criminal Justice Center, Sam Houston State University).

*Occupational Outlook Handbook*. This handbook describes the nature of occupations, places of employment, training qualifications and advancement, employment outlook, earnings and working conditions, and additional sources of information for nearly every field of employment and type of work. Annual. (Washington, DC: Bureau of Labor Statistics Division of Occupational Outlook).

In addition to the above guides, the following sources will also be helpful.

*Pathway to Your Future*. Kenneth R. Adler. This publication details elements of a job resume, preparation of a resume, and letters of application. (Arlington, MA: Bellman Publishing Company, 1971).

VGM Career Books:

*Opportunities in Law Enforcement and Criminal Justice*. James Stinchomb. (Lincolnwood, IL: National Textbook Company, 1994).

*Opportunities in State and Local Government Careers*. Neale Baxter. (Lincolnwood, IL: National Textbook Company, 1994).

*Opportunities in Federal Government Careers*, Second Edition. Neale Baxter. (Lincolnwood, IL: National Textbook Company, 1994).

*Why and How To Prepare An Effective Job Resume*. Juvenal L. Angel. This publication describes the various steps a job seeker must take in order to prepare an effective resume. (New York: World Trade Academy Press, Inc., 1972).

# 7

# Bibliographies

Bibliographies are compilations of sources relating to a particular subject. Bibliographies provide researchers additional sources of information on a topic, and also acquaint the researcher with major authors in the field. Most textbooks, articles, and encyclopedias will contain bibliographies. Unfortunately, students often overlook bibliographies as supplemental sources of information. There is a vast amount of literature published in the criminal justice field and numerous bibliographies attempt to organize and categorize it. The most important bibliography is *Bibliographies in Criminal Justice*.

The National Criminal Justice Reference Service (NCJRS) offers custom and prepackaged topical searches and bibliographies. Other major sources of bibliographies are *Bibliographical Index*, published by the H.W. Wilson Company, The American Correctional Association (for correctional related bibliographies), and *Criminological Bibliographies* published by Greenwood Press. The researcher should also check The Subject Guide of *Books in Print*.

*Abstracts on Crime and Juvenile Delinquency: Cumulative Index, 1968-1984*. (Buffalo, NY: William S. Hein and Company, 1986).

*Abstracts on Evaluative Research*. C.H. Weiss, J.A. Weiss, P.C. Kleinman, and S.T. Hillsman. (Washington, DC: National Criminal Justice Reference Service Microfiche Program, 1975).

*Abuse of Women: Legislation, Reporting, and Prevention*. Joseph J. Costa. (Lexington, MA: Lexington Books, 1983).

*The Administration of Justice in the Courts: A Selected Annotated Bibliography*. Fannie J. Klein. (New York: Oceana, 1976).

*After the Fact: The Art of Historical Detection*. James W. Davidson and Mark H. Lytle. 2 vols. 2nd ed. 1985, Vol. 1. Vol. 2. 1985.

*Alternatives to Institutionalization: A Definitive Bibliography*. James R. Brantley and Marjorie Kravitz. (Rockville, MD: National Institute of Law Enforcement and Criminal Justice, 1979).

*Alternatives to Institutionalization*. (Washington, DC: United States Department of Justice, Law Enforcement Assistance Administration, 1980).

*Annotated Bibliography of Alcohol and Other Drug Prevention Resources: Focus: Environmental Management Strategies*. Kimberly Kaphingst. (Newton, MA: Higher Education Center for Alcohol and Other Drug Prevention, 1997).

*Annotated Bibliography for Criminal Justice Planning*. Charles R. Davoli and Patrick J. Michaud. (Tallahassee, FL:Florida Bureau of Criminal Justice Planning and Assistance, 1975).

*An Annotated Bibliography of Homosexuality*. Vern L. Bullough, W. Dorr Legg, and Barrett W. Elcano. (New York: Garland, 1976).

*Annotated Bibliography of Research Reports and Program Studies*, Volume II, 1974; Volume III, 1975. (New York, NY: New York State Drug Abuse Control Commission).

*Auxiliary Police Forces; A Selected Bibliography*. Anthony G. White. (Public administration series, bibliography) (Monticello, IL: Vance Bibliographies, 1989).

*The Battered Child: A Review of Studies and Research in the Area of Child Abuse*. Emilio C. Viano. In Israel Drapkin and Emilio C. Viano, *Victimology: A New Focus*, v. 4. (Lexington, MA: Lexington Books, 1975).

*Battered Wives: A Comprehensive Annotated Bibliography of Articles, Books, and Statutes in the United States of America.* Nathan Aaron Rosen. (National Center for Women & Family Law, 1975).

*Behavior and Psychology as Related to Law Enforcement and Criminology: A Bibliography with Abstracts.* Mary E. Young and Edward J. Lehmann. (Springfield, VA: U.S. National Technical Information Service, 1975).

*Bibliographies in Criminal Justice.* This "bibliography of bibliographies" briefly describes more than 200 published bibliographies pertaining to criminal justice. Although it is not entirely comprehensive, its coverage represents almost all specialty areas within the field. The alphabetized subject index contains entries from adult offenders to work attitudes. An alphabetized title index is also included. This work is an important research tool, and should be consulted early in the research process if possible. Descriptive annotations of each bibliography provide the user with a concise summary of the contents. It is an excellent tool for scanning the majority of criminal justice bibliographies which in turn will lead the researcher to appropriate materials. (Washington, DC: United States Department of Justice. NCJRS, 1980).

The following five bibliographies are available from The Information Resource Center (IRC) of The American Society for Industrial Security (ASIS), 1655 North Fort Myer Drive, Suite 1200, Arlington, VA 22209: *Bibliography of Security Salaries and Wages* (November 1990); *Bibliography of Sources on Software/Security Applications* (June 1990); *Bibliography on Strikes* (September 1990); *Bibliography on Security for Multi-Tenant/High-Rise Buildings* (September 1990); *Bibliography on Security Lighting* (January 1991).

*A Bibliography of Correctional Law.* This is an excellent list of correctional legal materials. The titles reflect the opinions of nearly 25 councils representing correctional agencies, who were asked to list the research tools they found most useful. (Laurel, MD: American Correctional Association, 1987).

*Bibliography on Dangerousness: Its Prediction and Treatment.* United Nations. Social Defence Research Institute. (Washington, DC: National Criminal Justice Reference Service Microfiche Program, 1975).

*A Bibliography on General Deterrence Research.* Deryck Beyleveld. (Lexington, MA: Lexington Books, 1980.)

*Bibliography on Runaway Youth.* U.S. Department of Health, Education and Welfare. (U.S. Children's Bureau) Office of Youth Development. (Washington, DC: National Criminal Justice Reference Service Microfiche Program, 1975).

*A Bibliography of Selected RAND Publications: Criminal Justice.* This bibliography serves as a complete guide to all of the research completed by the RAND Corporation. This is an excellent source of state-of-the-art research being conducted in the field of criminal justice. This bibliography is a must for any serious researcher in criminal justice. (Santa Monica, CA: RAND Corporation, 1983).

*Bibliography on Shoplifting.* Final report. Patronic Systems Corp. Computer Science and Environmental Technology Division. Panorama City, CA, 19 September 1975.

*Capital Punishment in America: An Annotated Bibliography.* Michael L. Radelet and Margaret Vandiver. (New York: Garland 1988).

*Capital Punishment Dilemma 1950-1977: A Subject Bibliography.* Charles Triche. (New York: Whitson, Inc., 1979).

*Child Abuse: An Annotated Bibliography.* Dorothy P. Wells. (Metuchen, NJ: Scarecrow Press, 1980).

*Child Abuse and Neglect: An Annotated Bibliography.* Beatrice J. Kalisch. (Westport, CT: Greenwood Press, 1978).

*A Collection of Bibliographic and Research Resources.* (Dobbs Ferry, NY: Oceana, 1984-date).

*Correctional Law: A Bibliography of Selected Books and Articles.* William C. Collins. This bibliography covers a wide range of topics and legal issues related to corrections. Categories include criminal law, access to courts, counsel access to media, behavior modification, civil disabilities, and rights of ex-offenders, civil rights, litigation, cruel and unusual punishment and detainment, grievance procedures, habeas corpus, and several others. (College Park, MD: American Correctional Association, 1987).

*Community Crime Prevention: An Annotated Bibliography.* National Council on Crime & Delinquency Staff. (San Francisco, CA: National Council on Crime and Delinquency, 1987).

*Court Reporting; A Selected Bibliography.* By Kevin E. O'Brien, Marvin Marcus, and Robert J. Wheaton. (Washington, DC: National Institute of Law Enforcement and Criminal Justice, 1976).

*Crime,* Vol. 4. Eleanor C. Goldstein (ed.). (Incl. 1988-1992 Supplements) (Boca Raton, FL: Sirs, Inc., 1993).

*Crime Analysis, Selected Bibliography.* M.N. Emig, R.O. Heck, and M. Kravitz (eds.). This bibliography features 50 citations clarifying the role of crime analysis and presenting operational and administrative policies. The documents cited describe its application for resource deployment, investigation, and apprehension. There are three chapters: Tactical Use, Strategic Use, and Long-Range Planning. Microfiche. (Washington, DC: National Institute of Justice/NCJRS, 1980).

*Crime and Juvenile Delinquency: A Bibliographic Guide to the Basic Microform Collection.* This publication represents important or significant documents held in the library of the National Council on Crime and Delinquency (NCCD), which are not likely to be widely distributed in any other fashion. This is probably the largest single collection of reports and documents available from one source. (Glen Rock, NJ: Microfilming Corporation of America, 1977).

*Crime Prevention and Law Enforcement Through Community Relations: A Bibliography with Abstracts.* Mary E. Young. (Springfield, VA, U.S. National Technical Information Service, 1981).

*Crime and Punishment in America: A Historical Bibliography.* (Santa Barbara, CA: ABC-Clio, 1984).

*Crime and the Elderly; An Annotated Bibliography.* Ron H. Aday. (Westport, CT: Greenwood Press, 1988).

*Crime in the Black Community: An Exploratory Bibliography.* Lenwood G. Davis. Council of Planning Librarians. (Monticello, IL: Vance Bibliographies, 1975).

*Crime in the United States: A Selected Bibliography.* Robert Goehlert. (Monticello, IL:Vance Bibliographies, 1988).

*Criminal Investigation: A Selected Bibliography.* Robert Goehlert. (Monticello, IL: Vance Bibliographies, 1987).

*Criminal Justice Bibliography.* Marvin Marcus. This bibliography lists more than 6,000 entries and at the time of its publication was one of the most comprehensive bibliographies of criminal justice, consisting primarily of books, monographs, and government documents. (Atlanta: Georgia State University, School of Urban Life, 1976).

*Criminal Justice Evaluation: An Annotated Bibliography.* U.S. National Institute of Law Enforcement and Criminal Justice. (Washington, DC: National Criminal Justice Reference Service, 1975).

*Criminal Justice History: An International Annual.* Vol. 11. Louis A. Knafla (ed.). (Chicago: Greenwood Publishing, 1990).

*Criminal Justice Information Systems Selected Bibliography.* C. Klein and N. Arnesen (eds.). There are 197 citations in this bibliography addressing issues, concepts, and assessments of information systems; state plans developed in compliance with federal regulations; issues of individual rights and the Privacy Act of 1975; and security and privacy plans for information systems. Citations also cover computerized criminal histories, offender-based transaction statistics, and the Prosecutor's Management Information System (PROMIS). (Washington, DC: National Institute of Justice/NCJRS, 1980).

*Criminal Justice Research in Libraries: Strategies & Resources.* Marilyn Lutzker. (Westport, CT: Greenwood Press, 1986).

*Criminological Bibliographies and Uniform Citations to Bibliographies, Indexes and Review Articles of the Literature of Crime Study in the U.S.* Bruce L. Davis. (Westport, CT: Greenwood Press, 1978).

*Criminological Research: A Selected Bibliography.* (Public Administration Ser.: P 2369). (Monticello, IL: Vance Bibliographies, 1988).

*Criminology and Forensic Sciences: An International Bibliography.* Rudolfe von Ende. 1950-1980. (Detroit: K.G. Saur, 1981).

*Criminology Index: Research and Theory in Criminology in the United States, 1945-1972.* Marvin E. Wolfgang (ed.). 2 vols. (New York: Elsevier, 1975).

*Decision-Making In the Criminal Justice System.* Don M. Gottfredson. (New York: Plenum, 1987).

*Drug Abuse Bibliography.* (Troy, NY: Whitson Publishing Co., 1970-present).

*Drug Use and Abuse Among U.S. Minorities: An Annotated Bibliography.* Patti Iiyama, Setsuko M. Nishi, and Bruce D. Johnson. (New York: Praeger, 1976).

*Drugs of Addiction and Non-Addiction Their Use and Abuse: A Comprehensive Bibliography.* Joseph Menditto. 1960-1969. (Troy, NY: Whitston, 1970). NALU; supp., by Jean C. Advena. *Drug Abuse Bibliography for 1970.* 1971. 197p. NALU; supp., . . . *For 1971.* 1972.; . . . *For 1973.* 1975.; supp., by Charles W. Triche and Diane S. Triche. . . . *For 1974.* (Troy, NY: Whitson, 1976).

*Drug Addiction, Substance Abuse, and Narcotic Dependency: A Medical Subject Analysis and Research Index with Bibliography.* John C. Bartone. (Washington, DC: ABBE Publishers Association of Washington, DC, 1997).

*Education of Prisoners: A Selected Bibliography of Journal Articles, 1984-1987.* Verna Casey. (Monticello, IL: Vance Bibliographies, 1988).

*The Effectiveness of General Deterrents Against Crime: An Annotated Bibliography of Evaluative Research.* Deryck Beyleveld. (Cambridge, UK: University of Cambridge Institute of Criminology, 1978).

*Electronic Detention-House Arrest As a Correctional Alternative: A Selected Bibliography.* Verna Casey. (Monticello, IL:Vance Bibliographies, 1988).

*Ethics in Local Government: A Selected Bibliography.* Council of Planning Librarians. Anthony G. White. (Monticello, IL:Vance Bibliographies, 1977).

*The Etiology of Criminality: Non-behavorial Science Perspectives.* James R. Brantley. This is a bibliography which focuses on the efforts of bibligical and physical scientists to determine the underlying nature of criminality. Entries are representative of a biological approach to the study of criminality but are not intended to advocate biological influences at the expense of social factors. They make information available on those factors which may contribute to crime but which will rarely be included in social science literature. (Washington, DC: United States Department of Justice, Law Enforcement Assistance Administration, National Institute of Law Enforcement and Criminal Justice, 1979).

*Etiology and Treatment of Homosexuality.* Frank Acosta. Archives of Sexual Behavior. A Review. January 1975. (New York, NY: Plenum Press).

*The Female Offender.* Margery Velimesis. Crime and Delinquency Literature, March 1975. (New York, NY: National Council on Crime and Delinquency).

*The Female Offender: A Guide to Published Materials.* Eugen Doleschal. 1970. NALU; supp., Bibliography; The Female Offender: 1970-1974. (Hackensack, NJ: National Council on Crime and Delinquency, Information Center, 1975).

*Homicide: A Bibliography of Over 4,500 Items.* Bal K. Jerath, Paul E. Larson and Jesse F. Lewis. (Augusta, GA: Pine Tree Pubns., 1982).

*The Impact of Crime.* John E. Conklin. (New York: Macmillan, 1975).

*Index to Minorities & Criminal Justice: An Index to Periodicals and Books Relating to Minorities and Criminal Justice in the United States.* Scott Christianson (cumulative ed.). (Albany, NY: Center on Minorities and Criminal Justice, School of Criminal Justice, State University of New York at Albany, 1981).

*Indian Justice: A Research Bibliography.* Council of Planning Librarians. (Monticello, IL: Vance Bibliographies, 1976).

*International Bibliography & Medical Subject Index of Crime Publications.* American Health Research Institute Staff. John C. Barton. (ABBE Pubs Assn., 1982).

*International Terrorism: An Annotated Bibliography and Research Guide.* August R. Norton and Martin H. Greenberg. (Boulder, CO: Westview Press, 1980).

*Judicial Administration and the Legal Profession: A Bibliography.* Fannie J. Klein. *The Administration of Justice in the Courts: A Selected Annotated Bibliography Updating and Expanding Klein, Judicial Administration. . . .* (Dobbs Ferry, NY: Oceana, 1976).

*The Judiciary and The Criminal Justice System.* U.S. National Criminal Justice Reference Service. A report presented at the National Conference of State Criminal Justice Planning Adminstrators, annual meeting, July 18-20, 1976. (Seattle, WA: NCJRS, 1976).

*Juvenile Delinquency.* (Washington, DC: U.S. National Technical Information Service, 1975).

*Juvenile Delinquency: A Bibliography with Abstracts.* Mary E. Young. (Springfield, VA: U.S. National Technical Information Service, 1976).

*Juvenile Delinquency in the Black Community.* Council of Planning Librarians. Eleanor Dorton and Lenwood G. Davis. (Monticello, IL: Vance Bibliographies, 1975).

*Juvenile Diversion: A Selected Bibliography.* U.S. National Institute of Law Enforcement and Criminal Justice. Kevin E. O'Brien and Marvin Marcus. (Washington, DC: National Institute of Law Enforcement and Criminal Justice, 1976).

*Juvenile Gangs: A Bibliography.* U.S. National Criminal Justice Reference Service. C.A. Riccio. (Washington, DC: National Criminal Justice Reference Service Microfiche Program, 1975). NCJ-18039.

*Law Enforcement: A Selected Bibliography,* B.R. Felkenes and H.K. Becker. This bibliography contains thousands of listings which deal with the entire criminal justice system. Many of these are annotated. Books and articles are listed in alphabetical order by subject. (Metuchen, NJ: Scarecrow Press, 1977).

*Law, Medicine and Health Care: A Bibliography,* Dr. James T. Ziegenfuss, Jr. Malpractice suits and a multiplicity of other medical and health care issues today are of concern to lawyers, health care officials, and doctors. *Law, Medicine and Health Care* offers a complete listing of recent issues, their litigation and decisions both in and out of the courts. The book is divided into sections of specialty concern and each is supplemented with introductory text outlining the scope and relevance of the subject area to the overall health care field. Also provided is an essential listing of the lawyers involved in health care and medical issues throughout the 50 states. (New York: Facts on File, 1984).

*LEAA and Criminal Justice Planning: A Partial Bibliography of Documents and Articles.* Council of Planning Librarians. James C. Starbuck. (Monticello, IL: Vance Bibliographies, 1976).

*Legal Bibliography,* Current. (Cambridge, MA: Harvard Law Library).

*The Library Catalogue of the Radzinowicz Library*. Radzinowicz Library. Institute of Criminology, University of Cambridge, England. (Boston: G.K. Hall, 1979).

*The Literature of Higher Education in Criminology and Criminal Justice: An Annotated Bibliography*. Carolyn Johnson. (Chicago: Joint Commission on Criminology and Criminal Justice Education and Standards, 1979).

*The Literature of Police Corruption. Volume I: A Guide to Bibliography and Theory*. Anthony E. Simpson. (New York: The John Jay Press, 1980).

*The Literature of Terrorism: A Selectively Annotated Bibliography*. Edward F. Mickolus. "Mickolus has compiled the definitive bibliography on terrorism, superseding Augustus R. Norton's *International Terrorism*. Mickolus has been affiliated with the CIA for many years and knows his subject well. He provides extensive coverage . . . He has succeeded in imposing some order on the avalanche of material about terrorism. His tightly organized and well indexed bibliography is highly recommended for academic and large public libraries." (Westport, CT: Greenwood Press, 1980).

*Mafia: A Selected Annotated Bibliography*. Lloyd Trott. (Cambridge, U.K.: Institute of Criminology, 1977).

*Memoirs of American Prisons: An Annotated Bibliography*. Daniel Sunack. (Metuchen, NJ: Scarecrow Press, 1979).

*Observing the Law: Applications of Field Methods to the Study of the Criminal Justice System*. U.S. National Institute of Mental Health. Center for Studies of Crime and Delinquency. George J. McCall. (Washington, DC: National Institute of Mental Health, 1974).

*Organized Crime: A Bibliography*. This publication provides references of contemporary writings on the problems of organized crime. (Ottawa, Canada: Law Enforcement Reference Center, 1990).

*Physical Design and Urban Crime: A Selected Bibliography*. Council of Planning Librarians. Anthony G. White. (Monticello, IL: Vance Bibliographies, 1976).

*Physical and Sexual Abuse of Children: Causes and Treatment*. David R. Walters. (Bloomington, IN: University Press, 1975).

*Plea Bargaining: A Selected Bibliography*. U.S. National Institute of Law Enforcement and Criminal Justice. Marvin Marcus and Robert J. Wheaton. (Washington, DC: National Institute of Law Enforcement and Criminal Justice, 1976).

*Police Administration: A Bibliography*. This bibliography cites more than 1,100 references dealing with various aspects of police administration. Entries are listed alphabetically, and categories include accountability and discretion, corruption, detectives and criminal investigation, discipline, firearms and deadly force, job hazards, pedestrian and bicycle safety, police management, police chiefs and relationships with local government, productivity and performance measurement, recruitment, team policing, traffic and highway safety, and traffic engineering. An author index and an appendix listing publishers and periodicals is included. (Evanston, IL: Northwestern University, The Traffic Institute, 1979).

*Police Bibliography*. Jack E. Whitehouse. This comprehensive 500-page bibliography organizes approximately 17,000 published and unpublished criminal justice information sources into 1,100 subject headings with page references and cross indexes. (New York: AMS Press, Inc., 1980).

*Police Consolidation: A Selected Bibliography*. U.S. National Institute of Law Enforcement and Criminal Justice. Marvin Marcus, James M. Edgar, Robert J. Wheaton and Robert C. Hicox. (Washington, DC: National Institute of Law Enforcement and Criminal Justice, 1976).

*Police: Operations, Management, Training, Behavior, Equipment: A Bibliography with Abstracts (1964-March 1976)*. Mary E. Young. (Springfield, VA: U.S. Technical Information Service, 1976).

*Police Personnel Mangement: Selected References*. This publication annotates more than 700 citations from the following subject areas: personnel management, professionalization, employee and groups, labor relations, uniforms, problems on the job, and attitudes of police and public. (Evanston, IL: Northwestern University, The Traffic Institute, 1972).

*Police Research and Evaluation Studies: A Working Bibliography*. Council of Planning Librarians. Police Study Group, Northwestern University. (Monticello, IL: Council of Planning Librarians, 1976).

*Police Science, 1964-1984: A Selected Annotated Bibliography*. William G. Bailey. (New York: Garland Publishing, 1986).

*Police Training*. This publication highlights the literature on police training. The citations relate specifically to general issues of police training, descriptions of training programs in the United States and abroad, descriptions of modular programs, laboratory training, use of closed-circuit televisions, and evaluation of specific programs. The documents listed are part of the NCJRS collection and may be borrowed through interlibrary loan, or if available on microfiche, obtained free of charge. (Washington, DC: United States Department of Justice, NCJRS, 1980). (For more information on other government documents and NCJRS, please see Chapter 10, "Government Documents.")

*Police Unionization and Bargaining*. Selected references concern police unions, associations, and collective bargaining and public employee labor-management relations. (Evanston, IL: Northwestern University, The Traffic Institute, 1976).

*The Policewoman in American Society: A Preliminary Survey*. Council of Planning Librarians. Lenwood G. Davis. (Monticello, IL: Council of Planning Librarians) May 1976.

*Political Violence in the United States, 1875-1974*. Jarol B. Manheim and Melanie Wallace. (New York: Stein, 1975).

*The Politics of Rape: The Victim's Perspective*. Barbara Fagan, Diana E.H. Russell and Margaret Stone. Bibliography. (New York: Stein, 1975).

*A Preliminary Bibliography of Modern Criminal Law & Criminology*. xxi, Repr. of 1909 ed. lib. bdg. (Littleton, CO: Rothman, 1981).

*Poly Drug Use: Annotated Bibliography*. U.S. National Institute on Drug Abuse. National Clearinghouse for Drug Abuse Information. (Washington, DC: National Institute on Drug Abuse, 1975).

*Prescriptive Packages*. (Washington, DC: U.S. National Institute of Law Enforcement and Criminal Justice, 1975).

*Problems and Planning of Police Community-Relationships: A Selected Research Bibliography*. Council of Planning Librarians. Prakash C. Sharma. (Monticello, IL: National Council of Planning Librarians, 1975).

*Protecting the President: A Selective Bibliography*. Larry D. Benson. (Monticello, IL: Vance Bibliograhies, 1989).

*Protest and Crime in China: A Bibliography of Secret Associations, Popular Uprisings, Peasant Rebellions*. Ssu-yu Teng. (New York: Garland, 1981).

*Public Perceptions of Criminal Behavior: A Review of the Literature*. Graeme Newman and Carol Trilling. *Criminal Justice and Behavior*, September 1975. (Thousand Oaks, CA: Sage Publications).

*Publications of the National Institute of Law Enforcement and Criminal Justice*. This comprehensive bibliography is designed to provide criminal justice professionals with access to research sponsored and published by National Institute during 1968 and 1977. (Washington, DC: United States Department of Justice, Law Enforcement Assistance Administration, National Institute of Law Enforcement and Criminal Justice, 1979).

*Publication of the National Institute of Law Enforcement and Criminal Justice*, 1979 Supplement. This is a supplement to the 1978 catalog and contains citations for documents published in 1978 for distribution through the GPO or the NCJRS. Subject and title indexes are included. Part I lists citations in NCJ number order and abstracts are provided for each publication. Part II contains listings and annotations of several specialized types of publications such as program models, national evaluation programs, exemplary projects, and selected bibliographies. (Washington, DC: National Institute of Law Enforcement and Criminal Justice, 1979). (See Chapter 10, "Government Documents," under exemplary projects.)

*Readers Advisory Service: Selected Topics*. Leonard Cohan (ed.). (Broadway, NY: Science Associates International, 1983).

*Recidivism: A Selected Bibliography*. Robert J. Trudel, Marvin Marcus, and Robert J. Wheaton. (Washington, DC: National Institute of Law Enforcement and Criminal Justice, 1976).

*Rehabilitation of Criminals: A Bibliography*. Mary Vance. (Monticello, IL: Vance Bibliographies, 1988).

*Rehabilitation and the Retarded Offender*. Philip L. Browning. (Springfield, IL: Charles C Thomas, 1976).

*Research Approaches In Illicit Drug Use*. S.W. Sadava. A critical Review. Genetic psychology monographs, February 1975.

*Restitution As A Criminal Sentence*: Anthony G. White. (Monticello, IL: Council of Planning Librarians, 1977).

*A Selected Bibliography of Security and Loss Prevention*. This is an excellent bibliography of private security topics. It includes books, publications of the government, learned societies, and other organizations. Films and audiovisual materials, periodicals, related bibliographies and selected publishers. (Washington, DC: American Society for Industrial Security, 1981).

*Security and Privacy of Criminal Justice Information: A Bibliography*. This 126-page bibliography presents a wide range of literature dealing with various aspects of the subject of privacy and the security of information obtained on individuals who have had contact with the criminal justice system. (Sacramento, CA: Search Group, Inc., 1979).

*A Selective Bibliography on the Economic Costs of Crime*. Michael J. Slinger. (Monticello, IL: Vance Bibliographies, 1989).

*Selected Literature on Evaluation*. (Washington, DC: U.S. National Institute of Law Enforcement and Criminal Justice, 1975).

*Skid Row*. J. Randolph Gregson II. Council of Planning Librarians. This is a wide-ranging bibliography. (Monticello, IL: Vance Bibliographies, 1977).

*Social Class and Delinquency.* C.A. Riccio. U.S. National Criminal Justice Reference Service. (Washington, DC: National Criminal Justice Reference Service Microfiche Program, 1975).

*Soviet Prisons and Concentration Camps*, Zorin Libushe. An annotated bibliography, 1917-1980. (Newtonville, MA: Oriental Research Partners, 1980). (Russian bibliography Ser., no. 3).

*The Spatial Analysis of Crime.* Perry O. Hansen and Barbara Boehnke. (Monticello, IL: Council of Planning Librarians, 1976).

*Spies and All That . . . Intelligence Agencies and Operations: A Bibliography.* Ronald M. DeVore. Citing more than 500 monographs, reports, and articles this publication concerns espionage, intelligence operations, and related subjects. (Los Angeles: Center for the Study of Armament and Disarmament, California State University, 1977).

*Strategic Criminal Justice Planning.* Daniel Glaser. U.S. National Institute of Mental Health. Center for Studies in Crime and Delinquency. (Washington, DC: Center for Studies in Crime and Delinquency, 1975).

*Stress Factors As Identified By Research In Prisons.* Debra M. Hydge and Donald Conway. (Monticello, IL: Council of Planning Librarians, 1977).

*Suicide: A Guide to Information Sources.* David Lester and Betty H. Sell (eds.). (Detroit: Gale Research, 1980).

*Suicides In The Black Community: A Preliminary Survey.* Edward E. Hubbard. (Monticello, IL: Council of Planning Librarians, 1975).

*Toward the Prevention of Rape: A Partially Annotated Bibliography.* Marcia J. Walker. University of Alabama. Department of Psychology. Center for Correctional Psychology. (Washington, DC: National Criminal Justice Reference Service Microfiche Program, 1975).

*The Urban Police: An Annotated Bibliography of the Social Science Literature, 1960-1973.* Donald Ostrom. (Monticello, IL: Council of Planning Librarians, 1975).

*Victim Compensation and Offender Restitution; A Selected Bibliography.* Marvin Marcus, Robert J. Trudel and Robert J. Wheaton. (Washington, DC: U.S. National Criminal Justice Reference Service, 1975).

*Violence in the Family: An Annotated Bibliography.* Elizabeth Jane Kemmer. This publication comprises 1,055 citations to English-language publications, 1960-82. It has main-entry arrangement; subject and author indexes. (New York: Garland, 1984).

*Violence at Home.* Mary H. Lystad. A review of the literature. (*American Journal of Orthopsychiatry*, April 1975).

*Violence in the Home:Interdisciplinary Perspectives.* Mary H. Lystad. (New York: Brunner-Mazel, 1986).

## NCJRS CUSTOM SEARCHES

National Criminal Justice Reference Service (NCJRS) custom searches are a cost-effective way to gather complete, targeted information. Following a search strategy based on the researcher's needs, the NCJRS reference specialist conducts a database search to identify citations that address the area of interest. A search contains up to 400 citations including bibliographic information and summaries of content, and requester-specified areas and parameters ensure pertinent information.

Custom searches are available in hard copy as printouts or on diskette to use on an IBM-compatible personal computer.

The printouts include all abstracts and bibliographic citations in the NCJRS document database on a topic as well as instructions for interpreting the data.

NCJRS database searches provide overviews of published and unpublished materials compiled from almost 100,000 documents—the largest criminal justice database in the world.

Highly trained information specialists with direct online access to NCJRS's unparalleled criminal justice database can help answer information requests in all these areas:

- AIDS
- Corrections
- Courts
- Criminology
- Crime prevention
- Juvenile justice
- Law enforcement
- Victims
- Drugs
- Statistics

Three types of NCJRS database searches are available: topical searches, topical bibliographies, and custom searches. Researchers may call NCJRS to inquire if the desired information has already been compiled, or to request a custom search to meet specific needs.

## TOPICAL SEARCHES

Topical searches and topical bibliographies are prepackaged computerized searches of the NCJRS database. They provide reviews of published and unpublished materials on many criminal justice topics. Each includes bibliographic information, availability, and a summary. Topical searches contain 30 citations and are updated every six months. Topical bibliographies contain up to 200 citations with subject and title indexes and are updated annually. Following are samples of prepared topical searches with their topical search numbers (TS) and topical bibliographical searches (TB) available from NCJRS. They can be ordered from:

> NCJRS
> Attention: AIO
> Department F
> Box 6000
> Rockville, MD 20850

### AIDS

AIDS and Intravenous Drug Use
(TS011647)

AIDS and Its Impact on Corrections
(TS011644)

AIDS and Youth
(TS011651)

### Corrections

Adult Female Offender
(TS010103)

Capital Punishment
(TS010302)

Corrections Construction
(TS011105)

Corrections Personnel: Selection, Training,
and Performance
(TS011650)

Crowding in Prisons and Jails
(TS011108)

Educational and Vocational Programs in
Corrections
(TS011649)

Effectiveness of Probation and Parole
(TS011643)

Electronic Monitoring/House Arrest
(TS011662)

Health Care in Correctional Facilities
(TS011106)

Inmates and Their Families
(TS011103)

Intermediate Supervision
(TS011107)

Mentally Disordered/Disabled Offenders
(TS011627)

Prison Violence
(TS011633)

Private Sector Involvement in Corrections
(TS011628)

Recidivism
(TS011615)

Restitution
(TS011104)

Sex Offenses and Offenders
(TS011617)

Siting of New Correctional Facilities
(TS011663)

### Courts

Court Management
(TS011638)

Exclusionary Rule
(TS011620)

Habeas Corpus
(TS011646)

Insanity Defense
(TS010301)

Jury Selection
(TS011634)

Plea Bargaining
(TS011635)

Pretrial Issues
(TS011639)

Sentencing Disparity
(TS010303)

Sentencing Guidelines
(TS011654)

### Crime Prevention

Community Crime Prevention Programs
(TS010201)

Computer Crime and Security
(TS011602)

Crime Prevention Through Environmental
Design
(TS011210)

Crimes Against Business
(TS011205)

Employee Theft
(TS011203)

Evaluation of Crime Prevention Programs
(TS011201)

Private Police/Security Police
(TS011202)

Shoplifting
(TS011209)

## Drugs

Asset Seizure and Forfeiture
(TS011652)

Cocaine and Crack
(TS011648)

Drinking and Driving
(TS011619)

Drug Abuse Programs for Offenders
(TS011636)

Drug Law Enforcement
(TS011642)

Drug Legalization
(TS011653)

Drug Testing
(TS011640)

Drug Trafficking
(TS011641)

Drugs in the Workplace
(TS011645)

## Juvenile Classification

(TS021523)

Juvenile Correctional Education
(TS021524)

Juvenile Detention
(TS021511)

Juvenile Diversion Programs
(TS021513)

Juvenile Gangs
(TS020501)

Juvenile Probation Services
(TS021518)

Juvenile Restitution
(TS021508)

Juvenile Substance Abuse
(TS021504)

Juveniles in Adult Jails and Lockups
(TS021503)

Learning Disabled Youth
(TS021510)

Runaway, Missing, and Abducted Children
(TS021519)

Violence and Vandalism in Schools
(TS020503)

Serious Juvenile Offenders
(TS020502)

Waiver of Juvenile Court Jurisdiction
(TS020515)

## Juvenile Justice

Child Abuse and Its Link to Delinquency
(TS021516)

Child Sexual Exploitation
(TS021507)

Deinstitutionalization of Status Offenders
(TS021525)

## Law Enforcement

Campus Crime and Police
(TS011204)

Crime Analysis
(TS011610)

Criminal Investigations Management
(TS011637)

DNA (Deoxyribonucleic Acid)
(TS011655)

Foot Patrol
(TS011625)

Gun Control
(TS011621)

Minorities in Law Enforcement
(TS011660)

Motorcycle Gangs and Drugs
(TS011656)

One Officer Patrols and Take Home Vehicles
(TS011657)

Organized Crime
(TS011603)

Police Discipline and Internal Affairs
(TS011605)

Police Dogs
(TS011624)

Police Firearms Training
(TS011613)

Police/Fire Consolidation
(TS011611)

Police Manpower Allocations and Work
Scheduling
(TS011601)

Police Mobile Computers and Terminals
(TS011658)

Police Personnel Selection
(TS010601)

Police Physical Fitness
(TS011606)

Police Pistols and Revolvers
(TS011659)

Police Promotion/Career Development
(TS011604)

Police Pursuit Driving
(TS011614)

Police Stress and Stress Management
(TS011612)

Police Use of Force
(TS010604)

Search and Seizure
(TS011661)

Serial/Mass Murder
(TS011664)

SWAT and Hostage Negotiations
(TS010603)

Terrorism
(TS011631)

## Statistics

Prison Population Projections
(TS030001)

## Victims

Battered Women
(TS011213)

Bias-Related Violence
(TS040011)

Child Sexual Abuse: Programs and Curricula
(TS040008)

Crime and the Elderly
(TS010202)

Crime Victims and the Criminal Justice
System
(TS040003)

Effects of Violence on Children
(TS040014)

Homicide Victims
(TS040016)

Marital Rape and Date/Acquaintance Rape
(TS040010)

Police Response to Domestic Violence
(TS011622)

Psychological Effect of Victimization
(TS040004)

Rape
(TS040005)

Sexual Assault
(TS040013)

Survivors of Sexual Abuse
(TS040015)

Treatment of the Child Victim
(TS040002)

Victim Compensation
(TS040006)

Victims of Child Sexual Abuse
(TS040007)

Victims Rights
(TS040012)

Victim Services
(TS040001)

# TOPICAL BIBLIOGRAPHIES

## AIDS

AIDS and the Criminal Justice System
(TB010618)

## Corrections

Adult Female Offender
(TB010103)

Capital Punishment
(TB010302)

Crowding in Prisons and Jails
(TB010101)

Prison Industry
(TB010102)

Prison Violence
(TB010610)

Trends and Alternatives to Incarceration
(TB010619)

## Courts

Alternative Dispute Resolution
(TB050001)

Insanity Defense/Competency to Stand Trial
(TB010301)

Pretrial Issues and Practices
(TB010613)

Sentencing Disparity
(TB010303)

## Crime Prevention

Community Crime Prevention Programs
(TB010201)

Private Security: Training and Management
(TB010608)

## Drugs

Drugs and Crime
(TB010614)

Drug Law Enforcement
(TB010616)

Drugs in the Workplace
(TB010620)

Drug Treatment in Criminal Justice Settings
(TB010623)

## Juvenile Justice

Alternatives to Institutionalization
(TB020506)

Juvenile Illegal Drug Use
(TB020505)

Juvenile Gangs
(TB020501)

Juvenile Restitution
(TB020508)

Publications of the Office of Juvenile Justice and Delinquency Prevention
(TB020510)

Sexual Exploitation of Children
(TB020504)

Violence and Vandalism in Schools
(TB020503)

Serious Juvenile Offender
(TB020502)

## Law Enforcement

Arson
(TB010203)

Community Policing
(TB010621)

Computer Crime
(TB010622)

Police Personnel Selection
(TB010601)

Police Use of Force
(TB010604)

SWAT and Hostage Negotiations
(TB010603)

Terrorism
(TB010611)

White Collar Crime
(TB010615)

## Statistics

Publications of the Bureau of Justice Statistics, 1971-1984
(TB030012)

## Victims

Crime and the Elderly
(TB010202)

Crime Victims and the Criminal Justice System
(TB040002)

Criminal Justice Response to Child Abuse
(TB040005)

Victim Compensation
(TB040003)

Victim Services
(TB040001)

Victims: Family Violence
(TB040004)

# 8

# Directories

Directories are a major source of information for students. Directories are usually in book form, although now many directories also exist on computer disks and in computer databases. Directories most often will cover a specific subject matter and are listed in alphabetical order.

Thousands of directories provide direct information to addresses, phone numbers, and other useful data.

Following is a listing of directories related to criminal justice.

*Access: A Resource Guide to Legal Automation.* John C. Landis. Publishers of legal publications, consultants, seminars, bulletin board systems, and user groups involved in legal automation. (Chicago: American Bar Association, 1994).

*American Association of Motor Vehicle Administrators (AAMVA)—Membership Directory.* (Arlington, VA: American Association of Motor Vehicle Administrators).

*Almanac of American Politics.* Governors, United States senators, and members of the United States House of Representatives, voting records of major issues, ratings from liberal and conservative organizations, election votes, campaign contributions by source. Annual. (Washington, DC: National Journal Inc., 1995).

*American Academy of Forensic Sciences—Membership Directory.* 3,400 persons qualified in forensic sciences, including law, pathology, biology, odontology, physical anthropology, psychiatry, questioned documents, criminalistics, engineering, and toxicology. Entries include: Name, office address and phone, highest degree held, professional title, type of certification. Annual, May. (Colorado Springs, CO: American Academy of Forensic Sciences).

*American Academy of Matrimonial Lawyers—List of Certified Fellows.* 1,200 lawyers. Annual, July. Members only. (Chicago: American Academy of Matrimonial Lawyers).

*The American Bar.* 85,000 lawyers in the United States and over 100 countries abroad; selected state administrative offices. Entries include: Firm name, type of practice, address, phone, names, educational data, and memberships of partners and associates. State offices' listings include address, phone. Annual, March. (Sacramento, CA: Forster-Long, Inc.).

*American Correctional Association Directory: State and Federal Correctional Institutions.* (College Park, MD: American Correctional Association).

*American Lawyers Quarterly.* Semiannual, January and July; monthly supplements. (Cleveland: The American Lawyers Company).

*American Polygraph Association—Membership Directory.* Approximately 2,000 member individuals and companies involved in the polygraph field. (Chattanooga, TN: American Polygraph Association).

*American Society of Criminology—Membership Directory.* 2,200 professional and academic criminologists, students of criminology in accredited universities, psychiatrists, psychologists, and sociologists. Annual. (Columbus, OH: American Society of Criminology).

*Annual Directory of Sheriffs of the United States.* (Washington, DC: National Sheriffs' Association).

*Arms Control Fact Book.* Dennis Menos. (Jefferson, NC: McFarland & Company, Inc., 1985).

*Arson Control: Directory.* Latest edition 1992. (Washington, DC: United States Fire Administration).

*Arson Resource Directory.* National, state, and local anti-arson organizations and agencies, and information, research, courses, and training programs; publishers and producers of periodicals, audiovisuals. (Emmittsburg, MD: FEMA).

*Association of Federal Investigators Directory.* (Washington, DC: Association of Federal Investigators).

*Association of Former Agents of the U.S. Secret Service—Membership Directory.* (Alexandria, VA: Association of Former Agents of the U.S. Secret Service).

*Associated Public-Safety Communications Officers—Membership Directory.* Approximately 7,500 member firefighters, police officers, civil defense and governmental officials involved with public safety communications, as well as manufacturers and distributors of communications products. Annual, January. (New Smyrna Beach, FL: Associated Public-Safety Communications Officers).

*Attorneys and Agents Registered to Practice before the United States Patent and Trademark Office.* About 11,000 attorneys and agents. (Washington, DC: U.S. Patent and Trademark Office, Department of Commerce).

*Barron's Guide to Law Schools.* About 200 American Bar Association approved law schools. List of top law schools ranked for prestige is also included. Irregular; latest edition 1998. (Hauppauge, NY: Barron's Educational Series, Inc.).

*Barter Associations, Organizations & Businesses in the United States [Microfiche].* Association or company name and address. Triennial; latest edition 1997. (Houston, TX: Barter Publishing).

*Battered Women's Directory.* Over 2,000 shelters, hotlines, YWCA's, hospitals, mental health services, legal services agencies, and other organizations and agencies which offer services to abused women in the United States and abroad; includes listings of many educational resources on the problem. Irregular; latest edition spring 1989. (Richmond, IN: Terry Mehlman).

*Books on Trial: A Survey of Recent Cases.* List of about 25 attorneys who have participated in school district book censorship litigation. Irregular; latest edition October 1987; update, September 1989. Main content is narrative reporting of litigation surrounding attempts at censorship of published works, with recent decisions indexed by state and banned books indexed by author. [Censorship litigation]. (New York: National Coalition Against Censorship).

*Campus Gang Rape: Party Games?* List of about 10 publishers and organizations concerned with gang rape on college campuses. Published November 1992. (Washington, DC: Project on the Status and Education of Women, Association of American Colleges).

*Child Abuse and Neglect and Family Violence: Audiovisual Catalog.* Distributors of over 300 films, videotapes, filmstrips with tapes, slides with tapes, and audiovisual packages about child abuse and neglect and family violence. (Washington, DC: Clearinghouse on Family Violence Information).

*Child Find Photo Directory of Missing Children.* Nearly 570 children reported as missing in the United States. Name, photograph, description, date of birth, date abducted or became missing, location where last seen.(New Paltz, NY: Child Find of America).

*Congressional Yellow Book Directory.* Supplies up-to-date information on members of Congress, their key aides and nearly 300 Congressional committees and subcommittees. (Washington, DC: The Washington Monitor, Inc.).

*Contacts [Alcoholic beverage control].* Government officials in 19 control state jurisdictions concerned with alcoholic beverage regulation; association members in the alcoholic beverage industries; trade associations. Annual; updated quarterly. (Alexandria, VA: National Alcoholic Beverage Control Association).

*Correctional and Juvenile Justice Training Directory of North America.* A profile of training in each state and province as well as federal agencies in both the U.S. and Canada. Identifies training standards and oversight commissions, the number of full and part-time trainers in each jurisdiction and minimum annual training requirements. (Richmond, KY: Eastern Kentucky University).

*Crime Stoppers International—Directory.* Over 700 agencies and organizations which sponsor "Crime Stoppers," "Crime Solvers," or similarly named programs offering anonymity and rewards for information leading to the solution of serious crimes; coverage also includes Canada, Puerto Rico, Guam, Great Britain, Australia, the Netherlands, and West Africa. (Albuquerque, NM: Crime Stoppers International).

*Criminal Justice Agencies.* Names and addresses of all state and local criminal justice agencies in the U.S. (Washington, DC: National Criminal Justice Information and Statistics Service).

*Criminal Justice Education Directory.* Presents the number and types of institutions granting degrees in the field of criminal justice. Annual. (Gaithersburg, MD: International Association of Chiefs of Police).

*Criminal Justice Information Exchange Directory*. About 90 libraries that are members of the Criminal Justice Information Exchange Group; coverage includes Canada. (Rockville, MD: National Institute of Justice).

*Detective Agencies*. 4,300. Nationwide. (Omaha, NE: American Business Directories, Inc., American Business Information, Inc.).

*Directory of All Prison and Jail Addresses and Zip Codes*. Over 7,000 federal, state, county, and municipal correctional institutions and facilities; also includes drug and alcohol centers. (Boynton Beach, FL: Fraud and Theft Information Bureau).

*Directory of Automated Criminal Justice Information Systems*. Over 100 computerized information systems serving over 600 police, court, and correction agencies in federal, state, and local governments. (Washington, DC: Bureau of Justice Statistics).

*Directory of Bar Associations*. More than 55 state bar associations, 40 local bar associations represented in the American Bar Association House of Delegates, 170 other local associations with at least 300 members, and other associations represented in the ABA House of Delegates. (Chicago: Division of Bar Services, American Bar Association).

*Directory of British Associations*. Addresses and brief descriptions of both profit and nonprofit associations in England. (Croydon, UK: C.B.D. Research Ltd., 1996).

*Directory of California Justice Agencies Serving Juveniles and Adults*. (Sacramento, CA: Department of Youth Authority).

*Directory of Community Crime Prevention Programs, National and State Levels*. James Lockard, et al. Designed to facilitate dissemination of knowledge and ideas about crime prevention. (Washington, DC: United States Department of Justice, 1978).

*Directory of Computer Software Applications: Urban and Regional Technology & Development*. (Springfield, VA: National Technical Information Service, Commerce Department).

*Directory of Computerized Data Files*. (Springfield, VA: National Technical Information Service, Commerce Department).

*Directory of Corporate Counsel*. Kenneth B. Miller (ed.). For some 4,000 companies, subsidiaries, and divisions, provides details on: law department's address, telephone number, and staffing; area of legal specialization; biographical data on individuals listed. Companies include publicly held

corporations, privately owned businesses, utilities, insurance companies, and financial institutions. Annual. (New York: Aspen Law & Business, 1997).

*Directory of Correctional Service Agencies*. Lists voluntary, professional and private nonprofit agencies in the United States that provide assistance and job training to inmates, ex-prisoners, probationers, parolees, and their families. (Philadelphia: Correctional Services Federation, USA).

*Directory of Courses in the Field of Code Administration and Enforcement*. A listing for those seeking information about colleges and universities that offer courses and curricula in Fire Science, Architectural Design, Building Construction Technology, and related disciplines. (McLean, VA: National Academy of Code Administration, 1979).

*Directory of Criminal Justice Information Sources*. Lists 149 agencies throughout the country which provide sources of information in the criminal justice area. Notations are also made as to whether special services such as computerized literature search services, interlibrary loan programs, reference services, and technical assistance to criminal justice professionals are provided. An index by criminal justice specialty is provided. (Upland, PA: DIANE Publishing Co., 1994).

*Directory of Criminal Justice Issues in the States*. List of nearly 50 state Statistical Analysis Centers sponsoring about 420 criminal justice policy research studies. Annual, August. (Washington, DC: Criminal Justice Statistics Association).

*Directory of Surveillance Equipment Supplies*. Over 90 companies that supply equipment and services in the field of electronic surveillance. (Libertyville, IL: Full Disclosure).

*Directory of European Associations*. Address and description of each association. Annual. (Detroit: Gale Research).

*Directory of Expert Witnesses in Technology*. Suspended indefinitely, last published in 1985. (Woodbridge, CT: Research Publications).

*Directory of Federal Experts in Fire Technology and Related Fields*. Lists federal personnel with expertise in the field of fire safety technology. Provides addresses, telephone numbers, organizational affiliation, and fields of expertise. (Washington, DC: U.S. Fire Administration, 1979).

*Directory of Government Document Collections and Librarians*. Latest edition 1997. (Bethesda, MD: Congressional Information Service).

*Directory of Halfway Houses and Group Homes for Troubled Children*. A national directory of alternative treatment programs for youth. (Tallahassee, FL: Journal of Drug Issues, Inc.).

*Directory of Institutions for Mentally Disordered Offenders*. Lists mental health and correctional institutions providing psychiatric care to mentally disordered adult offenders in the United States. (Rockville, MD: Center for Studies of Crime and Delinquency, 1974).

*Directory of Intellectual Property Lawyers and Patent Agents*. More than 7,000 patent agents, lawyers, and law firms specializing in intellectual property law, including patents, trademarks, copyrights, unfair trade, and trade secrets. (New York: Clark Boardman Company Ltd.).

*Directory of International Terrorism*. Surveys more than a century of revolution, terror and counter-terror. Over 1,000 entries. (Upland, PA: DIANE Publishing Co.).

*Directory of Judges with Juvenile/Family Law Jurisdiction*. (Reno, NV: National Council of Juvenile and Family Court Judges).

*Directory of Juvenile and Adult Corrections Departments, Institutions, Agencies and Paroling Authorities*. 4,000 juvenile and adult state and federal correctional departments, institutions, agencies, paroling authorities, and military correctional facilities in the United States and Canada. (Laurel, MD: American Correctional Association).

*Directory of Juvenile Detention Homes*. (Dunbar, WV: National Juvenile Detention Association).

*Directory of Law Enforcement and Criminal Justice Associations and Research Centers*. More than 200 international, national, regional, and local organizations and associations, research centers and government agencies active in law enforcement and criminal justice within the United States. (Gaithersburg, MD: Law Enforcement Standards Laboratory, National Institute of Standards and Technology, Department of Commerce).

*Directory of Law Libraries*. Published for the American Association of Law Libraries . . . by the Commerce Clearing House, 1940-date. Biennial. Title varies: Law libraries in the United States and Canada, 1940-62/63. Geographical listing of law libraries in the United States, Canada, and other foreign countries that are members of the Association. Gives name, librarian, and number of volumes. Personnel index.

*Directory of Law Libraries*. (Chicago: American Association of Law Libraries).

*Directory of Law-Related Education Projects*. C.A. Kelly (ed.). Lists approximately 291 educational programs which focus on the law, legal system, and the legal process. (ABA Special Committee on Youth Education for Citizenship, 1978).

*Directory of Lawyer Disciplinary Agencies and Clients' Security Funds*. Disciplinary agencies responsible for handling complaints against lawyers; also covers agencies responsible for handling clients' security funds. (Chicago: Center for Professional Responsibility, American Bar Association).

*Directory of Legal Aid and Defender Offices in the United States, 1933-present*. Name of issuing body varies. Title varies slightly. Gives the names and addresses of all such known organizations in the United States, Canada, the Philippine Islands, and Puerto Rico, with a brief description of the types and limitations of the services provided by each. Annual. (Washington, DC: Legal Aid & Defender Association).

*Directory, Legal Aid and Defender Offices*. Attorneys that provide criminal representation to persons unable to retain a private counsel. Programs for special needs and legal support services. (Washington, DC: National Legal Aid and Defender Association, 1979).

*Directory of Legal Aid and Defender Services*. Annual directory listing names, addresses, and telephone numbers for sources of legal assistance and defender programs in the United States. (Chicago: National Legal Aid and Defender Association).

*Directory of Legal and Law Enforcement Periodicals*. (New York: Facts on File).

*Directory of Opportunities in International Law*. Several hundred possible employers of specialists in international law, United States and foreign law firms, United Nations agencies, governmental organizations and bodies; lists of law schools which include international law in their programs. (Charlottesville, VA: John Bassett Moore Society of International Law).

*Directory of Probation, Parole, and Correctional Associations*. Lists probation, parole, and correctional associations in the United States. (Hackensack, NJ: National Council on Crime and Delinquency, 1973).

*Directory of Published Proceedings, Series SSH-Social Sciences/Humanities*. Lists conference meetings on an international basis. Arranged by dates of conference meetings, a subject and sponsoring organization index. (Harrison, NY: Interdok).

*Directory of Residential Treatment Centers.* An annual, nationwide directory of juvenile and adult halfway houses. Halfway houses specializing in parole, probation, alcoholism, mental health, drug addiction pre-release, and work release. (Cincinnati, OH: International Halfway House Association).

*Directory of Sheriffs of the United States.* Annual. (Washington, DC: National Sheriff's Association).

*Directory of Social and Health Agencies of New York City.* Information about public and voluntary welfare and health agencies serving New York City (New York: Columbia University Press, 1981-82).

*Directory of State and Local Judges.* Furnishes an alphabetized state-by-state listing of state appellate, trial, county, and local judges within four jurisdictions of 50 states and the District of Columbia. The order of jurisdiction is as follows: court of last resort, intermediate appellate court, court of general jurisdiction, and court of special/limited jurisdiction. (Reno, NV: National College of the State Judiciary, United States Department of Justice, Law Enforcement Assistance Administration, National Institute of Law Enforcement and Criminal Justice, 1976).

*Directory of State Officials [Food and Drug Enforcement].* Officials of state health and agriculture departments, boards of pharmacy, and other state departments charged with enforcement of food, drug, device, feed, and cosmetic laws. Annual, February. (Rockville, MD: Division of Federal-State Relations, Food and Drug Administration).

*Directory for Successful Publishing in Legal Periodicals.* Publishers of about 450 legal journals, periodicals, and reviews; international coverage. Irregular; latest edition February 1987. (Charleston, IL: Qucoda Publishing Company).

*Directory Toward Criminal Justice.* A nationwide directory of organizations involved with the criminal justice system. National, voluntary, professional, nonprofit, and citizen organizations in the United States. (New York: National Council of Churches).

*Directory of United States Probation and Pretrial Services Officers.* Arranged by district, kind of prison, then by city. Free. Annual, September. (Washington, DC: Probation Division, Administrative Office of the U.S. Courts).

*Encyclopedia of Legal Information Sources.* Over 19,000 books, periodicals, newsletters, law reviews and digests, newspapers, audiovisual materials, and other publications; research centers, institutes, and clearinghouses; professional associations and societies; databases; and other organizations and sources of information on 460 legal topics. (Detroit: Gale Research).

*Federal Criminal Investigators Association—Directory.* 5,000 special agents and criminal investigators currently employed by or retired from the United States government). (Detroit: Federal Criminal Investigators Association).

*Federal Funding Guide.* About 220 major federal aid programs for which local, county, and state governments are eligible; nonprofit organizations are also eligible for about two-thirds of the programs. Programs are in the areas of community development, economic development, energy, housing, jobs, transportation, health, environment, emergency services, social services, senior citizens, arts, cultural activities, law enforcement, and substance abuse. (Arlington, VA: Government Information Services).

*Federal Information Centers.* (Washington, DC: General Services Administration).

*Federal Information Sources and Systems.* (Washington, DC: General Accounting Office).

*Federal Job Information Centers Directory.* (Washington, DC: Office of Personnel Management).

*Federal Prison System Facilities.* Reference guide to the institutions of the Federal Prison Service. (Washington, DC: U.S. Bureau of Prisons, 1980).

*Federal Regulatory Directory.* Contains each agency's history, responsibilities, powers, and authorities; biographies of commissioners; a detailed organizational description; sources of further information and location of regional offices. Annual. (Washington, DC: Congressional Quarterly Inc.).

*Federal Yellow Book Directory.* An organizational directory of the top level employees of federal departments and agencies. (Washington, DC: The Washington Monitor, Inc.).

*FEDFIND* (Information sources of U.S. government). List of nearly 140 government agencies and other publishers which are sources of the over 700 federal information publications and services described. (Springfield, VA: ICUC Press).

*Fire Marshals Association of North America—Membership Directory.* Over 1,200 municipal, county, state and provincial fire marshals and fire prevention bureau officials. (Washington, DC: Fire Marshals Association of North America).

*Fire Protection Reference Directory.* Equipment reports and addresses of all manufacturers of fire prevention materials. (Quincy, MA: National Fire Protection Association, 1982).

*Fire Research Specialists.* Names, addresses, and telephone numbers of specialists from the U.S. and Canada who have made significant contributions to the teaching of fire science, or have participated in fire research programs. (Quincy, MA: National Fire Protection Association, 1982).

*First Amendment Lawyers Association—Directory.* Approximately 125 member lawyers who support and defend cases involving the First Amendment to the U.S. Constitution. Annual. (Chicago: First Amendment Lawyers Association).

*Forensic Sciences Certification Program Directory of Diplomats.* (Colorado Springs, CO: Forensic Sciences Foundation).

*Forensic Services Directory.* About 5,000 individuals willing to serve as expert witnesses or consultants during litigation; also associations, societies, and institutes with specialized information. (Lawrenceville, NJ: National Forensic Center).

*Handbook of Federal Police and Investigative Agencies.* Over 60 federal police and investigative agencies. (Westport, CT: Greenwood Press, Inc.).

*Hazard Control Information Handbook.* (International Institute of Safety & Health, 1985).

*How and Where to Check Driving Records and Report Accidents.* Offices responsible for maintaining driving records and offices to which truck accidents are to be reported, in all states and Puerto Rico. (Alexandria, VA: American Trucking Association).

*IACP World Membership Directory.* A listing of the 15,000 IACP members. Includes the mailing addresses of thousands of the world's leading police executives, from Algeria to Zaire. Annual. (Arlington, VA: International Association of Chiefs of Police).

*Inside the Law Schools: A Guide by Students for Students.* About 100 law schools. School address, phone; median entrance scores and grade point averages; acceptance rate, transfer rate; enrollment; percentage minority and women students; student-faculty ratio, expenses, financial aid, library facilities; and a description of student life, faculty, curriculum, reputation, and placement success. (New York: Plume).

*Institute of Professional Investigators—Professional Register of Members in Private Practice.* Nearly 300 member investigators working in private practice worldwide. (Blackburn, UK: Institute of Professional Investigators).

*International Association of Arson Investigators—Constitution and Bylaws, Membership Directory.* 7,500 member arson investigators. Annual, May. (Louisville, KY: International Association of Arson Investigators).

*International Association of Assessing Officers—Membership Directory.* About 8,200 state and local officials concerned with valuation of property for tax purposes. Annual, December. (Chicago: International Association of Assessing Officers).

*International Association of Chiefs of Police—World Membership Directory.* 14,200 members in command and administrative positions in federal, state, and local law enforcement and related fields; includes county police and sheriffs; international, national, and regional law enforcement agencies and related organizations. (Arlington, VA: International Association of Chiefs of Police).

*International Association for Identification—Membership Directory.* About 2,500 police officials, identification personnel, and others engaged in forensic identification, investigation, and scientific crime detection work. Annual, September. (Alameda, CA: International Association for Identification).

*International Association of Law Libraries, Directory.* A list, arranged by country, of personal and institutional members. Indexed. (Marburg, Germany: International Association of Law Libraries, 1980-date).

*International Bar Association—Directory of Members.* About 12,000 members of the International Bar Association. (London, UK: International Bar Association).

*International Bibliography of Police.* 200,000 police officers, either on active service or retired, organized to establish ties of friendship and mutual aid. (Maidstone, UK: International Police Association).

*International Council of Environmental Law—Directory.* About 300 individuals and organizations in the fields of environmental law, policy, and administration organized to provide professional contacts and information on environmental conservation. Semiannual. (Bonn: International Council of Environmental Law).

*International Defense Directory.* About 15,000 suppliers of defense and military products and services; government armed forces, police, and customs agencies worldwide concerned with defense and procurement in 170 countries. (Geneva, Switzerland: Interavia S.A.).

*International Directory of Correctional Administrations.* Suspended indefinitely. Last edition published in 1987. (Laurel, MD: American Correctional Association).

*International Directory of Prisoner's Aid Agencies.* A worldwide directory which lists voluntary agencies concerned with providing aftercare for prisoners and their families. (Milwaukee: International Prisoner's Aid Association).

*International Exchange of Information on Current Criminological Research Projects in Member States of the Council of Europe.* Centers conducting about 200 research projects in criminology. English, French. (Strasbourg, France: Publications Section, Division of Crime Problems, Directorate of Legal Affairs, Council of Europe).

*International Institute of Comparative Linguistic Law—Membership Directory.* Approximately 550 law and linguistics professors, jurists, lawyers, judges, linguists, and social scientists worldwide, whose objective is to promote the study of comparative linguistic law. French, English. Annual. Members only. (Montreal: International Institute of Comparative Law).

*International Law and Practice—Directory.* Over 12,800 member lawyers, judges, law students, and law clerks; international coverage. Annual. (Washington, DC: International Law and Practice, American Bar Association).

*International Legal Aid Association.* Directory of legal aid and advice facilities available throughout the world. (London and New York: International Legal Aid Association).

*International Legal Aid Directory.* List of organizations able to give preliminary legal advice. (London, UK: International Bar Association).

*The International List.* Attorney firms with collection practices, address, phone. (Williston Park, NY: The International Lawyers Company, Inc.).

*International Narcotic Enforcement Officers Association—Directory.* 7,500. Name affiliation, address, phone. Annual, January. Members only. (Albany, NY: International Narcotic Enforcement Officers Association).

*International Security Directory.* Defense and security companies in the United Kingdom and selected other nations; ministries of defense, police, and fire in each country profiled; defense/security trade associations worldwide. 1990. (Henley-on-Thames, UK: R. Hazell and Company).

*International Society of Family Law—Directory of Members.* Approximately 650 member individuals and organizations. Irregular. (Cambridge, UK: International Society of Family Law).

*The Jeffers Directory of Law Enforcement Officers.* The most comprehensive listings available for all law enforcement agencies in the United States. More than 17,000 agencies. A total of more than 38,000 names of law enforcement officers. (New York: Pace Publications).

*Justice—Directory of Services.* Nearly 2,000 police commissions, Royal Canadian Mounted Police divisions, human rights commissions, legal aid services, police colleges, courts, parole boards, correctional authorities, prisoner aid agencies, and professional and voluntary associations. (Ottawa: Canadian Criminal Justice Association).

*Juvenile and Adult Correctional Departments, Institutions, Agencies and Paroling Authorities, United States and Canada.* Addresses, names of officials, and brief descriptions, with some statistical summaries. (College Park, MD: American Correctional Association, 1980).

*Law and Legal Information Directory.* Approximately 29,000 national and international organizations, bar associations, federal courts, federal regulatory agencies, law schools, firms and organizations offering continuing legal education, paralegal education, sources of scholarships and grants, awards and prizes, special libraries, information systems and services, research centers, publishers of legal periodicals, books, and audiovisual materials, speaker bureaus, lawyer referral services, legal aid offices, public defender offices, legislature manuals and registers, corporation departments of states, and law enforcement agencies. Biennial, October of even years. (Detroit: Gale Research).

*Law and Order Magazine—Police Equipment Buyer's Guide Issue.* List of manufacturers, dealers, and distributor products, and services for police departments. Entries include: Company name, address, phone, product codes, code showing what manufacturer or dealer. Annual, January. (Wilmette, IL: Hendon, Inc.).

*Law Books and Serials in Print.* List of publishers and producers of over 50,000 legal reference publications, periodicals, software, online databases, microforms, audio cassettes, and video cassettes. Base edition, annual, February; quarterly cumulative supplements. (New York: Bowker Legal Reference Publishing).

*Law Books in Print.* Approximately 900 publishers of law books in English; international coverage. Each volume of the six-volume set includes the publisher directory. Triennial; latest edition spring 1990. (Dobbs Ferry, NY: Glanville Publishers, Inc.).

*Law & Business Directory of Corporate Counsel.* About 5,000 corporations in the United States with in-house corporate counsel staff; includes parent companies and subsidiaries of industrial firms, utilities, financial institutions, insurance companies, and service firms. Annual, April. (Englewood Cliffs, NJ: Prentice-Hall Law & Business).

*Law Databases.* (ASLIB) Over 35 publicly available online data bases in the field of law, including full-text, referral, and indexing databases; international coverage. (London, UK: Association for Information Management).

*Law Directory [Solicitors in Ireland].* About 4,200 member solicitors, court officials, members of the Honourable Society of Kings Inns, circuit barristers, notaries public, and relevant government departments in Ireland; also includes solicitors in Northern Ireland. Annual, February. (Dublin, Ireland: Incorporated Law Society of Ireland).

*Law Enforcement Technology—Directory Section.* Each issue includes a directory of manufacturers and suppliers of one type of law enforcement equipment such as computers, weapons, training, Special Weapons and Tactics (SWAT) radio and communications equipment. Updated ten times during the year. (Woodbury, NY: PTN Publishing).

*Law Librarian's New Product Directory.* Publishers and suppliers of recently introduced law books and services. (New York: Garland Publishing, Inc.).

*Law Office Economics & Management—Directory Computers for the Law Office Issue.* List of about 100 suppliers of data processing equipment and software. Companies listed have more than one installation in a law firm or, if only one installation, have additional experience with law firm management needs. Annual, August; updated in quarterly issues. (Deerfield, IL: Callaghan & Company).

*Law Office Guide in Computers Directory.* Discontinued. (San Francisco: L.O.G.I.C. Publishing Company).

*The Law Schools of the World.* Henry P. Tseng. A specialized directory listing all existing law schools on a worldwide basis. (Buffalo, NY: William S. Hein).

*Law Services Information Book—Canadian Edition.* (Newtown, PA: Law School Admission Council/Law School Admission Services).

*Lawyers' and Creditors' Service Directory.* About 30,000 individuals and agencies involved in forwarding and collecting, including sheriffs, process servers, private investigators, repossessors, skip tracers, court reporters, litigation attorneys, courthouses, chambers of commerce, and collection agencies. Entries include: Firm name, address, phone. (Eau Claire, WI: Professional Education Systems, Inc.).

*Lawyers' List.* About 2,500 lawyers in practice in the United States. Annual, April. (Easton, MD: Commercial Publishing Company).

*Lawyer's PC—Legal Software Directory Issue.* List of more than 500 programs from 200 publishers designed for personal computer use by lawyers, including timekeeping and billing software. Annual, November. (Lexington, SC: Shepard's/McGraw-Hill, Inc.).

*Lawyer's Register International by Specialties and Fields of Law Including a Directory of Corporate Counsel.* Corporate legal staffs worldwide; legal firms; independent practicing attorneys each identified as specialist in one or more fields of law. Irregular. 1990. (Solon, OH: Lawyer's Register Publishing Company).

*Legal Information Alert.* List of publishers of books, databases, CD-ROM products, loose-leaf services, periodicals and journals, audio and videotapes, and microfilm covering the legal profession and reviewed or discussed in the issue. Ten issues per year. (Chicago: Alert Publications, Inc.).

*Legal Looseleafs in Print.* Over 320 publishers offering more than 3,500 loose-leaf legal information services; includes many publications of interest outside the legal field. Annual, March. (Teaneck, NJ: Infosources Publishing).

*Legal Newsletters in Print.* Over 1,750 legal, law related, legislative, or regulatory related newsletters, bulletins, and reporting services published in the United States. Annual, January. (Teaneck, NJ: Infosources Publishing).

*Legal Software Directory* [Law office software]. Over 300 suppliers of computer software used in legal offices. Annual, March. (Chicago: American Bar Association).

*Martindale-Hubbell Law Directory.* An annual publication since 1968, this directory provides biographical sketches of United States lawyers. (New York: Martindale-Hubbell).

*Municipal Yearbook.* Listing of city officials, including police and fire chiefs. Information on salaries of municipal employees and separate mini-directories for various city-run agencies nationwide. Annual. (Chicago: International City Manager's Association).

*National Council of Juvenile Court Judges Directory.* (Reno, NV: National Council of Juvenile and Family Court Judges).

*National Directory of Black Law Firms.* Discontinued. (Philadelphia: Drexel University).

*National Directory of Child Abuse Services and Information.* Child abuse services and sources of information are listed. Governmental and private agencies, volunteer and professional organizations, and specific intervention programs such as referrals, prevention programs, hotlines. (Chicago: National Committee for Prevention of Child Abuse).

*National Directory of Correctional Education—State Administrators.* Names and addresses of all state administrators in various agencies dealing with correctional education and social rehabilitation. (Vienna, IL: Correctional Education Association).

*National Directory of Corrections Construction.* Over 265 correctional institutions constructed since 1978. (Rockville, MD: National Criminal Justice Reference Service).

*National Directory of Drug Abuse and Alcoholism Treatment Programs.* "A compilation of over 9,000 federal, state and local agencies responsible for the administration of alcoholism or drug abuse services." (Rockville, MD: U.S. Department of Health, Education and Welfare, 1979).

*National Directory of Hotlines, Switchboard and Related Services.* Lists a variety of telephone intervention services, such as crisis hotlines and suicide prevention, free clinics for medical problems and legal assistance, and runaway programs and services. (Minneapolis: National Crisis Intervention Clearinghouse).

*National Directory of Law Enforcement Administrators and Correctional Institutions.* Police departments and police chiefs in cities and towns with populations of more than 1,600; sheriffs and criminal prosecutors in all counties in the nation; state law enforcement and criminal investigation agencies; federal criminal investigation and related agencies; state and federal correctional institutions; campus law enforcement departments. (Stevens Point, WI: National Police Chiefs and Sheriffs Information Bureau).

*National Directory of Prosecuting Attorneys.* (Chicago, IL: National District Attorneys Association).

*National Directory of Runaway Centers.* Runaway programs in the United States which accept runaways and provide them with housing in group homes or other residential facilities. (Washington, DC: National Youth Alternative Project).

*National Directory of Runaway Programs.* I.G. Miles, et al. 212 runaway centers located throughout the country. Also included are reviews of literature on the runaway problem, sociological explanations, responses of the government to the problem, and motives of the runaway. (Washington, DC: National Youth Work Alliance, 1983).

*National Directory of State Agencies.* Nancy Wright, comp. All state agencies organized by state and by function in 93 categories. Includes U.S. possessions. (Washington, DC: Information Resources Press, 1977).

*National District Attorneys Association Roster of Officers and Board of Directors.* (Chicago: National District Attorneys Association).

*National Ex-Offender Assistance Directory.* 1,000 programs assisting the ex-offender with such problems as employment, housing and vocational training. (Lincoln, NE: CONTACT Inc.).

*National Jail and Adult Detention Directory.* 3,000 facilities in the United States. Such vital data as operations budgets and capital expenditures, program and staff information, population size and movement, and more are included in an easy-to-use format. (Laurel, MD: American Correctional Association).

*National Legal Aid and Defender Association.* (Chicago: American Bar Association).

*National Prison Directory, Organizational Profiles of Prison Reform Groups in the United States.* M.A. Bundy and K.R. Harmon (eds). Describes the goals, objectives, programs, and activities of several hundred prisons. (College Park, MD: Urban Information Interpreters, Inc.).

*Nationwide Patrol* [Missing children/crime watch]. About 25 individuals concerned with locating missing children through search and rescue patrols. (Wilkes-Barre, PA: Nationwide Patrol, Inc.).

*National Victims Resource Directory.* The National Victims Resource Center, sponsored by the Office for Victims of Crime, has developed the National Victims Resource Directory, a central listing and service description of organizations that provide national victims information. This directory is a useful resource for making referrals and exchanging information between organizations. It also provides information about who is conducting research, tracking legislation, offering training programs, or providing victim assistance, counseling, and crisis intervention. In addition, the directory includes a summary appendix for quick reference. (Rockville, MD: National Victims Resource, 1990).

*Police Chiefs' Directory.* Names and addresses of members of the International Association of Chiefs of Police. (Published annually with the October issue of *Police Chief* magazine).

*Police Employment Guide.* Offers information about employment with police departments in all major U.S. cities. Entrance requirements, salaries, fringe benefits, training and application procedures are presented. Includes descriptions of all special programs. (Huntsville, TX: Sam Houston State University).

*Probation and Parole Directory.* Parole, pardon, and release boards; names, addresses, and telephone numbers of key personnel; data on probation and parole programs and services; statistics on budgets, beginning salaries, personnel, and client caseloads. (Laurel, MD: American Correctional Association).

*Research Centers Directory.* A guide to university-related and other nonprofit research organizations and support services. (Detroit: Gale Research).

*Risk Retention Group Directory and Guide.* (Pasadena, CA: Risk Retention Reporter).

*Sheriffs of the United States.* State by state listing of all law enforcement administrators and county sheriffs. Annual. (Washington, DC: National Sheriffs Association).

*State Drug Resources: A National Directory.* A comprehensive guide to state agencies that address drug abuse concerns. Organized by state, the directory provides agency names, addresses, and telephone numbers. Also included are listings of federal agencies that people frequently contact for information, as well as several quick references of state agencies by area of specialty. The directory was compiled by the Drugs & Crime Data Center & Clearinghouse, which is a national resource center for drug-related crime information. (Rockville, MD: National Criminal Justice Reference Service).

*A Survey of Educational Offerings in the Forensic Sciences.* K. Field, B. Lipskin and M. Reich. A guide to courses and degree programs in the forensic sciences offered at American colleges and universities. (Washington, DC: Law Enforcement Assistance Administration).

*U.S. Court Directory.* A comprehensive listing of each and every court in the U.S., and includes: the Court of Appeals, Claims Court, Special Courts, Sentencing Commission, and U.S. District Courts and much more. (Upland, PA: DIANE Publishing Co.).

*United States Government Manual.* The official handbook of the federal government; provides comprehensive information on the agencies of the legislative, judicial, and executive branches. Also includes information on boards, committees, commissions and international organizations in which the U.S. participates. Annual. (Washington, DC: Office of the Federal Register).

*Washington Information Directory.* Names, addresses, and all pertinent information on federal and nongovernmental organizations located in Washington, DC. Annual. (Washington, DC: Congressional Quarterly).

*Who's Who in American Law Enforcement.* (Miami, FL: American Law Enforcement Officers Association).

*World Association of Detectives, Membership Directory.* (San Mateo, CA: World Association of Detectives).

*A World Directory of Criminological Institutes.* 300 agencies in 53 countries. Gives addresses, names of staff members, projects and publications. (Rome: United Nations Social Defense Research Institute).

*World Legal Directory.* (Washington, DC: World Peace Through Law Center).

*World List of Forensic Science Labs.* Lists addresses, directors and fields of investigation for each lab. (North Yorkshire, UK: Forensic Science Society).

# 9

# Database Literature Searches

The prolific publication of books, journals, special reports, newspapers, and other written material since World War II has created an information explosion, resulting in the need for more sophisticated information handling systems. Computers are increasingly being used to meet this need. Most libraries have access to various computerized information systems. These systems are composed of categorized units of information known as databases, which relate to a given field or body of knowledge. Databases are created when indexing and abstracting services put their data into machine-readable form. Computerized information systems vendors then make the databases available to subscribers (e.g., libraries, industries, agencies) so they, in turn, can provide this information to researchers. Computerized literature searches also are referred to by librarians, information scientists, and researchers as "online information" searches. This denotes a comprehensive service in terms of the type and quantity of information available for searching. Access to many millions of records (books, directories, periodicals, reports, bibliographies, dissertations, newspaper features, patents, grants, reviews, legislative reports, conference proceedings, descriptions of documents, current research, pamphlets, and manuals) is possible via computer or online searches. Online searches fulfill many needs, including information gathering for reports, keeping up with developments in a particular field, determining important issues, reviewing literature, avoiding duplication of research, obtaining background material on court cases, and gathering resources for writing papers, theses, and dissertations.

When an online search is initiated, a computer scans the appropriate database and provides the researcher with a printed, annotated bibliography of citations on the topic. The larger the database, the more citations a researcher is likely to get from a computerized search. Students contemplating a computerized literature search typically will need to contact the reference librarian for assistance. The librarian will work with the student to develop a strategy for searching the databases appropriate for the topic and will then help perform the online search.

Some libraries absorb part of the cost for computerized literature searches, but the user may also be responsible for a portion of the fee. Charges vary according to the complexity of the search and the number of databases scanned, plus actual "online" computer usage time.

Literature searches through computers are faster and more efficient than manual searches of printed indices, especially when research involves searching several subjects. Computerized searches make available far more documents and information sources than most libraries and other information centers could possibly purchase in printed form. The computerized databases are also generally more current than printed abstracts and indices, so the researcher has access to the latest information before it appears in published form.

Obtaining information on topics related to criminal justice need not be limited to searching printed indices and other reference books. In fact, many departments and professors now expect or require students, particularly master's and doctoral candidates, to use computer literature search services. It should be kept in mind, however, that computerized searches are most suitable for certain types of questions. Research questions with one or more of the following characteristics are most effectively searched using a computer:

1.  Questions involving two or more distinct but interrelated topics. One example is the relationship of failure in school to drug abuse. Another example is the difference, if any, in the self-concept of male inmates of prisons that allow conjugal visits as opposed to male inmates of prisons that do not allow such visits. The first example has two topics—school failure and drug abuse. The second example involves three topics—self-concept, male inmates, and conjugal visits.

2.  Questions about topics so new that only limited material on the subject is available in printed form.

3.  Questions involving searching several different topic headings, or topics that could be stated in so many ways that searching printed indices and abstracts would be extremely time consuming. For example, a researcher studying an aspect of organized crime might find, using a computer, these subject headings: mafia, mob, mobsters, gangsters, professional criminals, subversive activities, underworld, syndicate, and even "family"—in a far shorter time than such a manual search of the literature could be accomplished.

Questions should be specific, so as to result in a fairly small number of citations. A broad or vaguely stated question can result in hundreds of citations, many of which may not directly refer to the problem the researcher is trying to solve. A librarian or other information specialist will usually ask the user to describe the topic in as detailed a fashion as possible. Key words likely to appear in titles or abstracts of articles are noted. The online search will involve the use of these key words to obtain bibliographic citations from one or more databases. The result is a printout and annotation of citations, usually more comprehensive than can be obtained by manual searching, and in a fraction of the time. Try more specific key words at first and then expand to a more general search as needed.

The major source available for information on computerized online databases is *The Directory of On-Line Data Bases*, published by Cuadra/Elsevier. This publication is updated on a regular basis and, at the time of this writing, listed and annotated 4,400 different computer databases. The directory classifies databases in the following way:

*Reference Databases*: These point the user to other sources of information.

*Bibliographic*: Contains citations, abstracts, and indices of journals, books, and other printed information.

*Referral*: Contains references to nonpublished information.

*Source Database*: These contain original source data.

*Numeric*: Contains survey data.

*Textual-Numeric*: Typically would contain databases with dictionary or handbook-type data most often in chemical or physical fields.

*Full-Text*: Contains the complete text of newspaper articles, court decisions, or newsletters.

*Software*: Contains computer programs that can be downloaded with local computers.

*Images*: Contains photographs, maps, trademark logos, and other graphics.

Another major source available for information on computerized online databases is *Access to Access: An On-Line User's Guide to IAC Databases*, 3rd Edition. This guide is the definitive source to searching all of Information Access Company's (IAC's) databases on BRS, Dialog, and LEXIS/NEXIS.

Another major source available for information on computerized databases is:

American Psychological Association
P.O. Box 0107
Washington, D.C. 20055-0107

There are many databases now in existence and more are being developed all the time. Most university and large public libraries subscribe to at least one of the following systems: ORBIT, by System Development Corporation (SDC); Bibliographic Retrieval Services, Inc.; Informatics, Inc.; and LEXIS and NEXIS from Mead and New York Times Information Bank. For more information on available resources, contact your librarian.

Various databases of potential interest to criminal justice students are alphabetically presented and described below. These are offered as suggestions—your library may have additional databases from which to choose.

*ABA/net Division for Public Services*
American Bar Association
Available Online
Covers law and policy in dispute resolution, legal help for the elderly and mentally handicapped, the electoral process, housing and urban development, and environmental and energy law. Includes publications, conferences, symposia, model legislation, policy development, internships for law students and references to products and services of the division.

*Academic American Encyclopedia*
Contains full text of the 20-volume *Academic American Encyclopedia.*

*Academic Index Database (AID)*
Information Acess Company
Provides access to 1,600 journals and newspapers. Also provides abstracts of many popular journals found in the general services, social sciences, and the humanities.

*ACAnet*
American Correctional Association
Contains a variety of information services for corrections professionals. Contents include citations, with abstracts, to approximately 500 reports on such topics as security and safety, prison crowding, personnel management, facility design, litigation, and juvenile corrections. Also contains about 250 unpublished reports from correctional agencies. ACAnet includes files such as AIDSNet, CI-Net, and Correctional Industries Information Clearinghouse. Earliest material from 1980.

*Acompline/Urbanline*
London Research Centre Research Library
Available Online
This is a merged file of the two London Research Centre databases, Acompline and Urbanline. It contains citations with abstracts to the worldwide literature related to urban studies. Database contains 200,000 citations with abstracts. Sources include press releases, journals, pamphlets, conference proceedings, reports, bibliographies, and theses. Coverage includes United Kingdom. Note: On entry, the file defaults to the merged database, but users can limit to either database.

*Addiction Letter*
Manisses Communications Group Inc.
Addiction Letter is a resource exchange on treatment and prevention of alcoholism, drug abuse and all other forms of chemical and behavioural addiction. Coverage is international.

*AgeLine*
Contains about 28,000 citations, with abstracts, to the literature on social gerontology, with a focus on the social, psychological, and economic aspects of middle age and aging. Approximately two-thirds of the citations are devoted to journals, the rest is made up of citations from books, book chapters, and reports.

*AIDS Abstracts from the Bureau of Hygiene and Tropical Diseases*
Contains about 11,000 citations, most with abstracts to the worldwide literature on Acquired Immune Deficiency Syndrome (AIDS).

*AIDSDrugs*
Contains references to over 80 drugs being tested for use against Acquired Immune Deficiency Syndrome (AIDS), AIDS-Related Complex (ARC), and related opportunistic diseases.

*AIDS In Focus*
Contains about 14,000 citations to the worldwide literature on Acquired Immune Deficiency Syndrome.

*AIDS Knowledge Base*
Contains full text of approximately 200 textbook chapters on Acquired Immune Deficiency Syndrome (AIDS) written by physicians and other health professionals associated with San Francisco General Hospital, the University of California, and affiliated institutions.

*AIDSLine*
Contains about 30,000 citations, with some abstracts, to the worldwide literature on Acquired Immune Deficiency Syndrome (AIDS) from CANCERLIT literature on AIDS and HEALTH PLANNING AND ADMINISTRATION.

*AIDS Newsletter*
Bureau of Hygiene & Tropical Diseases (Now part of CAB International)
Contains full text of the Aids Newsletter, covering news and developments about Acquired Immune Deficiency Syndrome (AIDS) and HIV infection. Approxiamatly 11,000 records with abstracts exist, from journals, newspapers, and newsletters. AIDS Newsletter is the online version of the printed *AIDS Newsletter* published by the Bureau of Hygiene & Topical Diseases (Now part of CAB International).

*AIDS Policy and Law*
Contains information on the legal and practical implications of Acquired Immune Deficiency Syndrome (AIDS) on government and private employment policies.

*AIDSScan*
Contains about 600 annotated citations to the holdings of Ryerson Polytechnical Institute on treating and interacting with Acquired Immune Deficiency Syndrome (AIDS) patients.

*AIDSQuest Online*
AIDS Periodical Information Database (AIDS P/D). Contents include full text of over 8,000 articles and book reviews on AIDS. AIDS Research Database (AIDS R/D). Contains descriptions of computer-readable and online AIDS databases. Includes contact addresses and telephone numbers.

*AIDSTrials*
Contains references to about 230 clinical trials of agents being evaluated for use against Acquired Immune Deficiency Syndrome (AIDS), AIDS-Related Complex (ARC), and related opportunistic diseases.

*Alcohol and Alcohol Problems Science Database*
Available Online
Contains 85,000 citations with abstracts to the worldwide literature on alcoholism research. Sources include books, monographs, journals, dissertations, proceedings, and conference papers. Start year: 1972.

*Alcohol & Drugs in the Workplace Costs, Controls, and Controversies*
Contains full text of *Alcohol & Drugs in the Workplace: Costs, Controls, and Controversies*, a special report covering drug and alcohol abuse in the workplace and strategies for employer and union responses.

*Alcohol Information for Clinicians and Educators Database*
Dartmouth Medical School
Contains about 9,000 citations to literature on alcohol use and abuse with an emphasis on educational materials for health-care providers. Sources include conference papers, reports, monographs, journals, and government documents. Also includes a controlled vocabulary developed by the Project Cerk Resource Center. Start year: 1978.

*Alcohol Outlook*
Contains full text of *Alcohol Outlook*, a monthly newsletter providing data and analyses of alcohol fuels, with an emphasis on oxygenated fuels.

*A.L.E.R.T. (A Law Enforcement Round Table)*
GE Information Service
Contains news and information of interest to people in law enforcement and related occupations at the local, state, and federal levels. A.L.E.R.T. covers Canada, Europe, Japan, and the United States. Includes "most wanted" lists, information on missing children, law enforcement careers, safety tips for "latchkey" children and senior citizens, and anti-fraud and home safety information. Database type is bulletin board, factual, and e-mail.

*America: History & Life*
Contains citations, with abstracts, to literature on all aspects of U.S. and Canadian history, culture, and current affairs from prehistoric times to the present. Start year: 1964.

*Applied Social Sciences Index & Abstracts*
Contains over 68,000 citations, with abstracts, to the worldwide literature on the applied social sciences. Start year: 1987.

*ASI (American Statistics Index)*
Contains citations, with abstracts, to publications containing social, economic, demographic, and other statistical data collected and analyzed by the U.S. government. Start year: 1973.

*ASSIA*
Bowker-Saur Ltd.
Coverage is international with 40 percent United Kingdom, 45 percent North America, and 15 percent rest of the world. Contains approximately 145,000 citations with abstracts. Sources include journals and newspapers. Database type is bibliographic. Start year: 1987.

*British Journal of Criminology*
Oxford University Press
Institute for the Study and Treatment of Delinquency
May also be known as the *British Journal of Delinquency*. Focuses on British and international criminology.

*Canadian Journal of Criminology*
Canadian Criminal Justice Association
Covers information on criminology in Canada. Start year 1958.

*Cendata*
Contains full text and selected numeric data from U.S. Census Bureau economic and demographic reports, press releases, and new product announcements.

*Child Abuse and Neglect*
U.S. National Center on Child Abuse and Neglect
Contains 17,000 citations, with abstracts, to materials concerned with the definition, identification, prevention, and treatment of child abuse and neglect. Coverage is primarily the United States. Sources include A-V material, project descriptions, laws/regulations, and journals. Start date: 1965.

*CINCH-The Australian Criminology Database*
Contains over 20,000 citations, with some abstracts, to the Australian literature on criminology.

*CIS (CIS/Index)*
Contains citations, with abstracts, to publications produced by the committees and subcommittees of the U.S. Congress.

*CJ Data*
Provides information on over 750 computer-readable data collections in the criminal justice area held by the ICPSR and other organizations in the U.S.

*Code of Federal Regulations*
U.S. Government Printing Office
This database is the U.S. government's secondary legislation: regulations made under the authority of Congress for the implementation of laws and government activity. Sources are laws and legislation. Coverage is the United States.

*Combined Health Information Database*
Contains 12 files of information on health education and health promotion topics for health professionals and the general public.

*Computer ASAP*
January 1988-present, with some titles going back to 1983. The most comprehensive full-text database covering the computer industry, providing a wide range of information on computers, electronics, and telecommunications.

*Computer Database*
Provides wide range of information on computers, telecommunications, and electronics. Contains abstracts to articles from 140 business and technical periodicals. Start year: 1983.

*Computer Data Security*
Contains full text of *Computer Data Security*, a special report covering security measures for prevention of computer theft, fraud, and viruses.

*Computer Fraud & Security Bulletin*
Contains full text of *Computer Fraud & Security Bulletin*, a monthly newsletter on computer crime and on prevention methods and related commercial products.

*Conference Papers Index*
Contains over 1.3 million citations to scientific and technical papers presented at regional, national, and international meetings.

*Congressional Record Abstracts*
Contains about 340,000 citations, with abstracts, to the *Congressional Record* (House, Senate, Extension of Remarks, and Digest sections), the official diary of the activities of the U.S. Congress.

*Consumer Drug Information*
Contains information on over 270 generic drugs that comprise over 4,000 brand name products marketed in the U.S.

*Corrections Today*
American Correctional Association
May also be known as *American Journal of Correction* or *Prison World*. Database covers the United States only. *Corrections Today* is a journal of prison facilities and prison administration. Selected articles are included full-text in ACAnet.

*Crime Bytes*
Contains public safety and crime information of interest to the general public and the law enforcement community. Includes hints on child safety, crime prevention, earthquake safety, "wanted" notices, and changes and additions to national and local laws.

*Criminal Justice Abstracts*
Willow Tree Press, Inc.
Contains full text of *Criminal Justice Abstracts* (Formerly *Crime and Delinquency Literature*), providing 46,000 citations, with abstracts, to journals, reports, books, dissertations, magazines, and newspapers. *Criminal Justice Abstracts* includes literature on crime trends, corrections, juvenile delinquency, crime prevention, and other criminal justice topics. Start year: 1968.

*Criminal Justice Periodical Index*
University Microfilms International/ Data Courier Inc.
Contains about 200,000 citations to articles in 120 magazines, journals, newsletters, and law reporting publications on the administration of justice and law enforcement. Subjects include penology, forensic science, abortion, commercial crime, organized crime, and crime prevention. Start year: 1975.

*Cross-Cultural CD - Volume 2: Family, Crime, and Social Problems*
CCCD contains the full text of the HRAF (Human Relations Areafile) material on 60 of these societies from around the world. Designed as a teaching aid for the social and behavioral sciences and humanities. Reliability of ethnographic sources is sometimes questionable—the user must attempt a determination of reliability.

*Current Contents Search*
Institute for Scientific Information
Contains citations to articles listed in the tables of contents of over 7,000 leading journals in the sciences, social sciences, and arts and humanities. 1990-present.

*D&B Dun's Electronic Yellow Pages*
Contains mailing and descriptive information on approximately eight million U.S. businesses.

*DHSS-Data*
Health Administration
Contains approximately 125,000 records, 40 percent with abstracts, to the holdings of the DHSS library, covering health services, social welfare, and social security. Coverage is primarily the United Kingdom. Sources include monographs, journals, government documents, reports, pamphlets, administrative circulars and official publications. 1983-present; earliest data from 1961.

*Dialog Information Retrieval Service (Dialog)*
Dialog now offers more than 290 databases. Dialog contains in excess of 80 million records, including references and abstracts of published literature, statistical tables, full text of selected articles, and directory, business, and financial data.

*Dissertation Abstracts Online*
University Microfilms International/ Data Courier, Inc.
*Dissertations Abstracts* is a definitive subject, title, and author guide to virtually every American dissertation accepted at an accredited institution. Contains 1,500,000 citations, with abstracts (since 1980), to dissertations accepted for doctoral degrees by accredited North American educational institutions and over 200 institutions elsewhere. Start year: 1861.

*DrugDex*
Contains about 775 monographs on drugs. Drug Consults. Contents include over 5,300 patient-based consultations, case histories, and documents from drug information centers and clinical pharmacology services worldwide. Coverage is international with primary emphasis on the United States. Sources include theses and dissertations.

*DrugInfo and Alcohol Use and Abuse*
University of Minnesota
Contains two files on alcohol and drug use/abuse that may be searched together or separately.
- DrugInfo. 1968-present. Contains citations, with abstracts, to monographs, journals, conference papers, instructional guides, and other materials that deal with the educational, sociological, medical, and psychological aspects of alcohol use and drug use/abuse.

- Alcohol Use and Abuse. 1968-1978. Contains citations to journal articles, reprints, unpublished papers, and chapters from books that deal with research in the area of chemical dependency.

*Drug Information Fulltext*
Contains full text of about 1,400 monographs covering about 50,000 commercially available and experimental drugs in the U.S.

*DrugLine*
Contains over 4,000 questions received and answers prepared by clinical pharmacologists and pharmacists at the Drug Information Center. Start year: 1982.

*DrugNews*
Contains citations, with evaluative summaries, to the worldwide literature on current developments in therapeutic drug research, including reports of significant adverse side effects. Start year: 1983.

*Educational Resources Information Center (ERIC)*
U.S. Department of Education
Objective is to make current educational research and related information available swiftly and inexpensively to researchers, teachers, administrators, and other users. Coverage is not limited to information on criminal justice education, but encompasses references on law enforcement issues, technologies, strategies, and legal responsibilities. There are 850,000 records with abstracts. Coverage is international with emphasis on the United States.

*Embase*
Elsevier Science B V
Contains over four million citations, with abstracts, from over 3,500 journals representing the worldwide biomedical literature on human medicine and areas of biological sciences related to human medicine. Sources include surveys, journals, conference proceedings, and reviews. Start year: 1974.

*Emforensic*
Contains citations, with abstracts, to the worldwide literature on forensic sciences. Start year: 1974.

*Encyclopedia of Associations*
Provides information on over 75,000 worldwide, nonprofit associations and organizations.

*The Expert and the Law*
Contains full text of *The Expert and the Law*, a newsletter covering the application of scientific, medical, and technical knowledge to litigation. Start year: 1981.

*Expernet*
Contains references to about 1,300 physicians who can serve as expert witnesses or consultants to attorneys.

*Facts on File World News Digest*
Contains full text of *Facts on File World News Digest*, providing news summaries of current events worldwide. Start year: 1975.

*Family Resources*
National Council on Family Relations
Provides more than 122,000 citations, with abstracts, to journal and nonjournal literature and references to other resources on marriage and family. Subjects covered include violence, child abuse and drug abuse. Coverage primarily is the United States. Sources include journals films, newsletters, A-V material, conference proceedings, and project descriptions. Start year: 1970.

*FBI's 10 Most Wanted Fugitives*
Contains descriptions of individuals named on the FBI's 10 Most Wanted Fugitives List.

*Federal Index*
Contains citations to the *Congressional Record, Federal Register,* and *Weekly Compilation of Presidential Documents.* Start year: 1982.

*Federal Procurement Data Center*
The Federal Procurement Data Center maintains a computerized compendium of the Federal Acquisition Regulations (FAR), many agencies' supplements to the FAR, and information relative to all active (and some completed) government contracts. It is accessible through DIALOG.

*Federal Register Abstracts*
Contains abstracts of each document published in the *Federal Register (FR).* Start year: 1986.

*Federal Research In Progress*
National Technical Information Service
Contains descriptions of and references to research in progress and recently completed research sponsored primarily by federal government agencies. Sources include research communication and project descriptions. 1982-present.

*Federal Sentencing Law and Practice*
Contains full text of *Federal Sentencing Law and Practice,* including supplemental appendices. 1989-present.

*Forensic Science Database*
Contains about 35,000 citations, with some abstracts, to the worldwide literature on forensic sciences. Start year: 1976.

*Forensic Services Directory*
Contains the names of thousands of scientific, medical, and technical experts available to serve as expert trial witnesses or consultants to attorneys, corporations, and the government.

*Foundation Directory*
Contains descriptions of over 26,000 currently active grant-making foundations.

*Foundation Grants Index and Grants Database*
Includes currently available grants and grant programs offered by federal, state, and local governments, commercial organizations, associations, and private foundations.

*General Accounting Office Documents Retrieval System (GAODOCS)*
GAODOCS contains experts from GAO reports and is searchable by subject, GAO division, and report name or number.

*General Services Administration Consolidated List*
The GSA Consolidated List is a computerized list of suspended and debarred bidders.

*GPO Monthly Catalog*
Contains approximately 305,000 citations to the publications of U.S. government agencies, including the U.S. Congress. Start year: 1976.

*GPO Publications Reference File*
Contains citations to about 21,000 public documents published by the executive, judicial, and legislative branches of the federal government and currently sold by the Superintendent of Documents. Start year: 1971.

*Grants*
Contains references to grants offered by federal, state, and local governments; commercial organizations; associations; and private foundations.

*Handsnet*
HandsNet Inc.
Contains news and information, with abstracts, on hunger, health care, housing, legal aid, and other poverty-related issues. Sources include newspapers, wire services, and government documents. HandsNet includes a bulletin board for postings. 1987-present.

*Historical Abstracts*
Contains citations, with abstracts, of the worldwide literature from approximately 2,000 journals, and, since 1980, books and dissertations on political, diplomatic, economic, social, cultural, and intellectual history and related areas of the social sciences and humanities. Start year: 1973.

*House Member Information Network (MIN)*
MIN is a group of online information-retrieval systems, which include the following: government statistics; the substance and present status of bills and resolutions; floor amendments; floor proceedings; pre-award grants; post-award grants; and available contracts and awarded contracts, listing every civilian contract of $10,000 or more and every defense contract of $25,000 entered into by the federal government over the last four quarters. MIN also provides full text of the *Congressional Record* since the 99th Congress.

*Industry Data Sources*
Provides access to sources of marketing, financial, and statistical data on 65 major industries, both American and foreign. 1979-present.

*Information and Technology Transfer Database*
Contains over three million citations, with some abstracts, to materials covering a wide variety of subjects: energy, law enforcement and justice, waste management, fiber optics and lasers, transportation, medicine, health, earth sciences, construction, civil engineering, and agriculture. 1892-present.

*The Information Bank Abstracts*
Contains abstracts of all news and editorial matter from the final Late Edition of *The New York Times* newspaper, the Eastern Edition of *The Wall Street Journal* newspaper, and selected material from approximately 40 other sources published in the U.S., Canada, and Europe.

*Judicial Conduct Reporter*
Contains full text of *Judicial Conduct Reporter*, a quarterly publication covering commentary and analysis of matters relating to judicial conduct. 1979-present.

*JURIS (Justice Retrieval and Inquiry System)*
Contains a family of files providing full text of federal court decisions, statutes, regulations, treaties, and other primary and secondary legal materials.

*Labor and Employment Law in Review*
Contains full text of articles summarizing developments in labor and employment law.

*Labor Law I*
Contains about 242,000 citations, with summaries, indexing, and other locator information, to federal and state court decisions, administrative agency rulings, and labor arbitration decisions published in seven Bureau of National Affairs printed information services.

*Labor Law II*
Contains about 3,300 citations, with summaries, indexing, and other locator information, to federal and state court decisions, administrative agency rulings, and labor arbitration decisions published in seven Bureau of National Affairs printed information services.

*Law Enforcement and Criminal Justice Information Database*
Contains citations, with some abstracts, to the literature on law enforcement and criminal justice. 1954-present.

*Legal Resource Index*
Contains over 325,000 citations to legal and law-related periodical literature. 1980-present.

*LEXIS Federal Sentencing Library*
Contains sentencing-related decisions from the Supreme Court since 1970, the Court of Appeals since 1789, and the District Courts since 1789.

*LEXIS Public Health and Welfare Library*
Contains selected Social Security case decisions from the Supreme Court, Courts of Appeals, District Courts, Claims Court, Bankruptcy Courts, and the Federal Tax Courts since 1790, United States Code Service Titles 26, 28, 29, 30, 42, and 45, sections of the Code of Federal Regulations related to the Social Security Administration, and Social Security Rulings since 1966.

*National Newspaper Index*
Contains citations to articles, news reports, editorials, letters to the editor, obituaries, product evaluation, biographical pieces, poetry, recipes, columns, cartoons, illustrations, and reviews from *The Christian Science Monitor, Los Angeles Times, The New York Times, The Wall Street Journal, The Washington Post.* 1970-present.

*NCJRS (National Criminal Justice Reference Service)*
Contains over 92,000 citations, with abstracts, to both print and nonprint information on all aspects of law enforcement, crime prevention and security, criminal justice, and juvenile justice. 1972-present.

*The National Law Journal*
1983-present. Contains full text of *The National Law Journal*, a weekly newspaper for the legal profession.

*The National Report on Substance Abuse*
Contents include full text of *The National Report on Substance Abuse*, a newsletter on corporate policies toward drug abuse in the workplace. 1987-present.

*National Texts and Periodicals (NTP)*
NTP consists of selected articles from over 200 law reviews and bar journals.

*Newssearch*
Contains citations to the current month's magazine, journal, and newspaper literature.

*Newswire ASAP*
Kyodo's, July 1987-present; PR Newswire, January 1985-present; and Reuters, June 1987-present. Database offering the complete text and comprehensive subject indexing of news from Kyodo's Japan Economic Newswire, PR Newswire, and Reuters Financial Report.

*New York Times Index*
This source is published semimonthly. It is an index giving exact reference to date, page, and column where articles will be found. It contains cross references to names and related topics and answers questions without having to reread the article.

*NEXIS*
NEXIS is a full-text database consisting of general news, business and financial information from more than 150 newspapers, magazines, and wire services. Magazine data dating from January, 1975; newspaper data dating from January, 1977.

*NIJ Drugs and Crime CD-ROM Library*
National Institute of Justice
National Criminal Justice Reference Service
A comprehensive collection of books, reports, articles, data sets, abstracts, graphics and images related to drugs and crime, including several of the most important scholarly works on drugs, crime and law enforcement, providing historical and international perspectives. Also includes research results, with statistics and case histories, from various government and private sector studies. Subjects include law and legislation, social sciences, banking, crime and criminal law, and drug information. 1970-1989.

*NTIS (National Technical Information Service)*
Contains about 1.4 million citations, most with abstracts, to unrestricted technical reports from U.S. and non-U.S. government-sponsored research, development, and engineering analysis. 1964-present.

*On-Line Retrieval of Bibliographic Information, Time-shared (ORBIT)*
ORBIT is an online, interactive retrieval system designed and implemented by the SDC Search Service Division Development Corporation, Santa Monica, California. The ORBIT user interacts directly with the retrieval program via a terminal and telecommunication line.

*Readers Guide to Periodical Literature*
This source is a reference guide to articles in over 125 popular magazines. It is published semimonthly, with a cumulative index every two years. This contains a full dictionary cataloging of all articles.

*Register of Stolen Art and Artifacts*
Contains information on 15,000 stolen art works. 1966-present.

*Scorpio*
This research service contains several different databases, and includes abstracts of the following: The Library of Congress Computerized Catalog, the Bibliographic Citation File, Congressional Statute Files, and the National Referral Center Master File.

*Securities Information Center (SIC)*
The SIC is operated by Itel Corporation under contract with the Securities and Exchange Commission. Banks and brokerage houses that receive bad securities are required to report this information to the SIC. 1977-present.

*Sentencing*
Contains full text of all reported and unreported British Columbia Court of Appeals sentencing decisions, full text of selected cases throughout Canada covering the law on sentencing, and about 120,000 citations, with abstracts, to British Columbia trial-level sentencing decisions.

*Social Justice*
*A Journal of Crime, Conflict, and World Order*
Global Options
Formerly known as *Crime and Social Justice*. Combines analysis of global issues (peaceful resolutions of conflicts, state terrorism, and human rights) with domestic policy concerns, such as reducing crime, as well as race and gender discrimination. Sources include journals. 1974-present.

*Social Sciences Index*
Social Sciences Citation Index—Institute for Scientific Information
Contains over 2,400,000 citations, with abstracts, to articles and book reviews in about 350 English-language periodicals in the social sciences. Subjects covered criminology and penology, sociology, political science, ethic studies, and business and finance. 1969-present.

All ISI databases have a linked service known as The Genuine Article which can deliver the full text of located articles by mail, facsimile transmission, or courier.

*Social Scisearch*
Contains over 2.2 million citations to significant articles from the 1,400 most important social sciences journals worldwide and social sciences articles from 4,500 journals in the natural, physical, and biomedical sciences. 1969-present.

*Social Work Abstracts*
National Association of Social Work
Also may be recognized as SWAB. Contents include about 31,000 records, with abstracts, to journal articles, doctoral dissertations, and other materials on social work and related fields. Areas covered include social work service methods, social policy, social work professional issues and related fields of knowledge such as economics, psychology, sociology, and psychiatry. Primary coverage is the United States. 1977-present.

*SSIE Current Research*
National Technical Information Service
A database containing reports of U.S. government and privately funded scientific research projects, either in progress or initiated and completed between 1978 and 1982. Covers projects funded from over 1,300 federal, state, and local government agencies, nonprofit associations and foundations, and colleges and universities. 1978-1982.

*Sociological Abstracts*
Sociological Abstracts, Inc.
Coverage includes literature in sociology and related areas in the social and behavioral sciences from 1963 to the present. Abstracts included in addition to the citations. The social, political, and even economic aspects of criminal justice can be successfully searched through the Social Scisearch and Sociological Abstracts databases. Contents include 332,000 citations with abstracts. Sources include book abstracts, thesis, monographs, journals, conference reports, and dissertaions.

*Standard & Poor's (S&P)*
S&P has several databases regarding corporations. These databases are available through DIALOG, including information on 36,000 corporations and 340,000 "key executives," with 74,000 profile biographies. S&P can provide substantial information on financial institutions, including a list of the corporate officers and directors, mailing addresses, total deposits, primary bank, and primary law firm.

*State Legislatures*
National Conference of State Legislatures
Articles on state tax reform, education, child welfare, criminal justice, health care and other public policy issues. Coverage is United States. 1975-present.

*Statistics Canada Catalogue Online*
Statistics Canada Library
May also be recognized as STATCAN or Statistics and Canada Catalogue. This database includes 6,500 citations with abstracts available. Sources include journals and monographs. This is a bibliographic database that covers recent periodicals and monographs published by Statistics Canada. Subjects of importance to the Criminal Justice

field are government, law enforcement and public safety, population and immigration, women, native peoples, the elderly, and handicapped persons.

*Statistics Canada Reference Database*
Statistics Canada
May also be known as ScatCan Reference Database. Coverage is Canada only. This database contains the Inventory of Catalogued Publications, bibliographic material on current and past Statistics Canada publications, the CANSIM Mainbase Series Directory, reference material for using the CANSIM Time Series Data Bank, the current Statistics Canada internal telephone directory, and the StatCan Thesaurus. 1989-present.

*Substance Abuse in the Workplace: An Employer's Prospective*
Contains information on employee substance abuse in the workplace. 1987 only.

*Technical Advisory Service for Attorneys*
Contains references to about 14,000 individuals in a variety of occupations available to serve as expert witnesses or as consultants to attorneys.

*Texts and Periodicals*

West Publishing Company
A database of legal periodicals, loose-leaf services and monographs. This is not an indexing or abstracting service. Contains 535 journals. Coverage in international with primary focus of the United States.

*United States Government Publications*
U.S. Government Printing Office
Reports, studies, fact sheets, maps, handbooks, and conference proceedings from various government agencies as well as congressional documents from 1976 to present. This database contains a catalogue of US GPO publications and subscription services, with online ordering facilities.

*Westlaw Criminal Justice Data Base*
Contains full text of articles and documents selected from a variety of law-related monographs and periodicals relating to federal criminal justice.

*Westlaw Criminal Justice Topical Highlights Data Base*
Contains summaries of significant recent state and federal cases covering criminal justice, including the nature, investigation, prosecution, and punishment of crimes.

*Westlaw Federal and Multistate Criminal J· .ice Data Bases*
Contains full text of case law and other documents related to U.S. state and federal law covering criminal acts and the investigation, prosecution, and punishment of crimes.

*Westlaw Federal Data Base*
Contains full text of U.S. federal laws, regulations, executive documents, and court decisions.

*West's Legal Directory*
West Publishing Company
This is a directory containing profiles of attorneys and law firms, including qualifications, representative cases and clients, and general contact information. Coverage includes the United States, Canada, United Kingdom.

*Wilson Social Sciences Abstracts*
H.W. Wilson Co.
This database offers indexing of about 350 English-language periodicals, with single subject headings that cover the applied and theoretical aspects of the discipline, extensive cross-referencing, verification of all corporate and personal names used a subjects complete bibliographic dates, title enhancement to clarity titles of articles or to indicate special features such as review articles or symposia, and a separate index to reviews of current books in the social services. Contents include 430,000 citations with abstracts. [Note: From March 1995, all new records were generated with abstracts, alongside Wilson Social Sciences Abstracts, which includes the entire file, with abstracts from March 1995.]

# 10

# Government Documents

Many people think that government publications are limited to huge piles of statutes and laws. But the truth is, government documents provide a wealth of information in almost every field, and criminal justice is no exception. Government documents include not only those published by the federal government (although it is the major source) but also those published by state and local governments. These publications help the public make better use of governmental services. Government publications include results of government research, annual reports, statistical information, congressional hearings, bibliographies, directories, special and irregular publications, audiovisual materials, maps, and charts. Federal publications are printed by the United States Government Printing Office (GPO), Washington, D.C., an independent body in the legislative branch of government. Distribution of the documents is the responsibility of the Superintendent of Documents, an office within the GPO.

Publications currently offered for sale by the Superintendent of Documents are listed in the *GPO Sales Publications Reference File (PRF)*. Anyone wishing to purchase a particular document need only look in this catalog to determine availability and ordering information.

The contents of the *PRF* are arranged in three ways: (1) by GPO stock numbers, (2) by Superintendent of Documents classification numbers, and (3) by alphabetical arrangement of subjects, titles, agency series and report numbers, key words and phrases, and authors. *PRF* is issued six times yearly, with monthly updates.

Most federal government documents are available through libraries that are also Federal Depository Libraries. For a partial list of these, see the section of this book titled Special Libraries.

## LOCATING GOVERNMENT DOCUMENTS

Government documents are usually in a separate collection in a designated section of the library. Many collections also include international, state, and local government documents. Most libraries organize government documents by a Superintendent of Documents number assigned to each publication. These numbers are listed in the *Monthly Catalog of United States Government Publications*. It is indexed by author, title, subject, and key word.

The governmental agency producing the majority of documents relating to criminal justice is the Department of Justice and its affiliated agencies, such as the FBI, Federal Bureau of Prisons, National Institute of Justice, Bureau of Justice Statistics, Immigration and Naturalization Service, and Drug Enforcement Administration.

Several different guides to government publications, plus some government publications themselves, are alphabetically annotated below.

*American Statistics Index.* A comprehensive index to statistical publications published by the federal government. (Washington, DC: Congressional Information Service, Inc.). (For additional information on this reference see Chapter 11, "Statistical Data.")

*Bibliographic Guide to Government Publications.* An annual publication with an alphabetized subject index. The work consists of two volumes, A through N, and O through Z. The main subject heading for government publications relating to criminal justice is Crime and Criminals. (Boston: G.K. Hall and Company).

*City and County Data Book.* Devoted to statistical analyses of many different characteristics of each county in the United States. (Washington, DC: U.S. Bureau of the Census). (For more information regarding this publication, see Chapter 11, "Statistical Data.")

*Comprehensive Index to the Publications of the United States Government 1881-1893.* John G. Ames. Mainly comprised of listings of congressional publications during the designated period. (Washington, DC: U.S. Department of Interior, 1905). (See also Chapter 15, "Historical Research Sources.")

*Congressional District Data Book.* A biennial publication since 1961 which makes it possible to examine congressional voting records in regard to district characteristics. It includes information on vital statistics, bank deposits, retail trade, local governments, housing, and so forth. (Washington, DC: U.S. Department of Commerce).

*Congressional Index.* Designed to provide assistance to researchers regarding the status of legislation pending in Congress. Public bills and resolutions are indexed, and subject and author indexes are included, as well as a Headline Legislation Index for bills which have received widespread publicity. Members of the House and Senate are listed in separate divisions with biographical data and committee assignments provided. Also included is a list of all permanent committees and their subcommittees, public hearings held by all committees, subjects not identified by their bill numbers, and reports of investigations and studies by committees as they are submitted to Congress. Progress of public bills and resolutions are reported from their introduction to their final resolution. (Chicago: Commerce Clearing House, Inc.).

*Congressional Information Service Index (CIS) Annual.* A basic index to information contained in the working papers of Congress. It includes information on almost every important area of public policy. Hearings, committee prints, House and Senate Reports and Documents, Executive Reports and Documents, and public laws are covered. Monthly indexes, cumulated annually, are provided. (Washington, DC: Congressional Information Service, Inc.).

*Congressional Record.* Published Monday through Friday while Congress is in session, this source contains primary sources of information on topics discussed on the Congressional floor. Indices include an alphabetical listing of subjects and names and a history of bills and resolutions arranged by their numbers. (Washington, DC: Congress).

*Consumer's Guide to Federal Publications.* A pamphlet which describes subject bibliographies of government publications that are available to the public free of charge from the Superintendent of Documents. Publications listed in the bibliographies are for sale. Subject bibliographies and their ordering numbers of interest to criminal justice students include: Accidents and Accident Prevention; Alcohol, Tobacco and Firearms; Courts and Correctional Institutions; Crime and Criminal Justice; Criminal Justice Agencies; Drug Education; FBI Publications; Firefighting, Prevention and Forest Fires; Grants and Awards (see also Grants section, Appendix III.); Juvenile Delinquency; Law Enforcement; Subversive Activities; Supreme Court Reports; Violence. (Washington, DC: Superintendent of Documents, GPO).

*Digest of Public General Bills and Resolutions.* Furnishes a summary of the essential characteristics and/or changes of public bills and resolutions made during sessions of Congress. It also shows the status of bills acted upon and enacted. Indexes include sponsor and co-sponsor, short title, and subject index. Supplements are issued irregularly and a final issue is published upon adjournment of Congress. (Washington, DC: Library of Congress).

*Federal Regulatory Directory.* Published biennially by *Congressional Quarterly*, this is a comprehensive guide to federal regulatory activities, describing developments in the regulatory process as well as the agencies and personnel and their functions. Includes addresses and phone numbers for regional and national offices (Washington, DC: Congressional Quarterly, Inc.).

*Government Publications Index.* An index to U.S. government publications by subject, title, author, and issuing agency. (Santa Monica, CA: Information Access Corp, 1980-present).

*Government Reports Announcements and Index.* This bi-weekly publication indexes government reports. Behavioral and social sciences, as well as physical and life sciences, are represented. (Springfield, VA: U.S. Dept. Of Commerce).

*Guide to Popular Government Publications.* Lists many documents in a wide variety of subjects, mainly popular in nature. (Englewood, CO: Libraries Unlimited).

*Guide to United States Government Serials and Periodicals.* John Andriot. An annual publication that guides the reader to serials, periodicals, and irregular publications of the United States Government. Contents are arranged alphabetically by branch of government, department, and agency. Agency, subject, and title indexes are provided. (McLean, VA: Documents Index).

*Index to Current Urban Documents.* Issued quarterly, covers the publications of 272 of the largest cities and counties in the United States. These publications include annual reports, audit reports, budgets, community development programs, demographic profiles, conference transcripts, consultant's reports, directories, economic studies, environmental impact statements, evaluations and analyses, feasibility studies, inventories, planning reports, policy statements, plus many more. Access is through geographic and subject indexes. (Westport, CT: Greenwood Press).

*Index to Government Periodicals.* Issued quarterly. Indexes 147 selected United States Government periodicals, including FBI Law Enforcement Bulletin, Drug Enforcement, and Federal Probation. (Chicago: Infodata International, Inc.).

*Introduction to United States Public Documents.* Joe Movebead. Intended as a textbook for library science students, but the chapters dealing with the publications of the various branches of government are exceptionally good for anyone researching public documents. (Littleton, CO: Libraries Unlimited, 1983).

*Monthly Catalog of United States Government Publications.* Lists the publications issued by the Government Printing Office each month. Detailed author, title, subject, and other specialized indexes are provided each month and cumulated semi-annually and annually. (Washington, DC: GPO).

*Monthly Checklist of State Publications.* A record of state documents issued during the last five years which have been received by the Library of Congress. Citations include monographs, periodicals, publications of associations of state officials and regional organizations and library studies, manuals, and statistical reports. (Washington, DC: Library of Congress).

*Municipal Yearbook.* Describes activities in and provides statistical data on major American cities. (Chicago: International City Managers Association). (See Chapter 11, "Statistical Data," for additional information on this reference).

*National Directory of State Agencies.* (Bethesda, MD: Cambridge Information Group Directory, Inc.).

*The National Union Catalog of Manuscript Collections.* Annual. Describes manuscript collections housed permanently in the Library of Congress. (Washington, DC: Library of Congress).

*Official Congressional Directory.* Published for each Congress elected; this official directory is a manual of Congressional committees as well as a guide to executive departments and the judicial branch. (Washington, DC: GPO).

*Popular Names of U.S. Government Reports.* Bernard A. Bernier. Many times "popular names" are given to government commissions. This book can be an excellent help in locating a specific government commission report. (Washington, DC: Library of Congress).

*Recent Publications on Governmental Problems.* Monthly. (Chicago: Merriam Center Library).

*A Reference List of Audiovisual Materials Produced by the United States Government.* (Washington, DC: GPO).

*State Government Research Checklist.* Bimonthly. (Lexington, KY: Council of State Governments).

*Statistical Reference Index.* (Bethesda, MD: Congressional Information Service).

*Subject Guide to Major United States Government Publications.* Ellen Jackson. Describes important United States Government publications from early periods to the present. (Chicago: American Library Association).

*Uniform Crime Reports for the United States.* Generally published annually. Analyzes crime in the United States. Statistical tables of offenses known, arrests, persons charged, and police employee data are included. This is a very important publication with a wide range of uses. (Washington, DC: Federal Bureau of Investigation).

*United States Government Manual.* Describes the objectives and activities of most government agencies and lists names of management personnel within each agency. (Lanham, MD: Bernan Associates).

*Washington Information Directory 1998-1999.* This publication gives information on the Executive Office of the President, executive offices, and federal agencies. Also included are chapters with information on specific departments. A ready reference list is also given. (Washington, DC: Congressional Quarterly, Inc.).

## NATIONAL COMMISSION REPORTS

In addition to various government publications and sources concerned with government publications, the National Commission Reports also are very good sources of information. Most of these, however, are out of print at the NCJRS and the GPO, but NCJRS has produced a "SLIM" (Selected Library in Microfiche) of Commission reports. The Wickersham Commission Reports (see Chapter 15) are included in the SLIM package. The full text of all reports are available for sale from the NCJRS (see Chapter 16). A brief annotation of each report produced by the respective Commission is provided below.

National Advisory Commission on Criminal Justice Standards and Goals, Washington, D.C.

National Advisory Committee on Criminal Justice Standards and Goals, Washington, D.C.

National Commission on Marijuana and Drug Abuse, Washington, D.C.

National Commission on the Causes and Prevention of Violence, Washington, D.C.

President's Commisssion on Law Enforcement and Administration of Justice, Washington, D.C.

National Planning Association

## National Institute of Justice

The National Institute of Justice (NIJ), a component of the office of Justice Programs, is the research agency of the U.S. Department of Justice. NIJ was created by the Omnibus Crime Control and Safe Streets Act of 1968 as amended. NIJ is authorized to support research, evaluation, and demonstration programs, development of technology, and both national and international information dissemination. Online NIJ publications are categorized into ten sections:

| | |
|---|---|
| Law Enforcement | Drugs and Crime |
| Courts | Victims |
| Corrections | Crime Prevention |
| Science and Technology | International |
| Investigative Sciences | Research Evaluation |

## Freedom of Information Act (FOIA)

The Freedom of Information Act was signed into law during Lyndon Johnson's administration. Essentially, this law provides that unclassified government information is available, and if it is not made available to a requesting individual, the burden of proof lies with the government agency to show why it should not be made available. Directions and rules on where and how to obtain information must be published by each government agency in the *Federal Register*. Types of information that must be made available are:

The results of administrative court cases and rulings

Policy statements not appearing in the *Federal Register*

Administrative staff manuals affecting the public

Types of information exempt under the Freedom of Information Act are:

Documents classified as secret, top secret, or confidential

Rules and procedures concerning the internal workings of the government

Information designated as exempted by statute

Trade secrets

Internal communications

Personal and medical files

Certain investigatory records

Regulatory records of a financial institution

Specific geological information

If you find it necessary to request government information under the Freedom of Information Act, you will need to determine the appropriate agency from which to request the information, and then describe what you want as specifically as possible. Information held by various federal, state, and local agencies is often extensive and covers a broad spectrum. Some of the materials these agencies possess is not generally known to the public, but most is accessible upon request. Most persons in charge of a particular agency will be glad to assist you in locating your requested information. The following publications are excellent sources of additional information on how to obtain government materials under the FOIA:

*Legally Available U.S. Government Information as a Result of the Public Information Act.* Matthew J. Kerbee. (Arlington, VA: Output Systems Corporation, 1970.)

*Your Right to Government Information: How to Use the FOIA.* Christine Marwick. (New York: Bantam, 1985). (This is part of the ACLU Handbook.)

Many government agencies are good sources of criminal justice information. These are described below. In addition to the printed matter that these agencies offer, don't forget the people you meet. They, too, are very good sources of information.

## Federal Field-Based Information

Several federal agencies may be visited or written to for information. Some, such as the FBI, have regional offices throughout the country that may be easily accessible to you. Federal courts are also sources of information, and one may be in close proximity to you.

## State Field-Based Information

The attorney general's office in most states is the top law enforcement agency, and it will maintain statewide records regarding criminal justice matters, including statistics on crime by city, county, type of crime, and so on. Information concerning new or proposed legislation or reforms to the judicial process may also be found here. The State Department of Corrections will maintain records on the number of persons in state prisons, on probation, or released on parole. Information can also be obtained regarding expenditures, number of staff, types of services, recidivism rate, etc. This agency is a good source through which original data from interviewing prisoners can be collected. This is usually possible, but permission should first be obtained in writing from the director of the department. Other agencies that will have information pertaining to criminal justice include the state highway patrol, and the state's bureau of investigation.

## Local Field-Based Government Information

Police departments and sheriffs' departments keep records of the different crimes that are reported to them, as well as data on the time of day, location, crimes cleared by arrest, unsolved cases, patterns or trends, traffic accidents, local manpower, and so forth. The county court house maintains records relating to trials, including transcripts of trials, court appearances, dispositions, bail, divorce and probate, land ownership, civil suits and other information relating to criminal justice and law. Other sources of local records include such community service organizations as rape crisis centers, mental health centers, welfare departments, the coroner's office, various courts, probation and parole offices, local correctional departments, juvenile detention centers, and museums. Addresses of local criminal justice agencies can be found in a publication entitled *Criminal Justice Agencies*. (Washington, DC: United States Department of Justice, LEAA, National Criminal Justice Information Statistics Service). Most libraries have a copy. It can also be purchased from the Government Printing Office.

# 11

# Statistical Data

## FEDERAL JUSTICE STATISTICS
(Excerpted from U.S. Department of Justice, Bureau of Justice Statistics, *Bulletin*.)

Fifty years ago the Wickersham Commission (see Chapter 15 of this book, titled Historical Research Sources), this country's first national crime commission, published a report on criminal justice statistics, noting as a basic principle that accurate statistics are a key to understanding and improving the administration of justice. The 1931 report, which bears the name of a former Attorney General, noted also that a compilation of such statistics did not exist at that time: "Accurate data are the beginning of wisdom in such a subject, and no such data can be had for the country as a whole, nor have they even been available hitherto with respect to many of the activities of the Federal government in the enforcement of Federal laws."

A comprehensive federal transaction database would reflect all transactions occurring in the investigative, prosecutorial, judicial, and correctional segments of the criminal justice system that describe successive actions taken with respect to the same criminal event. Ironically, while the federal government has, over the past decade, encouraged and assisted the states in developing comprehensive state-level transaction data, the federal justice system itself has not experienced comparable progress toward that end. There exists no body of comprehensive statistics about federal offenders and little information about the flow of cases from federal investigators to U.S. Attorneys to the federal court and corrections systems. Although a comprehensive system does not yet exist, partial data may be derived from the following sources.

*Comprehensive Criminal Justice Statistics: Uses, Barriers, and Methods.* Statistics describing the components of state criminal justice systems are now routinely maintained at the state level. Although the systems vary in comprehensiveness and data quality from state to state, they have become increasingly important in every jurisdiction as the needs have increased for improved criminal justice planning, fiscal control, policy assessment, and response to legislative requests for information (for example, to analyze the impact of determinate sentencing systems).

The needs to plan, to support the fiscal process, to assess policy, and to respond to legislative inquiry exist as well at the federal level. The data to meet these needs, however, have not been maintained at the federal level as they have at the state level.

Improved justice statistics for the federal system are needed for more than planning, control, and policy assessment. They are also essential to enable federal authorities to respond to the Attorney General's directive to balance coordination between the federal, state, and local criminal justice systems by establishing Law Enforcement Coordinating Committees. A prerequisite to effective coordination is a basic understanding of the magnitudes of case flow from one stage of federal criminal case processing to adjacent stages.

Barriers to developing comprehensive justice statistics that have been confronted at the state level exist at the federal level as well. Independent data systems have been developed and maintained by federal investigative agencies, the Executive Office for U.S. Attorneys, the Administrative Office of the U.S. Courts, the Federal Prison System, and ancillary federal agencies. As a result, data definitions vary from agency to agency, as do reporting periods and crime classification schemes. These barriers make the prospect of developing a comprehensive federal transaction database incorporating the various data sets maintained by federal agencies fairly difficult, at least for the near future. They also limit the inferences to be drawn from comparing the reports of different justice agencies.

Specific uses of available data to assess federal criminal justice policy are numerous, even prior to data linkage. Simple numeric descriptions of federal case flow and events can reveal the frequency with which specific problems, such as crimes committed while on bail, and bail jumping, actually occur. The data can also be used to assess a host of other issues: case referral policies and rates of case flow between federal and local agencies; the quality of evidence and investigations; rates of pretrial misconduct and the criteria used in making pretrial release decisions; rates of recidivism and chronic-offender case-targeting decisions; delays in case processing at each stage of the system; and consistency in case processing and sentencing practices. Although the case record can serve as the basis for many of these analyses, the data could be reorganized to allow other issues to be addressed. For example, studying recidivism and its predictors requires that the data be reorganized to describe offenders rather than current cases. Likewise, a study of arrest quality might require that the data be restructured to focus on federal investigative functions rather than on individual cases. Similarly, studying case backlogs may require a reorganization of the data by unit of time.

*The Federal System.* The federal criminal justice system is divided into 94 judicial districts. Each has a Federal District Court and a U.S. Attorney. According to the Administrative Office of the U.S. Courts, approximately 50,000 criminal cases enter this system each year. Basic similarities exist between the way these cases are processed and the way cases are usually handled at the state and local levels. At the federal level, as at the state and local levels, criminal justice responsibilities are divided into the components of law enforcement, prosecution, adjudication and sentencing, and corrections.

There are also some fundamental differences between the federal and state systems. The federal system is perhaps most readily distinguishable from state and local systems in terms of the kinds of crimes unique to federal jurisdictions, including major crimes (e.g., major drug offenses and crimes of serious fraud and corruption), crimes that cross state boundaries (e.g., interstate transport of stolen property, cargo theft), crimes involving federal money (e.g. counterfeiting, forgery of U.S. checks), and crimes committed on U.S. Government property.

Criminal offenses that are investigated and prosecuted at the federal level typically do not involve crimes of violence. These are commonly handled at state or local levels. Federal criminal cases usually result from long-term investigations of crimes such as embezzlement, fraud, drug dealing, or forgery. These cases may involve offenders who have committed many offenses over several months or years, or who have stolen large sums of money.

Five investigative agencies conduct a substantial majority of the investigative work done at the federal level: the Federal Bureau of Investigation, the Drug Enforcement Administration, the Secret Service, the Postal Inspection Service, and the Bureau of Alcohol, Tobacco, and Firearms. Other federal agencies, including the Customs Service, the Internal Revenue Service, the Food and Drug Administration, the Immigration and Naturalization Service, the Securities and Exchange Commission, and individual executive departments also employ investigators to monitor infractions that are the responsibility of those agencies. Investigative activities include crime detection, evidence collection, making arrests, presenting cases to federal prosecutors, and conducting follow-up investigations.

Prosecuting federal cases is the responsibility of the Department of Justice litigating divisions and the Office of the U.S. Attorney in each district. U.S. Attorneys are appointed by the President but generally have long-standing familiarity with the concerns of their districts. They are supported in Washington, D.C., by the Executive Office for the U.S. Attorneys.

Many, if not most, federal crimes are "dual jurisdiction" offenses that may be prosecuted either federally or locally. The decision by a U.S. Attorney to prosecute a bank robbery, for example, may rest on such factors as the seriousness of the offense, the prior record of the offender, policies of the agencies involved, and the degree of involvement of local law enforcement officials in investigating the offense. Generally, the federal government will prosecute cases brought by federal agents when the cases meet the U.S. Attorney's standards of seriousness and have enough evidence to merit prosecution.

In addition to the 94 U.S. Attorneys and the 94 Federal District Courts, there are 13 Circuit Courts of Appeal, and the Supreme Court of the United States. Statistical information about case processing in the judicial branch of the federal system is maintained by the Administrative Office of the U.S. Courts.

After receiving sentences, convicted offenders in the federal system may be turned over to the Division of Probation in the Administrative Office of the U.S. Courts or the Bureau of Prisons. Offenders sentenced to incarceration are confined in one of the 42 federal correctional facilities located throughout the country.

Eligibility for parole is determined by using guidelines developed by the Federal Parole Commission. These guidelines permit evaluating each federal inmate on the basis of offense seriousness and relevant aspects of the inmate's criminal history.

*Federal Data Sources.* The agencies that make up the federal criminal justice system maintain data that document the processing of cases and defendants within each agency and describe the criminal record of individual offenders. At the investigation stage there are several automated databases, including the FBI's Computerized Criminal History File (CCH); the Criminal Automated Reporting System of the Bureau of Alcohol, Tobacco, and Firearms; and the automated files maintained by the Drug Enforcement Administration and the Secret Service. Also, manual files are maintained by other agencies that engage in investigative work.

Information about the cases processed by U.S. Attorneys is maintained by the Executive Office for the U.S. Attorneys in its Docket and Reporting System. The system provides data about criminal (and civil) case rejections, filings, and dispositions.

Court data maintained by the Administrative Office of the U.S. Courts in the Automated Docket System provide information about criminal case filings and terminations in the federal courts. The "termination" file contains offense, disposition, and sentencing information.

Finally, the Federal Bureau of Prisons uses automated prison records to monitor the confinement and release of federal offenders.

In addition to the databases listed above, special-purpose data sets provide information about federal defendants, cases and practitioners. These include: the U.S. Parole Commission longitudinal recidivism files; pretrial release data maintained by the Federal Pretrial Services Agency; COURTRAN files designed by the Federal Judicial Center, that provide automated court records for 13 federal districts; Prosecutor's Management Information System (PROMIS) currently in two U.S. Attorney's offices, with plans to extend it to other offices; other data developed as part of specific studies sponsored by federal agencies (e.g., coded presentence investigation reports).

*Conclusion.* Maintaining statistical information about the federal criminal justice system is not an easy task. It is one that at present is done primarily within each district and aggregated nationally by the numerous agencies operating separately within the federal executive and judicial branches.

Movement toward a comprehensive system of federal criminal justice statistics would certainly help to improve understanding of federal case processing and enable the various agencies of the federal justice network to conduct analyses that are needed to enable them to carry out their mandates. It would also foster better coordination both within the federal government and between the federal and local systems.

The Bureau of Justice Statistics has undertaken to build toward these ends. Currently, efforts are being directed toward a comprehensive review of federal data sources to determine feasibility of developing an integrated database. BJS will also release a major Compendium of Federal Criminal Justice Statistics, which will provide a single-source reference to criminal justice statistics describing the federal criminal justice system. Additionally, reports will be issued that analyze statistical data relevant to particular priority issues associated with the federal offender and the federal criminal justice system.

## BUREAU OF JUSTICE STATISTICS

The Bureau of Justice Statistics (BJS) is an agency of the U.S. Department of Justice. It is mandated by Congress to collect, analyze, publish, and disseminate statistics on crime, victims of crime, criminal offenders, and operations of justice systems at all levels of government throughout the United States. It also is a source of financial and technical support to state and local statistical and operating agencies throughout the nation. It develops national policy on such issues as the privacy, confidentiality, and security of data and the interstate exchange of criminal records.

BJS began its work in 1969 as the National Criminal Justice Information and Statistics Service (NCJISS) of the Law Enforcement Assistance Administration, consolidating existing justice statistical programs throughout the federal government in a single agency and developing new programs to meet data needs. In 1979, the Justice System Improvement Act (JSIA) established the Bureau of Justice Statistics and mandated that it continue the NCJISS statistical programs. The act also created the Office of Justice Assistance, Research, and Statistics (OJARS), which coordinates the work of BJS, the National Institute of Justice, and the Office of Juvenile Justice and Delinquency Prevention. Collectively, these agencies are sometimes referred to as JSIA agencies or OJARS agencies.

More information about any BJS program can be obtained from BJS at 633 Indiana Avenue, N.W., Washington, D.C. 20531, (202) 724-7765. The Internet address for BJS is www.ojp.usdoj.gov/bjs.

### The BJS Data Collection Programs

BJS collects data about criminal justice agencies, victims of crime, and criminal offenders. Most of these data are collected for BJS by another organization, such as the Bureau of the Census (Internet address: www.census.gov/), professional associations, or research organizations, under contract to BJS.

### The BJS National Statistical Program

The largest part of the BJS program is national data collection, which includes:

- The National Crime Survey (NCS), which interviews a sample of households to determine the incidence and characteristics of criminal victimization

- The new Law Enforcement Management and Administrative Statistics (LEMAS) program

- The prosecution and adjudication program, which includes
  —two annual series, the National Judicial Reporting and the Prosecution of Felony Arrests Programs
  —periodic collection of data on public defense
  —a new statistical series being developed to cover the pretrial stage of criminal justice processing

- The corrections statistics program, which
  —periodically surveys persons held in local jails, state prisons, and juvenile facilities
  —enumerates correctional populations annually, including persons in prisons and jails, on probation and parole, and under sentence of death
  —conducts censuses of state prisons and local jails

- The justice expenditure and employment program, which produces annual data for the federal, state, and local justice systems

## Major BJS Surveys

*National Crime Survey.* Begun in 1973, produces annual national estimates of the amount of crime against persons and households; victimization rates; the characteristics of victims, criminal events, and offenders; reporting of crime to the police; and the reasons for not reporting.

*State Court Caseloads.* Begun in 1975, produces annual national and state-level data on state and local filings and dispositions of civil, criminal, juvenile, and traffic cases.

*Prosecution Statistics.* Compiles data for selected jurisdictions on felony case processing. The data cover case attrition, reasons for case rejection, pretrial release decisions, continuances, trial rates, time from arrest to disposition, guilty pleas, conviction rates, and sentences.

*National Indigent Criminal Defense Survey.* Begun in 1983, produces national and state-level data on public defender systems. The data cover costs, employment, organization, fees paid, caseloads, types of cases (felony, misdemeanor, juvenile, mental commitments, appeals), and disposition of cases.

*National Prisoner Statistics.* Produces annual and semiannual national and state-level data on the numbers of prisoners in state and federal facilities. Every five years, data are collected on detailed characteristics of state prisons, such as age of facility, security level, programs offered, confinement space, employment, and operating costs. Also at five-year intervals, data are collected from a survey of state prisoners; data collected include criminal histories, incarceration offense, drug and alcohol use, and demographic characteristics. Much of the information dates to the early 1900s.

*National Jail Statistics.* First conducted in 1970. It now produces annual national estimates of the number of jail inmates. Every five years, it produces detailed national and state-level data on the characteristics of inmates and jails similar to those produced by the National Prisoner Statistics program.

*Capital Punishment.* Yields annual national and state-level data on the numbers and characteristics of persons sentenced to death and those executed. Some of the information dates to 1930.

*Uniform Parole Reports.* Begun in 1965, produces annual national and state-level data on the number of persons on parole, the number released to parole during the year, and the number who were returned to prison while on parole. The characteristics of persons placed on parole and of persons who leave parole each year are also collected.

*National Probation Reports.* Begun in 1980, produces annual national and state-level data on the number of persons on probation, the number placed on probation, and the number leaving probation.

*National Corrections Reporting Program.* Begun in 1983, collects annual data from all states on all offender movements from prison admission through parole release, including demographic, offense, and sentencing data.

*White Collar Crime.* Begun in 1983, collects data from selected financial institutions on electronic-funds-transfer crime.

*Computer Crime.* Begun in 1983, collects data on prosecutions and prosecutorial experience under state computer crime statutes.

*Victim and Witness Assistance.* Summarizes recent federal and state laws. The report discusses the impact that proposed victim/witness programs may have on demands for criminal justice data and the extent to which such programs may require modifications of current information management policies.

## The BJS Data Analysis and Publication Programs

BJS has an extensive data analysis and publication program that produces different types of reports aimed at different audiences. Sometimes the organizations that collect data for BJS also analyze the data for BJS publication, but most frequently BJS personnel analyze the data from the BJS statistical series and author reports for BJS publication.

BJS also has an External Analysis Program, in which researchers analyze data of current topical interest for BJS publication. Analyses now under way address such topics as: career criminals; processing habeas corpus petitions; repeated victimization; recidivism; the deterrent effect of the criminal justice system; plea bargaining; causality in crime statistics; school crime; outcomes of state parole and incapacitation policies; civil and criminal dockets; the alternatives of rehabilitation, deterrence, incapacitation, and retribution.

Report series published by BJS include:

*BJS Bulletins.* Initiated in 1981, summarize data from the various statistical series. The bulletins are published monthly in a four-page, nontechnical format, suitable for a broad audience. Each bulletin addresses a topic on crime or the administration of justice.

*BJS Compendium of Federal Justice Statistics.* First issued in 1984, compiles data from agencies and courts that have federal jurisdiction. The report presents data on eight federal offenses for the whole federal system and for each district. Topics include investigations, arrests, prosecutions, trials, sentencing, and incarcerations.

*BJS Computer Crime Series.* Discuss subjects such as recent legislation, expert witness procedures, computer security techniques, and the prosecution of computer crime; a document describing the nature of electronic-fund-transfer crime is also available.

*BJS Detailed Findings Reports.* Detailed data collected through the various BJS statistical series. Extensive tabular material is presented along with technical details on the sample design, survey methodology, and statistical definitions used. The reports are suitable for users who desire more detailed and technical information than is available in the shorter bulletins and special reports.

*BJS Directory of Automated Criminal Justice Information Systems.* Serves as a current reference for data processors and criminal justice planners in developing new information systems and in enhancing present systems. It is intended to foster communication among developers and users of criminal justice information systems, to facilitate the transfer or adaptation of exemplary systems, and to minimize duplication of effort. The directory is issued periodically.

*BJS Privacy and Security Series.* Describes state legislative activity relating to the privacy and security of criminal justice systems and analyze emerging issues in the area of criminal justice information policy. A compendium of state privacy legislation is issued every two years.

*BJS Report to the Nation on Crime and Justice.* Comprehensive presentation of statistical information concerning crime and the administration of justice. In addition to BJS data series, the report draws on data from other federal, state, and local agencies as well as a variety of other research and reference materials. The report uses nontechnical language and graphic presentation suitable for a general audience.

*BJS Sourcebook of Criminal Justice Statistics.* Begun in 1972, it is compiled annually from more than 100 separate sources, presented with minimal text and extensive tables. An index and a list of sources guides users to data not published in the *Sourcebook* because of space considerations.

*BJS Special Reports.* Written in nontechnical language and aimed at a broad audience. Each special report focuses on a topic of current public interest and policy debate. Each addresses the selected topics in a comprehensive, but nontechnical, manner.

*BJS Technical Reports.* Present findings of BJS statistical series and technical research programs, and address issues of statistical methodology and special topics in a more detailed and technical format than do the *Bulletin* and *Special Reports* series. These reports are aimed at a technical audience.

## How to Obtain Data and Reports from the BJS

BJS distributes its reports through the National Criminal Justice Reference Service (NCJRS). The Reference Service notifies its mailing list of forthcoming publications, and users return a form requesting copies of desired publications. To obtain a registration form for the Reference Service mailing list or to order a BJS report, write to NCJRS, Box 6000, Rockville, MD 20849-6000, or call (800) 851-3420.

BJS sponsors the National Criminal Justice Data Archive at the Inter-University Consortium for Political and Social Research at the University of Michigan. The archive assists users whose needs are not satisfied by published statistics. All BJS data tapes (covering most of the BJS data series) and much other high-quality data are stored at the archive and are disseminated via magnetic tapes compatible with the user's computing facility. The archive also disseminates microfilmed National Crime Survey data for users who desire more detail than is contained in BJS publications, but who lack access to computing facilities. For more information, contact the National Archive of Criminal Justice Data , P.O. Box 1248, Ann Arbor, MI 48106, (800) 999-0960 or via e-mail at nacjd@icpsr.umich.edu.

## The BJS State Statistical and Systems Program

Statistical analysis centers have been established in about 40 states. The centers provide statistical information services and policy guidance to the governors, executive branch agencies, state and local agencies, the judiciary, the press, and the public. They also act as clearinghouses for statistical information among criminal justice agencies within the state; investigate specific issues in criminal justice and develop analytic methods and techniques; and provide the data they collect to BJS for compilation into multistate reports.

Users desiring data specific to single states may contact Criminal Justice Statistics Association at (202) 347-4608.

Through BJS funding, a catalog and library of statistical reports produced by the centers is maintained by the Criminal Justice Statistics Association, 444 North Capitol Street, N.W., Suite 122, Washington, D.C. 20001, (202) 347-4608.

BJS supports the development and operation of state uniform crime reporting systems in more than 40 states to facilitate the submission of and improve the validity and reliability of data submitted by local police agencies to the FBI's Uniform Crime Reporting Program. These data include offenses known to the police, arrests, offenses cleared, and employment data.

BJS supports the National Clearinghouse for Criminal Justice Information Systems, 925 Secret River Drive, Suite H, Sacramento, CA 95831, (916) 392-2550. The clearinghouse: operates an automated index of criminal justice information systems maintained by state and local governments throughout the nation; issues technical publications; and provides technical assistance and training for state and local government officials.

## Bureau of Justice Statistics Reports

Single copies are available at no charge from the National Criminal Justice Reference Service, Box 6000, Rockville, MD 20849-6000. Multiple copies are for sale by the Superintendent of Documents, U.S. Government Printing Office, P.O. Box 371954, Pittsburgh , PA 15250-7954.

## NATIONAL CRIME SURVEY

*Criminal Victimization in the United States (annual)*:
    1973-92 Trends, NCJ 147006
    1994, NCJ 162126
    1993, NCJ-151657
    1992, NCJ-145125
    1991, NCJ-139563

*Patterns of Criminal Victimization in the U.S.* (From victims of crime, pp. 9-26, 1997, Robert C. Davis, Arthur J. Lurigio, et al. See NCJ-167369), NCJ-167362.

*Intimate Victims: A Study of Violence Among Friends and Relatives*, NCJ-062319

*Crime and Seasonality-A National Crime Survey Report*, NCJ-064818

*Seasonality and Crime Victimization*, NCJ-111033

*Criminal Victimization of New York State Residents*, 1974-77, NCJ-066481

*Criminal Victimization of California Residents*, 1974-77, NCJ-070944

*Indicators of Crime and Criminal Justice: Quantitative Studies*, NCJ-062349

*Criminal Victimization Surveys in 13 American Cities* (summary report, 1 vol.), NCJ-018471
    Boston, NCJ-034818
    Buffalo, NCJ-034820
    Cincinnati, NCJ-034819
    Houston, NCJ-034821
    Miami, NCJ-034822
    Milwaukee, NCJ-034823
    Minneapolis, NCJ-034824
    New Orleans, NCJ-034825
    Oakland, NCJ-034826
    Pittsburgh, NCJ-034827
    San Diego, NCJ-034828
    San Francisco, NCJ-034829
    Washington, D.C., NCJ-034830

*Public Attitudes About Crime* (13 vols.):
    Boston, NCJ-046235
    Buffalo, NCJ-046236
    Cincinnati, NCJ-046237
    Houston, NCJ-046238
    Miami, NCJ-046239
    Milwaukee, NCJ-046240
    Minneapolis, NCJ-046241
    New Orleans, NCJ-046242
    Oakland, NCJ-046243
    Pittsburgh, NCJ-046244
    San Diego, NCJ-046245
    San Francisco, NCJ-046246
    Washington, D.C., NCJ-046247

*Criminal Victimization Surveys in Chicago, Detroit, Los Angeles, New York, and Philadelphia: A Comparison of 1972 and 1974 Findings*, NCJ-036360

*Criminal Victimization Surveys in Eight American Cities: A Comparison of 1971/72 and 1974/75 Findings-National Crime Surveys in Atlanta, Baltimore, Cleveland, Dallas, Denver, Newark, Portland, and St. Louis*, NCJ-036361

*Criminal Victimization Surveys in the Nation's Five Largest Cities: National Crime Panel Surveys in Chicago, Detroit, Los Angeles, New York, and Philadelphia, 1972*, NCJ-016909

*Crimes and Victims: A Report on the Dayton/San Jose Pilot Survey of Victimization*, NCJ-013314

*Public Opinion About Crime: The Attitudes of Victims and Nonvictims in Selected Cities*, NCJ-041336

*The Police and Public Opinion: An Analysis of Victimization and Attitude Data from 13 American Cities*, NCJ-042018

*An Introduction to the National Crime Survey*, NCJ-043732

*Compensating Victims of Violent Crime: Potential Costs and Coverage of a National Program*, NCJ-043387

*Rape Victimization in 26 American Cities*, NCJ-055878

*Crime Against Persons in Urban, Suburban, and Rural Areas*: A Comparative Analysis of Victimization Rates, NCJ-053551

*Criminal Victimization in Urban Schools*, NCJ-056396

*Restitution to Victims of Personal and Household Crimes*, NCJ-072770

*Myths and Realities About Crime*: A Nontechnical Presentation of Selected Information from the National Prisoner Statistics Program and the National Crime Survey, NCJ-046249

## NATIONAL PRISONER STATISTICS

*Capital Punishment* (annual) 1982, NCJ-070945

*Prisoners in State and Federal Institutions on December 31*, 1984, NCJ-103768
    1983, NCJ-099861
    1982, NCJ-099855

*Census of State Correctional Facilities*, 1974 advance report, NCJ-025642

*Profile of State Prison Inmates*: Sociodemographic Findings from the 1974 Survey of Inmates of State Correctional Facilities, NCJ-058257.

*Profile of State Prison Inmates, 1986*, NCJ-109926

*Census of Prisoners in State Correctional Facilities, 1973*, NCJ-034729.

*Census of Jails and Survey of Jail Inmates, 1978*, preliminary report, NCJ-055172.

*Historical Statistics on Prisoners in State and Federal Institution*, Year end 1925-1986, NCJ-116855

*Profile of Inmates of Local Jails*: Sociodemographic Findings from the 1978 Survey of Inmates of Local Jails, NCJ-065412

*The Nation's Jails*: A report on the census of jails from the 1972 Survey of Inmates of Local Jails, NCJ-019067

*Uniform Parole Reports*:

*Parole in the United States* (annual):
1985, NCJ-103208
1980-81, NCJ-087387

*A National Survey of Parole-Related Legislation*. Enacted During the 1979 Legislative Session, NCJ-064218

*Characteristics of the Parole Population*. 1978, NCJ-066479

*Children in Custody 1987*: A Comparison of Public and Private Juvenile Custody Facilities, NCJ-127675

*Children in Custody: Public Juvenile Facilities*, 1987, NCJ-113950

*Public Juvenile Facilities*: Children in Custody, 1989, NCJ-127189

*State and Local Probation and Parole Systems*, NCJ-041335

*State and Local Prosecution and Civil Attorney Systems*, NCJ-041334

*National Survey of Court Organization*:
1977 Supplement to State Judicial Systems, NCJ-040022
1975 Supplement to State Judicial Systems, NCJ-029433
1971 (full report), NCJ-011427

*State Court Model Statistical Dictionary*, NCJ-120938

*A Cross-City Comparison of Felony Case Processing*, NCJ-055171

*Trends in Expenditure and Employment Data for the Criminal Justice System, 1971-77*, (annual), NCJ-057463

*Justice Agencies in the U.S.*: Summary Report of the National Justice Agency List, NCJ-065560

*Dictionary of Criminal Justice Data Terminology*: Terms and Definitions Proposed for Interstate and National Data Collection and Exchange, 1981, NCJ-076939

# UTILIZATION OF CRIMINAL JUSTICE STATISTICS PROJECT

*Sourcebook of Criminal Justice Statistics 1995* (annual), NCJ-158900
1994, NCJ-154591
1993, NCJ-148211
1992, NCJ-143496

*Offender-Based Transaction Statistics*: Tracking Offenders, 1990, NCJ-148200

*Sentencing of California Felony Offenders*, NCJ-029646

*Crime-Specific Analysis*:
The Characteristics of Burglary Incidents. NCJ-042093
An Empirical Examination of Burglary Offender Characteristics, NCJ-043131
An Empirical Examination of Burglary Offenders and Offense Characteristics, NCJ-042476

*Sources of National Criminal Justice Statistics*: An Annotated Bibliography, NCJ-045006

*Federal Criminal Sentencing*: Perspectives of Analysis and a Design for Research, NCJ-033683

*Variations in Federal Criminal Sentences*: A Statistical Assessment at the National Level, NCJ-033684

*Federal Sentencing Patterns*: A Study of Geographical Variations, NCJ-033685

*Predicting Sentences in Federal Courts*: The Feasibility of a National Sentencing Policy, NCJ-033686

## OTHER SOURCES OF STATISTICAL DATA

Statistics are an important form of information to any field of knowledge, and they can help determine the scope of a problem or issue. The many sources of statistics, such as public opinion polls, journals, books, pamphlets, government reports, and newspapers, sometimes make the task of finding a source with mention of desired statistical data easier said than done. Today, though, several publications provide compilations of statistical information. The following annotations of statistical reference sources represent a sample of the sources that are likely to be available in most libraries. Your library may possess additional sources.

*American Statistics Index (ASI).* A comprehensive guide and index to the statistical publications of the U.S. Government. Includes indices by subject and name, category, title, and agency report number, and an index which tells the reader what publications have been abstracted in the *ASI Abstracts* Volume. Monthly. (Washington, DC: Congressional Information Service, 1974-date). (This is also available as a computerized database. See *American Statistics Index* in Chapter 9, "Database Literature Searches.")

*American Statistics Index: Abstracts Volume.* Abstracts many of the citations that appear in the *ASI Index Volume.* Broken down into categories of Executive Office of the President, Department of Agriculture, Department of Commerce, Department of Defense, Department of Health, Education, and Welfare, Department of Housing and Urban Development, Department of the Interior, Department of Justice, Department of Labor, Department of State, Department of Transportation, Department of Treasury, Independent Agencies, Special Boards, Committees, and Commissions, United States Courts and United States Congress. Each of these departments is further subdivided and publications of each agency are abstracted. (Washington, DC: Congressional Information Service, 1974-date).

*Bureau of the Census Catalog.* This is the current listing of publications available from the Bureau. A subject index leads to abstracts of subject content with ordering information. Annual. (Washington, DC: U.S. Bureau of the Census).

*California Statistical Abstract.* This annual covers all types of statistics for California, including those related to crime, prisons, and law enforcement. Index in back. The 1970 Abstract is a historical volume, incorporating data "as far back as availability or space limitations permitted." (Sacramento, CA: Department of Finance, 1970-date).

*County and City Data Book.* Regarded as a complement to the *Statistical Abstract of the United States,* and covers 144 items for each county in the United States and 148 items for each of the 683 cities having 25,000 or more population. Items include population, dwelling units, retail and wholesale trade, vital statistics, and so forth. (Washington, DC: U.S. Bureau of the Census, GPO).

*Compendium of Social Statistics.* Contains statistics relating to the environmental conditions of life and work in the nations of the world, e.g., infant mortality, dwelling size, expenditure levels, work force, and employment conditions. (New York: United Nations, 1963-date).

*Complaints and Arrests: Statistical Report.* Statistics by precinct. Monthly. (New York: Police Department, Office of Management Analysis, 1975-date).

*Congressional Directory.* Lists all members of Congress by state, alphabetically, and by term of office. A short biography is included for each senator and representative. In addition, you will find a complete listing of all federal agencies and commissions, including addresses, phone numbers, and names and titles of officials. Other features include a listing of diplomatic representatives to the U.S., maps of each state's congressional districts, and much more. (Washington, DC: U.S. Government Printing Office, 1983-date).

*Congressional District Data Book and Congressional District Data Book Supplement: Redistricted States.* A variety of statistical data from a number of sources are presented in this biennial supplement to the *Statistical Abstract of the United States.* Information is organized by congressional district and concerns such topics as bank deposits, elections, housing, local governments, retail trade, nonwhite populations, vital statistics, and so forth. (Washington, DC: U.S. Government Printing Office, 1961-date).

*Corrections Statistics in the United States.* Presents summary tables and commentary for published national government reports on correction statistics from 1850 to 1984. Includes statistics on: capital punishment, state and federal prisons, jails, institutions for juvenile delinquents, parole and probation, and information on incarceration. Hundreds of charts, tables and graphs. (Upland, PA: DIANE Publishing Co.).

*Crime and Delinquency in California.* An annual statistical compilation covering the following topics: crimes, arrests, adult felony arrest dispositions, adult corrections, the juvenile justice system, and criminal justice agency expenditures and personnel. Charts and graphs show trends for both crime rates and criminal justice administration. (Sacramento, CA: Bureau of Criminal Statistics, 1972-date).

*Crime, Courts, and Figures; An Introduction to Criminal Statistics*, N. Walker. Provides an in-depth look at statistics and the criminal justice system. (New York: Peter Smith, 1973).

*Criminal Justice Abstracts. 11:122-147.* "Sources of Basic Criminal Justice Statistics: A Brief Annotated Guide with Commentaries." Eugene Doleschal. March, 1979.

*The Criminal Justice Data Directory.* Describes Bureau of Justice Statistics-sponsored data collections as well as a number of other relevant data sets. This 152-page directory is a must for any serious criminal justice researcher. (Ann Arbor: Criminal Justice Archive and Inter-University Consortium for Political and Social Research, 1982).

*The Criminal Justice System in the City of New York —An Overview.* (Albany, NY: Commission of Investigation, 1974).

*Criminal Victimization in the United States.* In addition to information about the nature of the crime, and about the victim and perpetrator, these studies include the relationship between the victim and the perpetrator, income and the place of residence of victim, and whether or not the crime was reported to officials. Annual. (Washington, DC: U.S. Census Bureau, 1973-date).

*Demographic Yearbook.* Offers detailed world figures on population, projected trends, births, deaths, marriages, life expectancy, and so forth. (New York: Statistical Office, United Nations, 1949-date).

*Directory of Criminal Justice Issues in the States, Volume 1.* H. Saizow and J. Boneta (eds.). Summarizes all activities of the state statistical analysis centers (SACs) conducted during 1983. The directory is designed to inform national policymakers on critical criminal justice issues under debate in the states, inform state policymakers on the activities of other states, and strengthen awareness of the work of the SACs. Included for each of 259 activities performed in 1983 is the title, brief description, data sources used, date of completion, and contact person. Activities are indexed by substantive area. Appendix. (Washington, DC: Criminal Justice Statistics Association, 1984).

*Expanding the Perspective of Crime Data: Performance Implications for Policymakers.* K.M. Williams, et al. Examines apprehension, conviction, and incarceration performance measures for various crimes. Data from approximately 100,000 "street crime" cases, handled through normal prosecution and court operation in the District of Columbia over a six-year period, gathered by Prosecutor's Management Information System (PROMIS). This data was then analyzed by the Institute for Law and Social Research, and results provided the basis for this publication. (Washington, DC: Law Enforcement Assistance Administration, GPO Stock #027-000-00575-6, NCJ 40230, 1977).

*Expenditure and Employment Data for the Criminal Justice System.* Published annually. Documents expenditure data for criminal justice activities in the United States. Data concerns the federal government, each of the 50 states, and the aggregate local level of government within each state. Annual. (Washington, DC: U.S. Department of Justice, Bureau of Justice Statistics).

*Guide to United States Government Statistics.* John L. Androit. An annotated guide to over 1,200 U.S. government publications relating to statistics. (McLean, VA: Documents Index, 1973).

*Handbook of Resources for Criminal Justice Evaluators.* Designed to provide evaluators, planners, and decisionmakers with information about techniques that could improve the handling of problems encountered in criminal justice evaluation. Four problems are addressed: 1) technical and research problems, 2) types of evaluations to be done and what questions should be answered, 3) insuring privacy and confidentiality of data collected and protection of human subjects, and 4) providing documentation to newly hired evaluators about local resources, organizational structure of the office, administrative procedures, and sources of data. (Washington, DC: U.S. Department of Justice, Law Enforcement Assistance Administration, National Institute of Law Enforcement and Criminal Justice, 1978).

*Historical Statistics of the United States, Colonial Times to 1957.* Summarizes social and economic developments of the United States from 1610 through 1957. A subject index is provided as are notations of access to originally published sources. (Washington, DC: United States Bureau of Statistics, GPO, 1960). (See Chapter 15, "Historical Research Sources," for additional sources.)

*Index to International Statistics (IIS).* An index to statistical publications of international organizations, including the United Nations System. (Bethesda, MD: Congressional Information Service, 1983-date).

*International Crime Statistics.* A biannual publication which provides crime statistics on an international basis. (Saint-Cloud, France: International Criminal Police Organization, INTERPOL). (See Chapter 14, "Sources of International Data," for additional suggestions on obtaining data with international relevance.)

*Inter-University Consortium for Political Research.* An academic data source which includes results of current research projects, academic surveys, and similar information. Surveys reflect motivation and attitudes of the individuals surveyed. A nominal fee is charged for data. (Ann Arbor: The University of Michigan Press).

*An Inventory of Surveys of the Public on Crime, Justice, and Related Topics.* Addressed to the studies of crime, delinquency, criminal justice, law enforcement, and closely related areas by means of the sample interview survey method. Studies included for review had to involve interviews or a questionnaire given to a study population not preselected on the basis of roles within criminal justice institutions. (Washington, DC: U.S. Department of Justice, National Institute on Law Enforcement and Criminal Justice, Law Enforcement Assistance Administration, 1972).

*Judicial Criminal Statistics, 1933-1945.* (U.S. Bureau of the Census: Dependent and Delinquent Classes, microfiche #1502).

*Juvenile Court Statistics.* Contains estimates and analyses of juvenile delinquency cases and dependency and neglect cases disposed of by juvenile courts in 1974. (Washington, DC: United States Department of Justice, Law Enforcement Assistance Administration, 1974).

*Municipal Yearbook.* Primarily a statistical almanac, published annually since 1934. Provides information on most United States cities with populations in excess of 10,000, although some towns with populations in the 5,000-10,000 range are also included. (Chicago: International City Managers Association).

*National Crime Surveys: Criminal Victimization in the U.S.* Bureau of Justice Statistics. (Washington, DC: U.S. Government Printing Office, 1973-date).

*National Prisoner Statistics.* Bureau of Justice Statistics. (Washington, DC: U.S. Government Printing Office, 1926-date).

*National Statistical Compendiums.* Microfiche. (Washington, DC: CIS).

*New York State Felony Processing Quarterly Report: Indictment through Disposition.* Provides detailed statistics on felony arrests, indictments, dispositions, and processing times. (Albany, NY: Division of Criminal Justice Services, 1974-date).

*New York State Statistical Yearbook.* Section K, "Public Safety," making use of figures from the Department of Criminal Justice Services and the Department of Correctional Services, supplies tables dealing with arrests, offenses, and correctional institutions. Most tables separate New York City from upstate; some also provide breakdowns into large urban areas, small urban areas and suburbs. Annual. (Albany, NY: Division of the Budget, 1967-date).

*Office of Justice Assistance, Research, and Statistics (OJARS).* This office is a result of the Justice System Improvement Act of 1979, signed by President Carter 12/27/79. This Act will reorganize the way in which the federal government provides financial and technical aid to the nation's criminal justice system. Under this legislation OJARS will provide staff support and coordinate administrative activities of the Law Enforcement Assistance Administration, the National Institute of Justice, and Bureau of Justice Statistics.

*Periodicals and Sources.* A 20-page guide which lists almost 900 U.S. Government statistical publications. Periodicals listed contain facts and figures on topics such as business, crime, natural resources, foreign trade, health, and demography. (Washington, DC: Congressional Information Service).

*Police Practices: The General Administrative Survey,* John F. Heaphy (ed.). A general survey report of police administrative practices of 56 police departments which serve cities of more than 250,000. (Kansas City, MO: The Police Foundation with the Assistance of the Police Executive Research Forum, 1978).

*Police Source Book.* B. Swainton, G. Hannigan, and D. Biles. This overview provides descriptive and statistical material on the status and organization of the police in Australia. The authors discuss the history and background of the Australian police, the principal law enforcement establishments and expenditures, police structure and organization, legal powers, and the typical police officer. Other topics of discussion include discipline and accountability; working conditions, uniforms, and weapons; ranks and salary; recruitment; and education and training. The report also describes police transport, communications, internal security, traffic control, and criminal investigation. International participation, major police organizations, and improvements in police capabilities are outlined. Tables, bibliography. (Phillip, ACT, Australia: Australian Institute of Criminology, 1983).

*Prisoners in State and Federal Institutions.* Annual. (Washington, DC: U.S. Government Printing Office, 1967-date).

*Quantitative Studies in Criminology: 1978.* Charles Wellford (ed.). Discusses advanced statistical techniques used in criminology and compares recent research to demonstrate the value of a rigorous methodology and the areas to be considered for the application of advanced statistical techniques. Emphasis is given to the measurement of crime, deterrence, the use of longitudinal analyses, and empirical studies of police. (Beverly Hills, CA: Sage Research Progress Series in Criminology, Volume 8, 1978).

*Report to the Nation on Crime and Justice: The Data*. Comprehensive picture of crime and criminal justice in the U.S., represented in simple-to-understand graphs and charts. (Washington, DC: U.S. Government Printing Office, 1983).

*Social Indicators III: Selected Data on Social Conditions and Trends in the United States*. Combines colorful graphs and charts with authoritative statistics to give you a comprehensive picture of American life and society. Includes facts and figures on population and the family, our health and nutrition, the housing situation and our environment, income and productivity trends, and social security and welfare programs. (Washington, DC: U.S. Government Printing Office, 1980).

*Sourcebook of Criminal Justice Statistics*. U.S. Department of Justice, Bureau of Justice Statistics. Annual. (Washington, DC: U.S. Government Printing Office, 1973-date).

*Sources of National Criminal Justice Statistics: An Annotated Bibliography*. Annotates sources of criminal justice statistics including public opinion, literature pertaining to crime, drugs, law enforcement, diversion, courts, juveniles, corrections, furloughs, probation and parole, and general sources. Alphabetically lists sources, addresses of publishers, and subject index. (Washington, DC: U.S. Department of Justice, Law Enforcement Assistance Administration, National Criminal Justice Information and Statistics Service, GPO Stock #027-000-00681-7, 1977).

*State Court Caseload Statistics, Annual Report*. Provides data regarding the number and types of cases handled through state courts. (Washington, DC: U.S. Department of Justice.)

*State and Local Probation and Parole Systems*. Included in this volume are lists of state and local probation agencies, their functions, government affiliations, case loads, number of employees, activities, and funding sources. A separate section discusses the organization of each state's probation and parole system, and presents full descriptive profiles of the system. (Washington, DC: U.S. Government Printing Office, 1978).

*State and Metropolitan Area Data Book, 1986*. Gives variety of information for states and metropolitan areas of the U.S., derived mainly from censuses. Provides facts and figures on births and deaths, marriages and divorces, households and families, health, education, employment, personal wealth, crime, housing, banking, elections, land ownership, energy, wholesale trade. (Washington, DC: U.S. Government Printing Office).

*Statesman's Year Book; Statistical and Historical Annual of the States of the World*. Provides statistics and other information on international organizations and every country during the preceding year. Data covering each nation's con-

stitution, political and governmental structure, financial basis, gross national product, court system, and so forth is included. (London and New York: Macmillan, 1864-date).

*Statistical Abstract of the United States*. Published annually. Includes a comprehensive selection of data from several significant statistical sources. Reliable summary of statistics on the social, political, and economic organization of the United States. Also serves as a reference to other sources of statistical information, and is very good for locating statistics on just about any current problem. This publication is the most reliable source for data regarding births, deaths, marriages, divorces, number of physicians, dentists, nurses, immigration and naturalization, law enforcement, courts and prisons, geography and climates, public lands and parks, recreation and travel, elections, and incomes. Annual. (Washington, DC: U. S. Bureau of the Census).

*Statistical Reference Index (SRI)*. Aims to provide current access to selected statistical reference material on a wide spectrum of subject matter, representative of all types of data available from American sources. Provides access to over 2,000 publications, representing over 6,000 individual issuances from more than 1,000 associations and institutes, business organizations, commercial publishers, independent research organizations, state government agencies, and university research centers . . . all of the leading sources of published statistical information outside of the U.S. government, 1980-date. SRI covers:

- *National data* — production, costs, and earnings in major industries and business sectors, operating ratios and market characteristics of business and commerce, data related to key areas of social or public interest; public opinion and salary surveys; demographic data; and national economic trends.
- *State-wide data* — statistical compendiums and 20-40 additional selected basic reports for each state on areas such as vital statistics, health, agriculture, business conditions and economic indicators, employment, education, state taxation and finance, elections, construction, insurance, tourism, motor vehicles and accidents, and judicial systems.
- *Data on foreign countries* — world economic or demographic trends, and foreign country studies; international finance, investment, and trade data; foreign country social and economic indicators.
- *Local or otherwise narrowly focused data* — detail by county and municipality, provided in many state reports if the subject matter is judged to have research value beyond the limited area of coverage.
- *Locating information* — Brief annotations in SRI's multiple-access index section direct users to full publication descriptions in a separately bound abstracts section. To facilitate diverse research approaches, several indices are included: index by subjects and names, index by categories, and supplementary indexes.

*Statistical Services Directory*: A Guide to the Organizations, Corporations, Professional and Trade Associations, Research Centers, Universities, Publishers, Foundations and Government Agencies That Provide Statistical Services, Second Edition. (Detroit: Gale Research, 1984).

*Statistics Sources*. Paul Wasserman (ed.). Provides data on industrial, business, social, educational, financial, and other topics for the United States and selected foreign countries and also directs the user to other sources of statistical data. (Detroit: Gale Research, 1999).

*Uniform Crime Reports for the United States*. Offers an annual assessment of crime across the nation, based on police statistics since 1930. Seven offenses comprise the crime index: murder, forcible rape, robbery, aggravated assault, burglary, larceny-theft, and motor vehicle theft. Data consisting of narrative comments, charts, and tables on crime index offenses reported, crime index offenses cleared by arrest, persons arrested, and persons charged are offered. (Washington, DC: Federal Bureau of Investigation, 1930-date).

*United Nations Statistical Year Book*. Contains a summary of statistics for world population, manpower, agriculture, consumption, productivity, external trade, education, social statistics, etc. Subject and nation indices, written in French and English, are included. (New York: United Nations, 1948-date). (See also Chapter 14, "Sources of International Data.")

*The United States Government Manual 1998/99*. Pinpoints the exact official you need to contact. It provides comprehensive information on the agencies of the legislative, executive, and judicial branches, as well as the quasi-official agencies, boards, commissions, and committees in the federal sphere. A typical agency entry includes a list of principal officers, a summary of the agency's mission and history, a description of its programs and activities, and a list of addresses and telephone numbers. (Washington, DC: U.S. Government Printing Office).

*Vital Statistics in Corrections*. Provides numbers on corrections budgets, salaries, staff demographics, fringe benefits, incarceration rates, correctional unions, and employee groups, and more. (Laurel, MD: American Correctional Association).

## VICTIMIZATION REPORTS

Criminal justice statistics may also be found in victimization reports, presented by the Bureau of Justice Statistics, National Crime Survey. These victimization surveys differ from the FBI's Uniform Crime Reports (UCR) in that the UCR compiles crimes reported to local police, sheriffs' departments, and state police, which are in turn reported to the FBI. Also reported in the UCR are the number of crimes cleared by arrest. Therefore, the amount of crime committed each year is actually much greater than that reported in the UCR. The victimization surveys contain a wealth of information relating to characteristics of victims as well as crime rates. The following reports, available from the NCJRS (Box 6000, Rockville, Maryland 20850), or for purchase from the Superintendent of Documents (U.S. Government Printing Office, Washington, D.C. 20402), should be consulted for additional statistical information.

*The Cost of Negligence: Losses from Preventable Household Burglaries* (NCJ-0 53527).

*Crimes Against Persons in Urban, Suburban and Rural Areas: A Comparative Analysis of Victimization Rates* (NCJ-053551).

*Crimes and Victims: A Report on the Dayton-San Jose Pilot Survey of Victimization* (NCJ- 013314).

*Criminal Victimization in the United States*. Summary Findings of 1977-78, Changes in Crime and of Trends Since 1973 (NCJ-061368); A Description of Trends from 1973 to 1977 (NCJ-059898); 1977 (Final Report) (NCJ-058725); 1976 (NCJ-049543); 1975 (NCJ-044593); 1974 (NCJ-039467); 1973 (NCJ-034732).

*Criminal Victimization Surveys in 13 American Cities*, Summary Report, 1 Volume (NCJ-018471). Boston (NCJ-034818; Buffalo (NCJ-034820); Cincinnati (NCJ-034819); Houston (NCJ-034821); Miami (NCJ-034822); Milwaukee (NCJ-034823); Minneapolis (NCJ-034824); New Orleans (NCJ-034825); Oakland (NCJ-034826); Pittsburgh (NCJ-034827); San Diego (NCJ-034828); San Francisco (NCJ-034829); Washington, D.C. (NCJ-034830).

*Criminal Victimization Surveys in Chicago, Detroit, Los Angeles, New York, and Philadelphia*: A Comparison of 1972 and 1974 Findings (NCJ-036360).

*Criminal Victimization Surveys in Eight American Cities*: A Comparison of 1971/72 and 1974/75 Findings (National Crime Surveys in Atlanta, Baltimore, Cleveland, Dallas, Denver, Newark, Portland, and St. Louis) (NCJ-036361).

*Intimate Victims: A Study of Violence Among Friends and Relatives* (NCJ-062319).

*An Introduction to the National Crime Survey* (NCJ-043732).

## Additional Statistical Reports

*Capital Punishment*, (annual) 1994, (NCJ-153367).
   1993, NCJ-150042
   1992, NCJ-145031
   1991, NCJ-146126

*Census of Jails and Survey of Jail Inmates*, 1978, Preliminary Report (NCJ-055172).

*Census of Prisoners in State Correctional Facilities*, 1973 (NCJ-034729).

*Census of State Correctional Facilities*, 1974, Advanced Report (NCJ-025642).

*Children in Custody: Juvenile Detention and Correctional Facility*, 1977, Advance Report: Census of Public Juvenile Facilities (NCJ-060967); Census of Private Juvenile Facilities (NCJ-060968); 1975 (Final Report) (NCJ-058139); 1974 (NCJ-057946); 1973 (NCJ-044777); 1971 (NCJ-013403).

*Crime Specific Analysis: The Characteristics of Burglary Incidents* (NCJ-042093); An Empirical Examination of Burglary Offender Characteristics (NCJ-043131); An Empirical Examination of Burglary Offenders and Offense Characteristics (NCJ-042476).

*A Cross-City Comparison of Felony Case Processing* (NCJ-055171).

*Delinquency Dispositions: An Empirical Analysis of Processing Decisions in Three Juvenile Courts* (NCJ- 034734).

*Federal Criminal Sentencing: Perspectives of Analysis and a Design for Research* (NCJ-033683).

*Federal Sentencing Patterns: A Study of Geographical Variations* (NCJ-033685).

*The Judicial Processing of Assault and Burglary Offenders in Selected California Counties* (NCJ-029644).

*Juvenile Dispositions: Social and Legal Factors Related to the Processing of Denver Delinquency Cases* (NCJ-017418).

*Myths and Realities about Crime: A Non-technical Presentation of Selected Information from the National Prisoner Statistics Program and the National Crime Survey* (NCJ-046249).

*The Nation's Jails: A Report on the Census of Jails from the 1972 Survey of Inmates of Local Jails* (NCJ-019067).

*Offender-Based Transaction Statistics: New Directions in Data Collection and Reporting* (NCJ-029645).

*Parole in the United States*, 1978 (NCJ-058722); 1977 and 1976 (NCJ-049702).

*The Patterns and Distribution of Assault Incident Characteristics Among Social Areas* (NCJ-040025).

*Patterns of Robbery Characteristics and Their Occurrence Among Social Areas* (NCJ-040026).

*Pre-Adjudicatory Detention in Three Juvenile Courts* (NCJ-034730).

*Prisoners in State and Federal Institutions*, 1978. Advanced Report (NCJ-058324); 1977 Final Report (NCJ-052701).

*Profile of State Prison Inmates*: Sociodemographic Findings from the 1974 Survey of Inmates of State Correctional Facilities (NCJ-058257).

*Program Plan for Statistics 1977-81* (NCJ-037811).

*Sentencing of California Felony Offenders* (NCJ-029646).

*State Court Caseload Statistics: The State of the Art* (NCJ-046934); Annual Report, 1975 (NCJ-051885); Annual Report, 1976 (NCJ-056599).

*State Court Model Statistical Dictionary* (NCJ-062320).

*Survey of Inmates of Local Jails*, 1972, Advance Report (NCJ-013313).

*Variations in Federal Criminal Sentences*. A Statistical Assessment at the National Level (NCJ-033684).

*Who Gets Detained?* An Empirical Analysis of the Pre-Adjudicatory Detention of Juveniles in Denver (NCJ-017417).

## PUBLIC OPINION POLLS

Each year, thousands of polls are taken by private research companies that specialize in determining public opinion. For example, the Nielsen Ratings are used to determine the popularity of various television shows, and politicians regularly use polls to determine what issues are most important to the public. The pollsters also conduct a number of inquiries to determine public opinion regarding criminal justice issues. The findings from these polls are recorded and kept for future reference.

Polls, particularly the Gallup, Harris, and Roper Opinion Polls, are fairly well known, and their findings are published regularly in many newspapers. Even so, polls as a source of data are still often overlooked or neglected by many researchers. This may be due, in part, to the fact that there is difficulty in locating results of a particular poll in an unindexed newspaper, or because the importance of polls as a form of data is not recognized. There are simple means, however, of locating results of public opinion surveys, at least some of which will be available in most libraries for the asking, or by writing to the pollster. Sources providing information on polls include:

*Index to International Public Opinion*. Prepared by Survey Research Consultants International, Inc. Annual. See Chapter 14, "Sources of International Data," for a complete description.

*The ABC/Washington Post Poll*. (New York: ABC News Polling Unit).

*American Association for Public Opinion Research*. (Princeton, NJ).

*American Enterprise Institute for Public Policy Research*. (Washington, DC).

*American Public Opinion Index*. Annual. (Louisville, KY: Opinion Research Service, 1981-date).

*California Poll*. Public opinion poll, concentrated within the state, questions Californians on the hottest issues at any particular time. The results, which often indicate future trends for the nation, are published approximately 40 times a year. To date. (San Francisco: Survey Research Services).

*CBS News/New York Times Poll*. (New York: CBS News).

*Current Opinion*. A monthly publication that includes results of recent, selected surveys conducted by leading opinion research organizations in the United States and abroad. Topics vary from issue to issue. Criminal justice topics include the death penalty, legalization of marijuana, and gun control. (Williamstown, MA: Roper Public Opinion Research Center).

*Gallup Opinion Index*. (Formerly Gallup Political Index.) Includes monthly surveys, covering a wide range of topics such as the presidency, capital punishment, crime rates, and so forth. (Princeton, NJ: Gallup International, 1965-date).

*The Harris Survey*. A frequent press release appearing in newspapers across the country and includes results of public opinion research conducted by Louis Harris and Associates. (Chicago: *The Chicago Tribune*).

*Index to International Public Opinion*. See Chapter 14, "Sources of International Data," for a complete description. Annual. (Survey Research Consultants International, Inc.).

*Minnesota Poll*. Published weekly in the Sunday edition of the *Minnesota Star and Tribune*. Weekly. (Minneapolis: *Minneapolis Star Tribune*, 1964-date).

*Public Attitudes About Crime*. Boston (NCJ-046235); Buffalo (NCJ-046236); Cincinnati (NCJ-046237); Houston (NCJ-046238); Miami (NCJ-046239); Milwaukee (NCJ-046240); Minneapolis (NCJ-046241); New Orleans (NCJ-046242); Oakland (NCJ-046243); Pittsburgh (NCJ-046244); San Diego (NCJ-046245); San Francisco (NCJ-046246); Washington, D.C. (NCJ-046247). These publications represent results of crime surveys conducted in the designated cities. (Washington, DC: U.S. Department of Justice).

*Public Opinion About Crime*. Composed of three sections: (1) The Attitudes of Victims and Non-Victims in Selected Cities (NCJ-041336), (2) The Police and Public Opinion: An Analysis of Victimization and Attitude Data from 13 American Cities (NCJ-042018), and (3) Public Opinion Regarding Crime, Criminal Justice, and Related Topics (NCJ-017419). Available. (Washington, DC: U.S. Department of Justice).

*Roper Public Opinion Poll*. Contains a massive amount of poll data, concentrating on all academic and professional poll and survey groups worldwide. The surveys and studies are available to students on cards or tapes at reasonable rates. Currently available. (Williamstown, MA: Williams College).

## Newspaper and Magazine Indexes and Abstracts

*Public Opinion*. Bimonthly. (Washington, DC: American Enterprise Institute for Public Policy Research, 1978-date).

*Public Opinion Quarterly*. Quarterly. (New York: Elsevier Science Publishing, 1937-date).

*Roper Center for Public Opinion Research*. (Storrs, CT: University of Connecticut).

# ORGANIZATIONS THAT PRODUCE CRIMINAL JUSTICE STATISTICS

Administrative Office of the United States Courts, Washington, DC 20544.

American Correctional Association (ACA), 4380 Forbes Blvd., Lanham, MD 20706-4322. Web Site: www.corrections.com/aca/

Criminal Justice Statistics Association (CJSA), 444 N. Capitol Street, NW, Suite 122, Washington, DC 20001.

Justice Research and Statistics Association (JRSA), 777 N. Capitol Street, NE, Suite 801, Washington, DC 20002. Web Site: www.jrsainfo.org/

National Archive of Criminal Justice Data (NACJD), P.O. Box 1248, Ann Arbor, MI 48106. Web Site: icpsr.umich.edu/nacjd

National Center for State Courts (NCSC), 300 Newport Avenue, Williamsburg, VA 23185. Web Site: www.ncsc.dni.us

U.S. Bureau of Justice Statistics (BJS), 810 Seventh Street, NW, Washington, DC 20531.

U.S. Bureau of the Census, Fourteenth Street between Constitution Avenue and E Street, NW, Washington, DC 20230. Web Site: www.census.gov

U.S. Federal Bureau of Investigation, Ninth and Pennsylvania Avenues, NW, Washington, DC 20535. Web Site: www.fbi.gov/

The Urban Institute, Attn: Public Affairs, 2100 M Street, NW, Washington, DC 20037. Web Site: www.urban.org

## Statistical Analysis Centers

Most states now have Statistical Analysis Centers for criminal justice data. The following are state centers.

Alabama Criminal Justice Information Center
770 Washington Ave.
Montgomery, AL 36130-0660
agencies.state.al.us/acjis/pages/alacrime.htm

University of Alaska
3211 Providence Drive
Anchorage, AK 99508
www.uaa.alaska.edu/
aycamai@uaa.alaska.edu

Information Analysis Section
Department of Public Safety
PO Box 6638
Phoenix, AZ 85005-6638
www.dps.state.az.us/welcome.htm
arizdps@primenet.com

Special Services Section
Arkansas Crime Information Center
One Capitol Mall
Little Rock, AR 72201
www.acic.org/
acic@acic.org

Bureau of Criminal Statistics and Special Services
PO Box 903427
Sacramento, CA 94203-4270
(916) 739-5568

Division of Criminal Justice
Department of Public Safety
700 Kipling Street
Suite 1000
Denver, CO 80215
www.state.co.us/gov_dir/cdps/cdps.htm
wwoodwar@safety.state.co.us.

Justice Planning Division
Office of Policy and Management
80 Washington Street
Hartford, CT 06106
(203) 566-3522

Office of Criminal Justice Plans and Analysis
1111 E Street, NW
Suite 500C
Washington, DC 20004
(202) 727-6554

Florida Statistical Analysis Center
Florida Department of Law Enforcement
PO Box 1489
Tallahassee, FL 32302
www.fdle.state.fl.us/FSAC/index.asp
SueBarton@fdle.state.fl.us

Georgia Crime Information Center
PO Box 370748
Decatur, GA 30037
(404) 244-2601

Crime Prevention and Justice Assistance Division
Department of the Attorney General
425 South Queen Street
Honolulu, HI 96813
www.cpja.ag.state.hi.us/

Support Services Bureau
Department of Law Enforcement
6111 Clinton Street
Boise, ID 83704
(208) 334-2162

Information Resource Center
Criminal Justice Information Authority
120 South Riverside Plaza
Suite 1016
Chicago, IL 60606-3997
www.icjia.org/
irc@icjia.state.il.us

Indiana Criminal Justice Institute
150 West Market Street
Suite 200
Indianapolis, IN 46204
(317) 232-1619

Division of Criminal Justice and Juvenile Planning
Executive Hills East
Des Moines, IA 50319
(515) 242-5816

Kansas Bureau of Investigation
1620 Southwest Tyler
Topeka, KS 66612
www.ink.org/public/kbi/main.html

Office of the Attorney General
1024 Capitol Center Drive
Frankfort, KY 40601
www.law.state.ky.us/
oag@mial.law.state.ky.us

Louisiana Department of Public Safety
2121 Wooddale Boulevard
Baton Rouge, LA 70806
www.dps.state.la.us/
Webmaster@dpsmail.dps.state.la

Maine Criminal Justice Data Center
Department of Corrections
State House 111
Augusta, ME 04333
janus.state.me.us/corrections/homepage.htm
corrections@state.me.us

Maryland Justice Analysis Center
Institute of Criminal Justice and Criminology
University of Maryland
College Park, MD 20742
(301) 454-4538

Massachusetts Committee on Criminal Justice
Statistical Analysis Center
100 Cambridge Street
Room 2100
Boston, MA 02202
www.state.ma.us/ccj/
charles.kaufmann@state.ma.us

Office of Criminal Justice
Lewis Cass Building
PO Box 30026
Lansing, MI 48909
(517) 373-6510

Criminal Justice Center
Minnesota Planning
658 Cedar Street
St. Paul, MN 55155
www.mnplan.state.mn.us/cj/
crimjust.center@mnplan.state.mn.us

Department of Public Safety
P.O. Box 958
Jackson, MS 39205
www.dps.state.ms.us/

Department of Public Safety
Truman State Office Building
P.O. Box 749
Jefferson City, MO 65102-0749
www.dps.state.mo.us/dpshome.htm
lpaul@mail.state.mo.us

Research Planning Bureau
Board of Crime Control
303 North Roberts Street
Helena, MT 59620
(406) 444-3604

Commission on Law Enforcement and Criminal Justice
PO Box 94946
Lincoln, NE 68509
(402) 471-2194

Criminal Justice Assistance
Nevada Highway Patrol
Building 107
Stewert Center
Carson City, NV 89711
www.state.nv.us/dmv_ps/cja.htm

Office of the Attorney General
33 Capitol Street
Concord, NH 03301-6397
(603) 271-3658

Office of the Attorney General
Hughs Justice Complex
25 Market St.
P.0. Box 080
Trenton, NJ 08625-0080
www.state.nj.us/lps/
citizens@oag.lps.state.nj.us

Institute for Criminal Justice Studies
Onate Hall
University of New Mexico
Albuquerque, NM 87131
(505) 277-4257

Division of Criminal Justice Services
Executive Park Tower
Stuyvesant Plaza
Albany, NY 12203
info.dcjs@DCJS.mailnet.state.ny.us

Criminal Justice Analysis Center
Governor's Crime Commission
Department of Crime Control
1201 Front St., Suite 200
Raleigh, NC 27609
www.gcc.state.nc.us/
DYearwood@gcc.dcc.state.nc.us

Office of the Attorney General
State Capitol Building
600 E. Blvd. Ave.
Bismarck, ND 58505-0040
(701) 328-2210

Office of Criminal Justice Services
400 E.Town St.
Suite 300
Columbus, OH 43215
(614) 466-7782
www.ocjs.state.oh.us/

Planning and Research
Oklahoma Department of Corrections
PO Box 11400
Oklahoma City, OK 73136
(405) 425-2590
www.doc.state.ok.us/

Department of Justice
Justice Building
Salem, OR 97310
(503) 378-8056
www.doj.state.or.us/welcome.htm

Bureau of Statistics and Policy Research
Pennsylvania Commission on Crime and Delinquency
PO Box 1167
Harrisburg, PA 17108
(800) 692-7292)
www.pccd.state.pa.us/

Governor's Commission on Justice
222 Quaker Lane
Suite 100
West Warwick, RI 02893
(401) 277-2620

Office of Research and Statistics
1000 Assembly St.
Suite 425
Columbia, SC 29201
(803) 734-3793
www.state.sc.us/drss/
wwworss@www.orss.state.sc.us

State Statistical Center
Criminal Justice Training Center
Division of the Attorney General
Pierre, SD 57501
(605) 773-3331

State Planning Office
307 John Sevier Building
500 Charlotte Avenue
Nashville, TN 37219
(615) 741-1676

Criminal Justice Policy Council
PO Box 13332
Capitol Station
Austin, TX 78711-3332
(512) 463-1810
www.texas.gov/agency/410.html

Commission on Criminal and Juvenile Justice
101State Capitol
Salt Lake City, UT 84114
(801) 538-1031
www.justice.state.ut.us/
cnanayak@state.ut.us

Vermont Criminal Information Center
103 South Main St.
Montpelier, VT 05671-2101
(802) 244-8727
www.dps.state.vt.us/cjs/vcic.htm

Department of Criminal Justice Services
805 East Broad Street
Richmond, VA 23219
(804) 786-4000
www.dcjs.state.va.us/

Office of Financial Management
Forecasting and Estimation Division
Insurance Building
MS AQ-44
Olympia, WA 98504
(206) 586-2501

West Virginia State Troopers
725 Jefferson Road
South Charleston, WV 25309
(304) 746-2100
www.wvstatepolice.com/
troopers@wvstatepolice.com

Office of Justice Assistance
30 West Mifflin Street
Suite 330
Madison, WI 53702
(608) 266-7646

Division of the Attorney General
123 Capitol Building
Cheyenne, WY 82002
(307) 777-7841
www.state.wy.us/~ag/index.html
webmaster@www.state.wy.us.

Office of the Attorney General
PO Box 192
San Juan, PR 00902-0192
(809) 721-7700

Office of Attorney General
Department of Justice
G.E.R.S. Complex
48B-50C KronprinsdenGade, VI
(809) 774-5666

# National Criminal Justice Reference Service (NCJRS)

## THE NATIONAL INSTITUTE OF JUSTICE (NIJ)

The National Criminal Justice Reference Service( NCJRS) is sponsored by the National Institute of Justice, the research branch of the U.S. Department of Justice. The Institute's mission is to develop knowledge about crime, its causes, and control. In carrying out this mandate, the National Institute of Justice established NCJRS in 1972 to disseminate information from research, demonstrations, evaluations, and special programs to federal, state, and local governments, and to serve as an international clearinghouse of justice information. NCJRS maintains the Juvenile Justice Clearinghouse for the National Institute for Juvenile Justice and Delinquency Prevention, operates the Dispute Resolution Information Center for the Federal Justice Research Program, and distributes publications and statistical information for the Bureau of Justice Statistics through the Justice Statistics Clearinghouse.

This chapter is a fingertip reference to the many ways the NCJRS provides professional information quickly, comprehensively, and in tune to the everyday needs of a criminal justice practitioner, policymaker, or scholar. To become a registered NCJRS user and receive the bimonthly *NIJ Reports*, special product announcements and notifications of new NCJRS services, contact NCJRS for a registration form. Note, though, that you do not have to be a registered user to take advantage of NCJRS products and services. For the investment of only a few minutes of time, substantial information can often be gained.

The bimonthly journal of the National Institute of Justice offers a regular column by the Director of the National Institute, a Research in Action section, a Selective Notification of Information section (abstracts of significant new publications in criminal justice with information on how to obtain them), a Calendar of Events (meetings, conferences, and seminars on the national and regional scenes), and announcement pages (information on new ways to use NCJRS services).

The following description of the services of NCJRS was provided by Kris Rose and is excerpted from that information.

## NCJRS Clearinghouses for Specific Information

NCJRS offers toll-free access to highly trained criminal justice reference specialists who can assist in finding answers to specific questions. The NCJRS Customer Service Center is staffed from 8:30 a.m. until 7:00 p.m. (Eastern Standard Time), Monday through Friday. Specialists also will return after-hour message left on the Customer Service Center telephone answering machine or on the web site. The NCJRS Customer Service Number is: 800-851-3420; 301-251-5500. The web site for NCJRS is www.ncjrs.org.

NCJRS also maintains clearinghouses that respond to specialized information needs:

*NIJ AIDS Clearinghouse.* Sponsored by the National Institute of Justice, this clearinghouse is the only centralized source of information on how AIDS affects criminal justice professionals and their work. Staff specialists with a broad knowledge of AIDS issues are available to answer questions, make referrals, and suggest publications pertaining to AIDS as it relates to the criminal justice system.

*Construction Information Exchange.* NIJ created the Construction Information Exchange to exchange data and information about prison and jail construction. The exchange has three components: the construction database of facilities built since 1978, the *National Directory of Corrections Construction*, and the *Construction Bulletin* series.

*Justice Statistics Clearinghouse.* The Bureau of Justice Statistics supports this clearinghouse for those seeking crime and criminal justice data. In addition to distributing BJS publications, the clearinghouse responds to statistics requests by offering document database searches, statistics information packages, referrals, and other related products and services.

*National Victims Resource Center.* Sponsored by the Office for Victims of Crime, the National Victims Resource Center (NVRC) responds to requests from researchers, practitioners, and individual victims for victim-related information. It has more than 7,000 victim-related books and articles covering child physical and sexual abuse, victims services, domestic violence, victim-witness programs, and violent crime. NVRC also maintains a legislation database containing state crime victim compensation statutes categorized by common search elements.

*Bureau of Justice Assistance Clearinghouse* (1-800-688-4252). The Bureau of Justice Assistance Clearinghouse informs state and local criminal justice practitioners about BJA products and programs. It disseminates BJA program briefs and reports to help criminal justice practitioners in their daily work. The Bureau of Justice Assistance Clearinghouse may be contacted via the Internet at www.ojp.usdoj.gov/BJA/

NCJRS reference specialists are prepared to respond to your criminal justice information needs. Drawing on their subject expertise and NCJRS resources, the reference specialists can answer questions about a whole range of criminal justice issues, such as:

- AIDS information
- Law enforcement
- Drugs and crime
- Courts
- Corrections
- Juvenile justice
- Statistics
- Criminology
- Victims
- Corrections construction
- Other criminal justice topics
- Asset forfeiture
- Drug control
- Drug testing
- Drug recognition programs
- Drug Education Programs
- Electronic monitoring programs
- Intensive probation/parole supervision programs
- Court delay reduction
- Information sharing and outreach systems
- Jail capacity programs

# THE BUREAU OF JUSTICE ASSISTANCE

Under the Anti-Drug Abuse Act of 1988, the Bureau of Justice Assistance (BJA) provides funds and technical assistance to state and local units of government to control crime and drug abuse and to improve the criminal justice system.

In support of these activities, BJA has created the Bureau of Justice Assistance Clearinghouse, now a component of the National Criminal Justice Reference Service. The clearinghouse informs state and local criminal justice practitioners about BJA products and programs.

The following BJA publications may be obtained from the Bureau of Justice Assistance Clearinghouse. They provide useful information on some of the most critical issues of the day related to criminal justice and will be valuable additions to your criminal justice library.

Adjudication, Brochure. BC000114

An Invitation to Project DARE: Drug Abuse Resistance
Education, Program Brief, June 1988. 10 pp.   DD114802

Building Integrity and Reducing Drug Corruption in
Police Departments, September 1989. 126 pp. DD120652

Drug Recognition Program, Monograph,
April 1989. 24pp. DD117432

Electronic Monitoring in Intensive Probation and Parole
Programs, Monograph, February 1989. 24 pp.   DD116319

Estimating the Costs of Drug Testing for a Pretrial Service
Program, Monograph, June 1989. 34 pp.   DD118317

FY 1988 Report on Drug Control, 1989. 136 pp. $6.50.
Call for ordering information. DD117435

FY 1988 Report on Drug Control, Executive Summary,
1989. 9 pp. DD118277

Intensive Supervision Probation and Parole (ISP),
 Program Brief, November 1988. 28 pp.   DD106663

Prosecution Management Support System,

Program Brief, March 1989. 25 pp. DD117093

Reducing Crime by Reducing Drug Abuse:
A Manual for Police Chiefs and Sheriffs,
January 1989. 166 pp. DD113110

Treatment Alternatives to Street Crime (TASC),
Brochure. BC000113

Treatment Alternatives to Street Crime (TASC),
Resource Catalog, October 1989. 161 pp.   DD119847

Treatment Alternatives to Street Crime (TASC):
Implementing the Model, Implementation Manual,
September 1988. 322 pp. DD116322

Treatment Alternatives to Street Crime (TASC):
Participant's Manual, Training Manual,
September 1988. 108 pp. DD116321

Treatment Alternatives to Street Crime—TASC Programs,
Program Brief, January 1988. 31 pp. DD116323

Urinalysis as Part of a Treatment Alternative to
Street Crime (TASC) Program, Monograph,
July 1988. 22 pp. DD115416

## Drugs and Crime Data Center and Clearinghouse

This service was begun in 1987 and is funded by the Bureau of Justice Assistance (BJA) and managed by the Bureau of Justice Statistics (BJS).

> Drugs & Crime Clearinghouse
> Box 6000
> Rockville, MD 20849-6000
> (800) 666-3332
> www.ncjr.org/

This service responds to policymakers' urgent need for the most current data about:

- Illegal drugs
- Drug law violations
- Drug-related crime
- Drug-using offenders in the criminal justice system
- The impact of drugs on criminal justice administration.

The Data Center & Clearinghouse serves the drugs-and-crime information needs of:

- Federal, state, and local policymakers
- Criminal justice and public health practitioners
- Researchers and universities
- Private corporations
- The media
- The public

Special attention is given to the needs of state and local government agencies, especially those seeking data to meet the statistical requirements of the Anti-Drug Abuse Grant Program of the Bureau of Justice Assistance (BJA).

# 13

# The National Archive
# of Criminal Justice Data

The National Archive of Criminal Justice Data (NACJD) is the world's largest single source of quantitative data on criminal justice, criminology, and general social science. The following information about the archive was originally provided by Victoria W. Scheider as Archival Assistant Director of NACJD.

Sponsored by the Bureau of Justice Statistics (BJS) within the U.S. Department of Justice, the National Archive of Criminal Justice Data was established in 1978 under the auspices of the Inter-university Consortium for Political and Social Research (ICPSR). Headquarters of the Criminal Justice Archive are located, along with the central staff of the ICPSR, in the Institute for Social Research at the University of Michigan.

The central mission of the Criminal Justice Archive is to facilitate and encourage research in the field of criminal justice through the sharing of data resources. Specific goals include:

- Providing computer-readable data for the quantitative study of crime and the criminal justice system through the development of a central data archive that disseminates computer-readable social science data

- Supplying technical assistance in selecting data collections and the computer hardware and software for analyzing data efficiently and effectively

- Offering training in quantitative methods of social science research to facilitate secondary analysis of criminal justice data

## ICPSR: MEMBERSHIP AND ACCESS TO DATA

Since 1962, ICPSR has served the academic community by acquiring, processing, and distributing data relevant to a broad spectrum of academic disciplines including criminology, law, political science, sociology, history, economics, gerontology, public health, and education. The Consortium maintains the world's largest repository of computer-based research and instructional data for the social sciences.

ICPSR is a membership-based organization with over 350 member colleges and universities in the United States and abroad. Payment of an annual institutional fee entitles faculty, staff and students at member schools to take advantage of the full range of ICPSR services. Because ICPSR is structured as a "partnership" with its member institutions, it is able to provide facilities and services to researchers and scholars that no single college or university could offer independently. Most ICPSR services are provided at no charge to the individual user.

## To Order Data

Individuals at member institutions can order data through their campus representative. Individuals at non-member institutions may obtain ICPSR data by paying an access fee. The Bureau of Justice Statistics supports the use of criminal justice data by individuals working in government or under grants from the U.S. Department of Justice.

Users at nonmember institutions or in government agencies wishing to order criminal justice-related data collections can contact Criminal Justice Archive staff members directly. Individuals at member schools also can contact staff regarding substantive and technical issues. Inquiries can be made to:

National Archive of Criminal Justice Data
Inter-university Consortium for Political and Social Research
Institute for Social Research
P.O. Box 1248
Ann Arbor, Michigan 48106-1248
(734) 764-2570
Homepage: www.icpsr.umich.edu/
E-mail: netmail@icpr.umich.edu

## ARCHIVAL DEVELOPMENT

The National Archive of Criminal Justice Data routinely receives data from four agencies within the U.S. Department of Justice:

- Bureau of Justice Statistics

- National Institute of Justice

- Office of Juvenile Justice and Delinquency Prevention

- Federal Bureau of Investigation

Many of the data files sent by these agencies are made available for public release in their original form. For other collections, additional data processing and documentation work is completed by Archive staff. Additional processing may include:

- Generating machine-readable documentation with full question text and code explanations

- Producing printed documentation that includes a copy of the original data collection instrument

- Providing SPSS, SAS, or OSIRIS control cards in machine-readable form

- Removing blanks and nonnumeric codes in the data file

- Performing consistency checks on variables in skip patterns within the original question-naire

- Making univariate frequencies and other descriptive statistics available in either printed or machine-readable form

- Performing recodes to preserve the confidentiality of survey respondents or to facilitate use of the data for analysis

The National Archive of Criminal Justice Data releases several major serial data collections sponsored by agencies within the U.S. Department of Justice. For example, the Archive routinely distributes data from the Juvenile Detention and Correctional Facility Censuses, sponsored by the Office of Juvenile Justice and Delinquency Prevention. The Federal Bureau of Investigation provides Uniform Crime Reporting Program Data which are then processed and released by the Archive. Collections from the Bureau of Justice Statistics include:

- National Crime Surveys

- Capital Punishment in the United States

- Censuses of State Adult Correctional Facilities and Local Jails

- National Corrections Reporting Program

- National Surveys of Jails

- Surveys of Inmates of State Adult Correctional Facilities and Local Jails

- Offender Based Transaction Statistics (OBTS)

- Censuses of State Felony Courts

- National Judicial Reporting Program

- Expenditure and Employment Data for the Criminal Justice System

- National Surveys of Law Enforcement Agencies

Individual scholars and researchers also deposit data with the Archive. For more information about depositing data or about any of the specific collections listed above, contact the National Archive of Criminal Justice Data.

# 14

# Sources of International Data

Researchers may often need to locate international data on a topic. The following sources can be good starting points for such a search:

*Bibliography on Afghanistan, The Sudan and Tunisia.* John J. Vidergar. (Monticello, IL: Vance Bibliographies, December 1978).

*Bibliography of Canadian Bibliographies.* Updated periodically. (Toronto, ON: Bibliographical Society of Canada).

*Bibliography on Crime and Juvenile Delinquency in Africa.* National Council on Crime and Delinquency. (New York: NCCD, 1963).

*Canadian Government Publications.* (Ottawa, ON: Department of Public Printing and Stationery, 1953-date).

*Crime in Foreign Countries: A Selected List of Recent Selections.* U.S. Library of Congress, Division of Bibliography. (Washington, DC: Library of Congress, 1935).

*Criminology and Forensic Sciences: An International Bibliography, 1950-1980.* Rudolf Vom Ende. (Detroit: Gale Research, 1982).

*Government Publications.* (London: Stationery Office, H.M.S.P., 1936-date).

*Index to International Public Opinion, 1982-1983.* Elizabeth Hann Hastings and Philip K. Hastings (eds.). The fifth volume of the annual *Index to International Public Opinion, 1982-1983* contains data drawn from surveys conducted and/or referenced in most parts of the world. All major regions are represented, with more than 125 individual nation states covered. The materials are selected on the basis of their widespread present and continuing interest to researchers and the public at large in their persistent quest for understanding the peoples of the world. Much of the data herein are not only of topical, present day interest, but also deal with problems and issues that are of sustaining concern over time and transcend geographical boundaries. With the publication of Volume V, the *Index to International Public Opinion* now covers the highlights of world events over a five-year period in relation to over 12,000 questions asked in more than 100 countries. The 1982-83 edition covers public reaction to events such as the Iranian hostage crisis, the Russian invasion of Afghanistan, and the Israeli invasion of Lebanon. Over 700 pages in length, Volume V contains a wider range of substantive content. It contains a significantly greater number of tables than previous volumes, presenting breakdowns by such demographics as age, sex, race, religion, education, and economic level, among others. Almost 30 new topical subcategories have been added. The section on "Multinational Surveys" contains an extraordinary study, "Fundamental Values: A Global Perspective," including close to 100 tables. The subject index has been enhanced to provide greater access to the contents of the volume. (Westport, CT: Greenwood Press, 1983).

*Index to International Public Opinion, 1981-1982.* 684 pages. Includes bibliographies.

*Index to International Public Opinion, 1980-1981.* 548 pages. Includes bibliographies.

*Index to International Public Opinion, 1979-1980.* 484 pages. Includes bibliographies.

*Index to International Public Opinion, 1978-1979.* 386 pages. Includes bibliographies.

*International Bibliography on Crime and Delinquency*. P.G. Van der Watt. "Six Decades of Crime Research in South Africa, 1900-1962," 2: 481-94 January, 1965.

*International Bibliography of Police Literature*. F. Andreotti. (London: M. & W. Publications, 1963).

*International Bibliography of Selected Police Literature*, Second Edition. International Police Association. Contains bibliographical data and list of periodicals from a number of foreign police agencies. In English and foreign languages. (Liverpool: M. &W. Publications Ltd., 1968).

*International Bibliography of the Social Sciences: Sociology*. (Chicago: Aldine, 1951-date).

*International Exchange of Information on Current Criminological Research Projects in Member States*. (Strasbourg, France: European Committee on Crime Problems, Directorate of Legal Affairs, Division of Crime Problems, Council of Europe, 1991).

*International Criminology and Criminal Justice: A Selected Bibliography*. Thomas R. Lagergreen and Kathleen A. Pitt. Abstracts 75 books and articles from other countries. All are in English. (Washington, DC: National Criminal Justice Reference Service, 1976).

*International Handbook of Contemporary Developments in Criminology*. Elmer H. Johnson (ed.). Volume 1: General Issues and the Americas; Volume 2: Europe, Africa, the Middle East and Asia. In his introductory chapter, Johnson establishes a conceptual scheme for integrating the contributions of resident experts who analyze the crime patterns, socio-political system and criminological enterprise of their respective countries. The first part of Volume 1 includes articles on transnational trends, international organizations, radical criminology, the feminist movement and crime, white collar crime, and other general issues. Country studies of the Americas follow. Country studies of Europe, Africa, the Middle East, and Asia continue in Volume 2. Bibliographies, with many annotated entries, accompany virtually every chapter. The product is a reference work essential to criminologists, criminal justice practitioners, social and economic planners, and students in universities and colleges throughout the English-speaking world. (Westport, CT: Greenwood Press, 1983).

*International Organizations, 1918-1945: A Guide to Research and Research Materials*. George W. Baer (ed.). (Guides to European Diplomatic History Research and Research Materials.). Part I of this book provides a general introduction to international organizations and the international system. Part II presents a section on the archives of the League of Nations, United Nations Organization, Permanent Court of International Justice and Permanent Court of Arbitration, International Labor Organization, Unesco, and some of the other international organizations, conferences, and institutes. The details include a description of the main units of the archives, its holdings, and its publications; information on regulations and procedures for admission is sometimes included. Part III treats pertinent archival material in Great Britain, France, and the United States. For each of these countries there is a short summary of materials available of published and documentary series, and a selected list of significant private papers and their locations. Records in Germany, Italy, and Belgium are also noted. The remaining chapters are bibliographies. (Wilmington, DE: Scholarly Resources, 1981).

*International Policing: A Selected Bibliography*. Mark Shanley and Marjorie Kravitz. 168 annotated entries. (Washington, DC: NCJRS, February, 1978).

*International Fire and Security Directory*. (London, UK: Blenheim Group Plc, 1993).

*A London Bibliography of the Social Sciences*. Eighteenth Supplement, 1983, Volume 41. Compiled and edited at the British Library of Political and Economic Science under the direction of D.A. Clarke. "The most extensive subject bibliography in the field. . . ..An essential addition to any major collection in the social sciences."—*American Reference Books Annual*. This annual publication catalogs the holdings of the British Library of Political and Economic Science (BLPES) and the Edward Fry Library of International Law. (BLPES is a depository for the publications of many governmental and international bodies throughout the world.) International in scope, the holdings encompass the whole range of the social sciences and are especially rich in economics; commerce and business administration; transport; statistics; political science and public administration; law; and the social and economic aspects of history. (Bronx, NY: H.W. Wilson Co., 1984).

*National Bibliography of Chinese Publications*, National Central Library Taipei (ed.). Annual. (New York: International Publication Service).

*The Okhrana: The Russian Department of Police: A Bibliography*, Edward E. Smith. (Stanford, CA: Hoover Institution on War, Revolution and Peace, 1967).

*Parole in Foreign Countries: Bibliography*. (Hackensack, NJ: National Council on Crime and Delinquency, 1969).

*Police Studies: The International Review of Police Development*. (Cincinnati, OH: Anderson Publishing Co.) Now: *Policing: An International Journal of Police Strategies and Management*. (Bradford, England: MCB University Press Ltd.)

*Regency International Directory of Private Investigators, Private Detectives and Debt Collecting Agencies.* Annual. (Folkestone, UK: Regency International Publications, 1981 to date).

*Selected and Annotated Guide to the Government and Politics of Egypt*, Robert B. Harmon. (Monticello, IL: Vance Bibliographies, 1978).

*A Selected International Bibliography on Capital Punishment.* (Chicago: University of Chicago Law School, 1968).

*Social Control and Deviance in Cuba*, Luis Salas Calero. (New York: Praeger Publishers, 1979).

*Sociology.* An International Bibliography of Serial Literature 1880-1980. Jan Wepsiec. This bibliography lists 2,300 current and ceased serial publications in sociology and the related areas of deviance and crime, social geography and psychology, social work, and community development. It includes periodicals, numbered research reports, and monographs, as well as abstracting, indexing, and bibliographic publications. (Bronx, NY: H.W. Wilson Co., 1983).

*Soviet Intelligence and Security Services, 1964-1970: A Selected Bibliography of Soviet Publications with Some Additional Titles from Other Sources.* (Washington, DC: Library of Congress, 1972).

*The Soviet Secret Police.* Simon Wolin and Robert M. Slusser (eds.). (Studies of the Research Program on the U.S.S.R., No. 14.). The most detailed picture yet publicly available of the history of the Soviet secret police, of its founder, the late Feliks Dzerzhinski, and of the organization and operation of the secret police and associated agencies. This very useful work was financed by the Research Program on the USSR which has many other useful collections and distillations of emigré knowledge to its credit. (Westport, CT: Greenwood Press).

*Statesman's Year Book: Statistical and Historical Annual of the States of the World.* (London and New York: Macmillan, 1864-date). (See Chapter 11, "Statistical Data," for additional information on this source.)

*World Encyclopedia of Police Forces and Penal Systems.* G. T. Kurain. (New York: Facts on File, 1989).

## UNITED NATIONS PUBLICATIONS

In addition to the above publications, the United Nations and United Nations Social Defence Research Institute have been very active in the criminal justice area, and have published many sources pertaining to the field. The United Nations web site is www.un.org/. This web site includes a United Nations periodical index, in which you can search and order publications.

> United Nations Publications
> 2 UN Plaza
> Room DC2-853
> New York, NY 10017
> (800) 253-9646
> E-mail: publications@un.org

A sample of some of the publications you might find particularly helpful in the criminal justice field are:

*Bulletin on Narcotics: The Family and Drug Abuse.* (1994).
    E.1994      Vol.XLVI      No.1

*Compendium of UN Standards & Forums in Crime Prevention and Criminal Justice.* (1992)
    E.92.IV.1      92-1-130148-3

*Crime Prevention and Control.* (1990)
    M.90, I.17      92-1-002052-9      No.340

*Criminal Victimization in the Developing World.* (1994)
    E.94.III.N.4      92-90-78-030-4

*Development and Policy Use of Criminal Justice Information.* (1994)
    E.94.III.N.2      92-9078-028-2

*Effectiveness of the International Drug Control Convention Supplement to the Report of the International Narcotics Control Board.* (1995)
    E.95.XI.5      92-1-148095-7

*Human Rights and Law Enforcement: A Manual of Human Rights training for the Police.* (1996)
    E.96.XIV.7      92-1-154121-2      No.5

*International Review of Criminal Policy.* (1997)
    E.97.IV.4        92-1-130186-6

*Sexual Exploitation of Children.* (1996)
    E.96.XIV.7      92-1-154123-9    No.8

*Strategies for Confronting Domestic Violence: A Resource Manual.* (1994)
    E.94.IU.1        92-1-130158-0

*Trends in Crime and Criminal Justice, in the Context of Socio- economic Change.* (1992)
    E.92.IV.3        92-1-130150-5

# SELECTED LIST OF INTERNATIONAL CRIMINAL JUSTICE PERIODICALS

*British Columbia Police Journal.* (Vancouver, BC: British Columbia Federation of Peace Officers).

*British Journal of Criminology.* (Littleton, CO: Fred B. Rothman & Co.).

*Canadian Journal of Criminology.* (Ottawa, ON: Canadian Association for the Prevention of Crime).

*Canadian Police Chief.* (Ottawa, ON: Canadian Association of Chiefs of Police, Inc.).

*Canadian Police College Journal.* (Ottawa, ON: Canadian Police College).

*Criminologie.* (Montreal, QUE: Universite de Montreal).

*International Annals of Criminology.* (Paris, France: Societe Internationale de Criminologie).

*International Center for Comparative Criminology Annual Report.* (Montreal, QUE: Universite de Montreal).

*International Directory of Detective Agencies.* (Neosho, MO: Inter State Service Co., Inc.).

*International Drug Report.* (Albany, NY: International Narcotic Enforcement Officers Association).

*International Juvenile Officers' Association Conference Journal.* (Holland, IL: International Juvenile Officers Association).

*International Juvenile Officers' Association Reporter.* (Holland, IL: International Juvenile Officers Association).

*International Prisoners Aid Association Newsletter.* (Louisville, KY: University of Louisville).

*International Review of Criminal Policy.* (New York: United Nations Department of Social Affairs).

*Journal of the Canadian Society of Forensic Science.* (Ottawa, ON: Canadian Society of Forensic Science).

*RCMP Quarterly.* (Ottawa, ON: Royal Canadian Mounted Police).

## Guides to Periodicals Relating to International Criminal Justice

*Guide to Foreign Legal Materials Series.* (Dobbs Ferry, NY: Oceana Publications, Inc.).

*Index to Foreign Legal Periodicals.* (Chicago: American Association of Law Libraries).

*International Center for Comparative Criminology Annual Report.* (Montreal, QUE: University of Montreal).

*International Guide to Periodicals in Criminal Justice.* (Greensboro, NC: Sandy Ridge Press).

## International Periodicals Offering a Broad General View of International Events

*ASILS Newsletter*. (Washington, DC: Association of Student International Law Societies).

*Amnesty Action*. (New York: Amnesty International, USA).

*Annual Review of United National Affairs*. (Dobbs Ferry, NY: Oceana).

*Conflict Quarterly*. (Fredericton, CAN: University of Brunswick).

*Countries of the World and Their Leaders, Yearbook 1982*. (Detroit: Gale Research).

*Department of State Bulletin*. (Washington, DC: U.S. Government Printing Office).

*Department of State Newsletter*. (Washington, DC: U.S. Government Printing Office).

*Facts on File Weekly World News Digest*. (New York: Facts on File).

*Foreign Affairs*. (New York: Council on Foreign Relations).

*Foreign Affairs Research*. (Washington, DC: U.S. Department of State).

*International Journal of Politics*. (White Plains, NY: M.E. Sharpe, Inc.).

*Police Studies: The International Review of Police Development*. (Cincinnati, OH: Anderson Publishing Co.). Now published as *Policing: An International Journal of Police Strategies and Management* (Bradford, England: MCB University Press)

*U.N. International Law Commission, Yearbook*. (New York: United Nations Publications).

*UN Monthly Chronicle*. (New York: United Nations Department of Public Information).

# 15

# Historical Research Sources

Historical research is the study of the past. It is the study of events that took place, what people said, wrote, and did, and the study of the trends that developed. As with other types of research, the main objective of a historical research project should be to make a contribution to knowledge on a particular subject of interest or significance. Historical research should be original. This does not mean that you have to study a subject or problem never before touched, but it does mean that you should handle the research in an original way. Remember that historical matters cannot be changed but the evidence of them is variable and their description and interpretations are often revised. Old ground can be covered again, and new evidence that will correct errors or improve interpretations can often be found. Facts overlooked by previous investigators, or new relationships between old facts, can be discovered by researchers re-examining the same material but with different perspectives and purposes in mind.

Two types of sources can be used to obtain historical data: primary and secondary. Both are important contributors to historical research. Primary sources are the actual materials, whether they be printed matter, rare items, or photographs, that were created in connection with the topic or event the researcher is studying. The information an investigator derives from these materials is firsthand, or from the primary source. Primary sources allow for documentation of authenticity and for firsthand examination and interpretation.

Secondary sources are works of other researchers who are studying a primary source. For example, what have other sociologists written about Karl Marx or Emile Durkheim? Secondary sources can provide important contributions to background and preparatory study of the primary sources.

## PRIMARY SOURCES

Before setting out to examine primary sources, a historical researcher needs to do some preparatory work in the library that involves searching out secondary sources. As with other styles of research, a tentative bibliography needs to be developed and preliminary reading should be done. Students should learn as much as possible about the people, events, or developments they are studying. Use the pertinent references in the library such as books, directories, journal articles, dissertations, newspapers, and encyclopedias. This process of information gathering from secondary sources will help identify names of persons, locations, significant events and dates for which you need more data, and may also lead to primary sources.

After doing some preliminary investigation of the appropriate secondary sources, you should be ready to examine any of the pertinent primary sources that might be accessible to you. These are found in a variety of places including private businesses, private organizations, government institutions, religious organizations, and private family collections. The Manuscript Division of the Library of Congress has the largest selection of primary sources, and a visit to this institution would almost certainly be an asset to any primary source search. However, not everyone undertaking historical research will be able to visit Washington, D.C. If this is the case for you, do not despair. Assistance in locating and using primary sources may also be obtained from the following sources:

*American Judicial Proceedings First Printed Before 1801: An Analytical Bibliography.* Compiled by Wilfred J. Ritz. This is the first bibliography to list every law report, trial, or separate event of judicial significance occurring in or relating to what is now the United States, and for which there was material other than a newspaper account printed before 1801. It includes rules of court applicable to judicial proceedings, proceedings in England relating to the English colonies, and American reprints of reports and European trials. The volume fills a gap in legal and historical literature, which has virtually ignored the pre-1789 period, the first 182 years of American jurisprudence. The bibliography is analytical in that the materials are arranged chronologically by jurisdiction, including states and the United States, and by major subject. An index of parallel entries gives cross references to 66 other bibliographic sources. Researchers will find this an invaluable tool for identifying, for any year through 1801, all printed materials relating to American judicial proceedings: those of any state or the federal government. All common law judicial decisions, grand jury charges, confessions and dying speeches of convicted criminals, and sermons on their executions are included. The compilations show the status of American common law in 1776 when independence was declared, in 1787 when the federal Constitution was drafted, and in 1789 when the federal government was organized. (Westport, CT: Greenwood Press, 1984).

*Combined Retrospective Index to Book Reviews in Scholarly Journals, 1886-1974.* This set provides author and title access to more than one million book reviews that appeared in complete backfiles of 459 scholarly journals in the social sciences. Most of the reviews were never included in any retrospective multi-title book review index. Review citations may be located in either of the separate author and title indices. (Arlington, VA: Carrollton Press, 1979-1982).

*Cumulated Magazine Subject Index, 1907-1949.* An index to approximately 175 English, Canadian, and American periodicals. Approximately one-half of the indexed journals are concerned with the national and local history of Anglo-American countries. Other major fields covered include travel, mountaineering, exploration, fine arts, and literature. Review references are entered under the subject of the book, with the exception of fiction which appears under the author's name. Reviews are distinguished from other entries by the word "review" enclosed in parentheses. (Boston, MA: G.K. Hall, 1964).

*Directory of Historical Societies and Agencies in the United States and Canada.* (Madison, WI: American Association for State and Local History, 1956-date).

*Historical Statistics of the United States. Colonial times to 1970.* (Washington DC: Government Printing Office, 1975). (See also Chapter 11, "Statistical Data.")

*Keepers of the Past.* Clifford L. Lord (ed.). (Chapel Hill: University of North Carolina Press, 1965).

*Materials and Methods for Historical Research.* Carla Staffle. (New York: Libraryworks, 1979).

*Nineteenth Century Reader's Guide to Periodical Literature, 1890-1899.* An author and subject index to 51 general British and American journals. Review references are cited under the author of the book reviewed. (New York, NY: H.W. Wilson Co., 1911).

*Poole's Index to Periodical Literature, 1802-1906.* A subject index to 470 British and American periodicals. References to reviews of books with definite subjects appear under those subjects. It reviews references to works of fiction, poetry and drama which appear under the author of the book reviewed. (Boston, MA: Houghton, Mifflin, 1972).

*Research in Archives: The Use of Unpublished Primary Sources.* Philip Brooks. (Chicago: University of Chicago Press, 1969).

*Research on the Propensity for Crime at Different Ages, 1831.* (Adophe Quetelet, translated by Sawyer F. Sylvester). This was the first scientific study of crime. Early in the 19th century, Adolphe Quetelet began an empirical approach to the study of crime as a sociological phenomenon which was concerned with the use of present findings to predict future events. Quetelet took from such sources as the Compte general de l'administration de la justice en France the number of crimes seen regularly for several years and uses these figures as the bases for prediction of the number of crimes in succeeding years. He then goes on to relate the rate of crime to certain other social factors. (Cincinnati, OH: Anderson Publishing Co.).

*The Wellesley Index to Victorian Periodicals, 1824-1900.* A listing of the contents of eight major British journals published during the years 1824-1900; one title, *The Edinburgh Review*, is indexed back to 1802. There is not an index to authors of books reviewed. To locate a review, ascertain the date of publication of the book in question and then consult the listing of each journal for that year and one or more additional years. (New York, NY: Routledge, 1999).

*Where Are the Historical Manuscripts: A Symposium.* (Sturbridge, MA: American Association for State and Local History, 1950).

## SECONDARY SOURCES

For students undecided on a topic or merely contemplating historical research, several secondary sources on criminal justice topics have been listed below. This may assist you in choosing a topic or in locating additional secondary sources that may in turn cite primary sources. Also, following this list, the Wickersham Commission reports have been annotated and included. (For additional historical sources, see Chapter 9.)

*Administration of Criminal Justice, 1949-1956*. (Berkeley, CA: University of California, Institute of Government Studies, reprinted by Patterson Smith, Montclair, NJ, 1970).

*Albions Fatal Tree*. Douglas Hay. (New York: Pantheon Books, 1975).

*The American Criminal: An Anthropological Study*. Ernest A. Hooton. With the collaboration of the Statistical Laboratory of the Division of Anthropology, Harvard University. (Westport, CT: Greenwood Press, 1939).

*American Doctoral Dissertations*. (Ann Arbor: University Microfilms International, 1964).

*American Newspapers 1821-1936: A Union List of Files Available in the United States and Canada*. (New York: H.W. Wilson, 1937).

*American Prisons: A History of Good Intentions*. Blake McKelvey. Text with bibliography. (Montclair, NJ: Patterson Smith, 1977).

*Anglo-American Legal Bibliographies: An Annotated Guide*. William L. Friend. (Washington, DC: U.S. Library of Congress, 1944).

*The Annals of Murder: A Bibliography of Books and Pamphlets on American Murders from Colonial Times to 1900*. Thomas M. McDade. (Norman, OK: University of Oklahoma, 1961).

*Bibliography of Crime and Criminal Justice*. Dorothy C. Culver. (A) 1927-1931, and (B) 1932-1937. (New York: H.W. Wilson Company, [A] 1934 and ([B] 1939).

*Bibliography Manual for the Students of Criminology*. Thorsten Sellin and J.P. Shaloo. (Philadelphia: The Authors, 1935).

*Bibliography: Works on Criminal Law, Penology and Prison Discipline*. Text with bibliography. (New York: Annual Report of The Prison Association of New York, 1870).

*Bloodletters and Badmen: A Narrative Encyclopedia of American Criminals from the Pilgrims to the Present*. Jay R. Nash. (Philadelphia: Lippincott, 1973).

*The Blue and the Brass: American Policing 1890-1910*. A unique collection of 64 articles, actually written by law enforcement officials before 1910, which provides the student of law enforcement with a vivid portrayal of policing at the turn of the century. (Gaithersburg, MD: International Association of Chiefs of Police, 1976).

*Brief Outline of the History and Organization of the R.C.M.P. Musical Ride*. Royal Canadian Mounted Police. Text with bibliography. (Ottawa: RCMP, 1978).

*Broadmoor: A History of Criminal Lunacy and Its Problems*. Ralph Partridge. (Westport, CT: Greenwood Press).

*Catalog of Law Books Published Prior to 1894*. G.E. Griswold. (New York: William S. Hein, 1977).

*Catalog of the Public Documents of Congress and of All the Departments of the Government of the United States for the Period March 4, 1893 — December 31, 1940*. (Washington, DC: Government Printing Office, 1896-1945). (See also Chapter 10, "Government Documents.")

*Comprehensive Index to the Publications of the United States Government, 1881-1893*. John G. Ames. (Washington, DC: Government Printing Office, 1905). (See also Chapter 10, "Government Documents").

*The Concise Encyclopedia of Crime and Criminals*. Sir Harold Richard Scott. (Englewood Cliffs, NJ: Prentice-Hall, 1961).

*Conquest of Violence: Order and Liberty in Britain*. Thomas A. Critchley. Text with bibliography. (New York: Schocken Books, 1970).

*A Contribution Towards a Bibliography Dealing with Crime and Cognate Subjects*. John Cumming. (Montclair, NJ: Patterson Smith, 1970, reprint of 1935 edition).

*Cops and Bobbies: Police Authority in New York and London*. Wilber R. Miller. Text with bibliography. (Chicago: University of Chicago Press, 1973).

*Crime and Authority in Victorian England: The Black Country, 1835-1860*. David Phillips. Text with bibliography. (Totowa, NJ: Rowman and Littlefield, 1977).

*Crime and Law Enforcement in the Colony of New York, 1691-1776.* Douglas Greenberg. Text with bibliography. (Ithaca, NY: Cornell University Press, 1976).

*Crime and Law in Nineteenth Century Britain.* W.R. Cornish and others. Text with bibliography. (Dublin: Irish University Press, 1978).

*Criminology.* Arthur MacDonald. Text with bibliography. (New York: Funk & Wagnalls, 1893).

*Criminology.* M.F. Parmelee. Text with bibliography. (New York: Macmillan, 1918).

*Criminology: A Bibliography of Research and Theory in the United States, 1945-1972.* (Philadelphia: University of Pennsylvania, 1974).

*Critical History of Police Reform: The Emergence of Professionalism.* Samuel Walker. Text with bibliography. (Lexington, MA: Lexington Books, 1977).

*Descent into Madness: An Inmate's Experience of the New Mexico State Prison Riot.* Mike Rolland. (Cincinnati, OH: Anderson Publishing Co., 1997).

*A Descriptive Catalog of the Government Publications of the United States, September 5, 1774 — March 4, 1881.* Benjamin P. Poore. (Washington, DC: Government Printing Office, 1881).

*Discipline and Punish: The Birth of the Prison.* Michel Foucault. Text with bibliography. (New York: Pantheon, 1977).

*Doctoral Dissertations Accepted by American Universities, 1935-55.* (New York: H.W. Wilson).

*Encyclopedia of Criminology.* Vernon Branham and Samuel Kutash (eds.). (New York: Philosophical Library, 1949).

*The English Police: Its Origin and Development.* E.H. Glover. Text with bibliography. (London: Police Chronicle, 1934).

*The Evolution of Criminology.* William V. Pelfrey. (Cincinnati, OH: Anderson Publishing Co., 1980).

*The Foundation of Australia, 1786-1800: A Study in English Criminal Practice and Penal Colonization in the Eighteenth Century.* Eris Michael O'Brien. (Westport, CT: Greenwood Press, 1970).

*The Growth of Criminal Law in Ancient Greece.* George Miller Calhoun. (Westport, CT: Greenwood Press, 1973).

*To Guard My People: The History of the English Police.* Percival Griffiths. Bibliography. (London: Benn, 1971).

*A Guide to Material on Crime and Criminal Justice (through 1926).* Augustus F. Kuhlman. (Montclair, NJ: Patterson Smith, 1969, orig. 1929).

*Hatchet Men: The Story of the Tong Wars in San Francisco's Chinatown.* Richard H. Dillon. Text with bibliography. (New York: Coward McCann, 1962).

*Henry and Sir John Fielding: The Thief Catchers.* Patrick Pringle. Text with bibliography. (London: Dobson, 1968).

*Historical Approaches to Crime, Research Strategies and Issues.* James A. Inciardi, et al. (Beverly Hills, CA: Sage Publications, 1977).

*Historical Criminology: The Evolution of Criminological Ideas.* Israel Drapkin. (Lexington, MA: Lexington Books, 1980).

*Historical Statistics of the United States.* (Washington, DC: United States Bureau of the Census, 1960). (See Chapter 11, "Statistical Data," for additional sources of statistical data.)

*History and Bibliography of American Newspapers 1690-1820.* Clarence S. Brigham. (Worcester, MA: American Antiquarian Society, 1947).

*History of the British South Africa Police.* Volume 1, *The First Line of Defence, 1899-1903.* Peter Gibbs. Text with bibliography. (Salisbury, Rhodesia: BSAP, 1972).

*History of Criminal Justice,* Second Edition. Herbert A. Johnson and Nancy Travis Wolfe. (Cincinnati, OH: Anderson Publishing Co., 1996).

*A History of English Criminal Law and Its Administration from 1750.* Volume 3, Cross Currents in the Movements for the Reform of the Police. Leon Radzinowicz. Text with bibliography. (London: Stevens, 1956).

*History of Police in England and Wales.* Thomas A. Critchley. Bibliography. (London: Constable, 1978).

*The Houston Police, 1878-1948.* Louis J. Marchiafava. (Houston: Rice University Press, 1977).

*Hue and Cry, The Story of Henry and John Fielding and Their Bow Street Runners.* Patrick Pringle. (Bungay, Suffolk, Britain: William Morrow and Company, 1955).

*Identification Wanted: Development of the American Criminal Identification System.* Published by The International Association of Chiefs of Police. Using articles and correspondence written by police officials who were directly involved in events, this book tells the dual story of the development of identification technology and the little known 50-year struggle by the nation's police chiefs to organize a national identification system. (Gaithersburg, MD: International Association of Chiefs of Police, 1977).

*"I'm Frank Hamer": The Life of a Texas Peace Officer.* Gordon Frost and John H. Jenkins. Text with bibliography. (New York: Pemberton Press, 1968).

*Intemperance: The Lost War Against Liquor.* Larry Engleman. (Riverside, NJ: The Free Press, 1979).

*Iron Men: A Saga of the Deputy United States Marshals Who Rode the Indian Territory.* C.H. McKennon. Text with bibliography. (Garden City, NY: Doubleday, 1967).

*Issues in Criminology,* 9:111-14, Spring, 1974, M.B. Miller. "At Hard Labor: Rediscovering the 19th Century Prison."

*Just Measure of Pain: The Penitentiary in the Industrial Revolution, 1750-1850.* Michael Ignatieff. Text with bibliography. (New York: Macmillan, 1978).

*Juvenile Court Laws of the U.S.: Topical and State by State Summaries.* Gilbert Cosulich. (New York: National Probation Association, 1939).

*Juvenile Delinquency: A Critical Annotated Bibliography.* Philippe S. Cabot. (New York: H.W. Wilson Company, 1946).

*Law & Order in American History.* Joseph Hawes (ed.). (Port Washington, NY: Kennikat Press, 1979).

*Law and Order in the Capital City: A History of the Washington Police, 1800-1886.* Kenneth G. Alfers. Text with bibliography. (Washington, DC: George Washington University, 1976).

*Law-Finders and Law-Makers in Medieval England: Collected Studies in Legal and Constitutional History.* Helen Maud. (Cambridge, UK: Merlin Press, 1962).

*List of American Doctoral Dissertations Printed in 1912-38.* (Washington, DC: United States Library of Congress).

*List of Investigations into Police Conditions in New York City Made By State and City Authorities and Private Organizations, 1831-1948.* James Katsaros. (New York: Municipal Reference Library, 1949).

*List of References on Crime and Criminals in the U.S. with Special Reference to Statistics.* U.S. Library of Congress, Division of Bibliography. (Washington, DC: USLC, 1922).

*List of Works Relating to Criminology.* New York Public Library. (New York: NY Public Library, 1911).

*Lynch Law: An Investigation into the History of Lynching in the United States.* James Elbert Cutler. (Westport, CT: Greenwood Press, 1905).

*Mafia and Mafiosi.* Henner Hess. A history of the Mafia. (Lexington, MA: Lexington Books, 1970).

*Maintain the Right: The Early History of the Northwest Mounted Police, 1873-1900.* Ronald Atkin. Text with bibliography. (New York: Stein & Day, 1973).

*The Medieval Underworld.* Andrew McCall. (North Pomfret, VT: Hamish Hamilton, 1979).

*Memoirs of American Prisons: An Annotated Bibliography.* D. Suvack. Lists almost 800 references to works published between the late 1700s and 1978. (Metuchen, NJ: Scarecrow Press, 1979).

*Nineteenth Century Crime, Prevention, and Punishment.* J.J. Tobias. (Newton Abbot, UK: David and Charles Publishers, 1972).

*Peel.* Norman Gash. Text with bibliography. (Harlow, UK: Longman, 1976).

*Penology: The Evolution of Corrections in America.* George C. Killinger, et al. (eds.). (St. Paul, MN: West Publishing, 1979).

*Personality, Social Class, and Delinquency.* John J. Conger and Wilbur Miller. (New York: Wiley, 1966).

*Pioneering in Penology: The Amsterdam Houses of Correction in the Sixteenth and Seventeenth Centuries.* J. Thorsten Sellin. Text with bibliography. (Philadelphia: University of Pennsylvania Press, 1944).

*Pioneers in Criminology.* Hermann Mannheim (ed.). Text with bibliography. (New York: Quadrangle, 1960).

*Pioneers in Policing.* Philip John Stead (ed.). Text with bibliographies. (London: McGraw-Hill, 1977).

*The Police Encyclopedia.* 8 vols., H.L. Adam. (London: Waverley, 1925).

*Police and Prison Encyclopedia.* G.W. Hale. (Boston: Richardson, 1894).

*Poole's Index to Periodical Literature.* Indices by subject; almost 600,000 articles from 470 American and British periodicals during 1802-1907. (Mongolia, MA: Peter Smith Publications, 1963).

*Prison Books and Their Authors*. John A. Langford. (Detroit: Gale Research, 1970, reprint of 1861 edition).

*Professional Criminals of America*. (New York: Chelsea House, originally published in 1886, reprinted in 1969).

*The Queen's Peace: The Origins and Development of the Metropolitan Police 1829-1979*. David Ascoli. (London: Hamish Hamilton, 1979).

*The Reformers: An Historical Survey of Pioneer Experiments in the Treatment of Criminals*. Torsten Eriksson. (New York: Elsevier North Holland, 1976).

*The Repression of Crime: Studies in Historical Penology*, Harry E. Barnes. Text with bibliography. (New York: Doran, 1926).

*The Rise of Scotland Yard: A History of The Metropolitan Police*. Douglas G. Browne. Text with bibliography. (London: Harrap, 1956).

*Rural Disorder and Police Reform in Ireland, 1812-1836*. Galen Brocker. Text with bibliography. (Toronto, ON: University of Toronto Press, 1970).

*The San Quentin Story, as Told to Dean Jennings*. Clinton T. Duffy. (Westport, CT: Greenwood Press, 1950).

*Secret Societies in China In the Nineteenth and Twentieth Century*. Jean Chesneaux. (Ann Arbor: University of Michigan Press, 1972).

*A Selected Bibliography on Juvenile Delinquency*. (Washington, DC: United States Department of Health, Education and Welfare, Social Security Administration, Children's Bureau, 1954).

A *Short History of the British Police*. Sir Charles Reith. (London: Oxford University Press, 1948).

*Silent Witness: The Emergence of Scientific Criminal Investigations*. Published by The International Association of Chiefs of Police. The story of crime laboratory development and various investigative aids is told through articles written by key participants in events. Covers ballistics, forensic sciences, the lie detector and similar technological advances in 62 articles. (Gaithersburg, MD: International Association of Chiefs of Police, 1977).

*Sources for the Study of the Administration of Criminal Justice 1938-1948, A Selected Bibliography*. Dorothy C. Tompkins. (Montclair, NJ: Patterson-Smith, 1970, orig. 1949).

*State Reports on Correction and Punishment, Poverty, and Public Welfare, Prior to 1930*. In microform. (Westport, CT: Redgrave Information Resources, 1973).

*Statesman's Year Book: Statistical and Historical Annual of the States of the World*. (London and New York: Macmillan, 1864). (See Chapter 11, "Statistical Data," for further information on this reference.)

*The Stranglers: The Cult of Thuggee and Its Overthrow in British India*. George L. Bruce. Text with bibliography. (New York: Harcourt, Brace & World, 1969).

*Studies in Juvenile Delinquency: A Selected Bibliography*. (Washington, DC: United States Department of Health, Education and Welfare, Social Security Administration, Children's Bureau, 1956).

*The Super Crooks*. R.M. Williams. Short history, 1584-1973. (Chicago: Playboy Press, 1973).

*The Sutherland Papers*. Albert Cohen, Alfred Lindesmith and Karl Schuessler (eds.). Selected bibliography of Sutherland's writing. (Bloomington: Indiana University Press, 1956).

*A Systematic Source Book of Juvenile Delinquency*. Walter A. Lunden. (Pittsburgh: University of Pittsburgh, 1938).

*They Have No Rights: Dred Scott's Struggle for Freedom*. Walter Ehrlich. (Westport, CT: Greenwood Press, 1979).

*They Were in Prison: A History of the Pennsylvania Prison Society, 1787-1937, Formerly the Philadelphia Society for Alleviating the Miseries of Public Prison*. Negley K. Teeters. Text with bibliography. (Philadelphia: Winston, 1937).

*Thief Taker General: The Rise and Fall of Jonathan Wild*, Gerald Howson. Text with bibliography. (New York: St. Martin's Press, 1971).

*Thirty Years of Lynching in the United States, 1889-1918*. (Westport, CT: Greenwood Press, 1919).

*The Victorian Railway Murders*. Arthur and Mary Sellwood. (North Pomfret, VT: David and Charles Publishers, 1979).

*Violence in America: Historical and Comparative Perspectives*. Hugh Davis Graham and Ted R. Gurr. (Beverly Hills, CA: Sage Publications, Inc., 1979).

*Wayward Puritans: A Study In the Sociology of Deviance*. Kai T. Erikson. (New York: John Wiley, 1966).

## MISCELLANEOUS SOURCES

A valuable source of historical statistical data can be found in the early editions (1967 and later) of the Uniform Crime Reports (Washington, DC: United States Department of Justice, Federal Bureau of Investigation). However, there have been serious problems relating to the methods used to collect data for these reports. (see explanation under victimization surveys in Chapter 11, "Statistical Data.")

## Out-of-Print Books

Many older books that are desirable for historical research are also out of print and therefore no longer available from the publisher. There are, however, sources specifically designed to assist researchers in determining the availability of out-of-print books. Two of these sources are briefly described below.

*Guide to Reprints.* An annual cumulative guide, alphabetically arranged, to books, journals, and other materials which are available in reprint form. (Kent, CT: Guide to Reprints, Inc., 1996).

*Books on Demand.* Makes available approximately 84,000 selected books as on-demand reprints in the broad categories of General and Reference Works, Humanities, Social Sciences, Sciences, and Technology and Applied Science. (Ann Arbor, MI: University Microfilms International, 1994).

## Wickersham Commission Reports

Another good source of historical information regarding criminal justice topics can be found in the Wickersham Commission Reports, formerly known as the National Commission on Law Observance and Enforcement. The Commission, under the leadership of George W. Wickersham, a former Attorney General, studied all aspects of law enforcement. Each of the resultant 14 reports addresses a particular problem, and ways to improve the administration of justice are suggested. These reports, reprinted by Patterson-Smith of Montclair, New Jersey in 1968, are also available for sale in microfiche from the NCJRS. Each is briefly annotated below:

Report #1: Preliminary Report on Prohibition. Contains proposals for the improvement of enforcement of the prohibition laws. The scope of the problem and the administrative and legal difficulties are outlined.

Report #2: Enforcement of the Prohibition Laws of the United States. A review of difficulties encountered in enforcing prohibition laws, along with proposals for more effective enforcement. Liquor control is traced from colonial times. Many sources of illegal liquor are described, as are corruption, negative public opinion, economic difficulties, and the strain on the courts and penal institutions.

Report #3: Criminal Statistics. Discusses the importance of statistics and provides a survey of criminal statistics of the United States.

Report #4: Prosecution. Examines the administration of criminal justice in the United States during 1931. Included are recommendations concerning organizations, methods, and basic principles as well as information on the public prosecutor, the public defender, and the grand jury.

Report #5: Enforcement of the Deportation Laws of the United States. Examines the 1931 laws concerning the deportation of aliens. Included are recommendations for improvement of the system.

Report #6: Child Offender in the Federal System of Justice. Examines methods used by police, courts, probation, and penal institutions in dealing with minors who have violated federal laws. Recommendations include that the federal government recognize the concept of juvenile delinquency and that youthful offenders be dealt with at the local level.

Report #7: Progress Report on the Study of the Federal Courts. Concerned with the efficiency of the administration of justice in federal courts. Data presented regards the daily business of the federal courts, including the kinds and numbers of cases coming before these courts, the various statutes bringing those cases into those courts, the kinds of parties involved in such cases, the various methods and devices which were employed in the courts to delay or expedite trials, and the various dispositions made of the cases.

Report #8: Criminal Procedure. Presents a 1931 investigation into criminal procedure and includes recommendations for reorganization of the administration of federal law and court procedure.

Report #9: Penal Institutions, Probation, and Parole. Concerned with three principal methods of penal treatment: imprisonment, probation, and parole. Brings to light the inadequacies and inefficiencies of the prison system and recommends wage incentives for prisoners, educational opportunities in prisons, and indeterminate sentences for the development of a proper institutional program and the establishment of an adequate system of parole.

Report #10: Crime and the Foreign-Born. Analyzes the extent of criminal involvement by foreign-born Americans, their relations with the criminal justice system in general, and public attitudes toward the immigrant population and crime. Statistics relating nationality to crime rate, type of crime, and number of arrests in various cities is presented. Various factors which could cause foreigners to violate the law, but which do not affect native Americans, such as language, foreign law and customs, are analyzed.

Report #11: Lawlessness in Law Enforcement. Illegal law enforcement practices such as the use of cruel treatment by police to force confessions of guilt from prisoners are examined. Other violations discussed include actions which jeopardize personal liberty, the right to bail, the presump-

tion of innocence until conviction of guilt by due process, and the right to employ counsel. Actual cases of prisoner beatings and torture by police are documented, and actions taken by cities to eliminate unlawful treatment by police are describe.

Report #12: Cost of Crime. Presents data on economic loss as a result of crime, and analyzes the problem of determining the cost of crime.

Report #13: Causes of Crime, Volumes 1 and 2. Morphological, physiological, mental, social, economic, and political factors in crime are explored in the first volume. The second volume deals with the relationship between unemployment and crime, along with the special problems of the black population as it relates to both work and crime.

Report #14: Police: Conditions in the United States. Examines the state of police departments in 1931. Deficiencies in organization, recruitment, training, and performance are given special attention. Prevention of crime as a recently recognized responsibility of the police officer is discussed, as is the status of the woman police officer and her contribution to crime prevention.

Report #15: The Mooney Billings Report. Suppressed by the Wickersham Commission. (New York: Gotham House, 1932.)

## John Jay College of Criminal Justice Library Special Collections

One of the finest sources of historical information on criminal justice is located at the special collections section of The Library of The John Jay College of Criminal Justice in New York City. Here, some of the most important works ever compiled in criminal justice can be found. Contact the Chief Librarian for additional information, and permission to use this material. A partial annotated list of some of these special collections is as follows:

*American Correctional Association, Annual Congress on Corrections.* The papers and debates that make up the proceedings of this Association document the gradual evolution of the science of penology from the point of view of both the scholar and the practitioner. The first four indexes covering the period 1870-1946 have been reprinted in one volume. Discussions as well as formal presentations are indexed.

*Anti-Saloon League of America, 1880, 1894-1938.* "The Saloon Must Go" was the motto of this nonpartisan pressure organization which sought to mobilize church forces against the liquor traffic. The collection includes correspondence, financial records, historical sketches, audits, news clippings and legal briefs. Records have been arranged according to provenance except with material in the Press Release, Book Reviews, and Press Statement sub-

series. The Guide to the Microfilm Edition of Temperance and Prohibition Papers contains background information on the League plus a general description of the Series and a detailed reel description.

*Bureau of Social Hygiene: Project and Research Files — 1913-1940.* The working papers of one of the earliest privately funded social science research institutions in the United States document the approach of experts to subjects of interest to the criminal justice researcher. Among the documented studies are Abraham Flexner's study of commercialized prostitution and Raymond Fosdick's study of police systems in the United States and Europe. A hidden treasure is Reel 9 which documents efforts during 1927-28 to establish a system of uniform crime reporting. The Guide provides a brief history of the Bureau and describes the organization and contents of the files.

*Center for Knowledge in Criminal Justice Planning. Records. (1974-78)* Spec. Coll. X 102. (Approximately 75 linear feet). The "Center" was established in 1975 to work on an LEAA funded follow-up to the provocative and controversial book, *The Effectiveness of Correctional Treatment* (1975) by Douglas Lipton, Robert Martinson and Judith Wilks. Martinson and Wilks were, respectively, Director and Associate Director of the follow-up project. The materials in the collection include scattered files from a 1974 project on deterrence in which Martinson was involved, files associated with *The Effectiveness of Correctional Treatment*, and the administrative and working files of the "Center" during the grant period. For additional information, and permission to use the material in this collection, see the Chief Librarian.

*COINTELPRO: The Counterintelligence Program of the FBI.* This FBI program was established to "expose, disrupt, and neutralize" extremist and radical groups perceived as threatening to the internal security of the U.S. The files contain intensive investigative reports made during the 1960s of the American Communist and Socialist Workers parties, the Ku Klux Klan, the Black Panthers, the SDS, plus many others. The material is arranged under such operational headings as Black Nationalist Hate Groups, White Hate Groups, New Left, etc. These files are revealing of both the organizations investigated and the FBI.

*G. Tyler Mairs (fl. 1914-1951).* In addition to correspondence between G.T. Mairs, Fingerprint examiner of the Magistrate's Court (Brooklyn), and students and specialists in dactyloscopy, this collection contains charts, photographs, and newspaper clippings which provide valuable information for the study of criminal identification by fingerprints. Finding aid in preparation.

*International Penitentiary Congress, 1st-9th (1872-1925). International Penal and Prison Congress, 10th-12th (1930-1950).* Transactions of the original congresses have been reprinted, including official documents, discussions, and papers presented. This material demonstrates on the international level an interchange of thought and experience similar to that found in the proceedings of the American Correctional Association. English summaries are provided where the presentation was not in English. Accompanied by subject and name indexes.

*John Howard.* Original works by and about this eighteenth century English prison reformer whose assiduous studies of British prisons and European lazarettos prompted significant reform legislation. The biographies are either by contemporaries or by close contemporaries. In addition to detailed descriptions of prison conditions, Howard's works contain exquisite plates of the facades and floor plans of institutions visited. Also included are tables indicating the number of prisoners by type of crime, punishments, executions, pardons, fees charged, and so on. Access is provided through the card catalog.

*Lewis E. Lawes (1883-1947).* Papers. Spec. Coll. X 101 (13 Boxes). Lawes was best known for his 21 years as Warden of Sing Sing, and for his ability to keep himself and his ideas in the public eye. The collection includes extensive correspondence with political and cultural figures, photographs, several volumes of Sing Sing publications, and over 1,000 pages of scrapbook material dealing with crime in general and Lawes' career in particular.

*Newgate Calendar of Malefactor's Bloody Register* (5 volumes). An eighteenth century publication of illustrated true sagas of the "most notorious criminals (of both sexes)" from 1700 to 1773. It was designed, in part, to guide the young of eighteenth century England, Scotland, and Ireland. The name index includes a list of all the capital convictions at the Old Bailey for that time period.

*New York City Court of General Sessions.* Typewritten transcripts of the complete proceedings of some 2,700 criminal trials from the 1880s through the 1920s. These transcripts contain primary material important not only in the study of the interaction between persons accused of crimes and the criminal justice system but in the study of immigration patterns and urban development during this period. A preliminary index has been prepared for each transcript indicating defendant's name, judge, prosecuting attorney, defense attorney, and charge. The library has received an NEH grant to preserve the transcripts on microfilm and produce and index. Finding aid in preparation.

*New York (State), Legislature, Joint Committee on Crime, Its Causes, Control and Effect on Society. The Voices of Organized Crime.* This cassette contains conversations of actual voices of members of organized crime syndicates taped by various police and prosecutive agencies throughout New York during the years 1963 to 1965. Conversations refer to the activities of organized crime — gambling, loansharking, murder, grand larceny, fraud, extortion — and its methods of operation — mobs, internal security, intelligence, counter-intelligence and discipline. The cassette is accompanied by printed material identifying the voices, transcribing the conversations, and describing their usefulness in obtaining indictments. The published Report of Legislative Recommendations by the Committee provides complementary research material.

*Police Department Annual Reports.* Beginning with the historic Bruce Smith Collection, the library has assembled reports representing some one hundred cities and counties. A significant portion of the reports date from the early part of the century. The library is engaged in a project to update the collection. Access is provided through the public catalog by department name. For ease of research, shelf arrangement is alphabetical within jurisdiction.

*Police Department Surveys.* The collection of police department surveys not only contains a more detailed description of specific departments than is found in annual reports but also provides recommendations from experts to improve operations. Consultants for these surveys include Bruce Smith, August Vollmer, and Donal MacNamara. Access is provided through the Public catalog by department name and by the subject heading POLICE SURVEYS.

*Police Handbooks.* A collection of well-worn pocket size handbooks and manuals containing the rules and regulations of forty-five police departments in the United States and Great Britain, 1816-1934.

*Public Order, Discontent and Protest in England, 1820-1850.* Series I: 1820-1830. A collection of letters, papers, and reports concerning crime and public order from the Home Office manuscript collection held in the Public Record Office. The documents contain information on criminal cases involving persons in the King's service, disturbances in the countryside, turmoil in the cotton mills, and plans to deal with the increased political agitation. This material is particularly useful for the study of public unrest in the years before the Great Reform Bill of 1832. Although no external finding aid is available, a contents list precedes the items on each reel.

*Richard Louis Dugdale, 1841-1883.* Documents written in Dugdale's hand have recently been received from the New York Correctional Association. Large worksheets from which Dugdale compiled tables for his studies contain raw data on over 800 individuals. The handwritten preface to an early edition of *The Jukes* describes the preparatory reading and circumstances which led to his conclusions about the relation of family history to crime and poverty. Also included are stray pages discussing criminal characteristics.

*Richard O. Hankey, 1915-1979.* Recently acquired from the University of Oregon are the correspondence and subject files of this well-known criminal justice educator and past president of the Academy of Criminal Justice Sciences. The files document Hankey's attempts to bridge practical law enforcement experience and the study of law enforcement and police administration. The files contain evidence of Hankey's association with August Vollmer and O.W. Wilson. Also included are documents from the California Peace Officers Training Program which reveal the state of police training in California during the 1950s and 1960s.

*State Reports on Corrections and Public Welfare, Prior to 1930.* This collection of documents from eleven of the oldest and most populous states contains valuable raw data available in no other sources, the United States census notwithstanding. It consists primarily of annual reports of state departments, boards, and commissions. Although the bulk of the reports focus on the first three decades of the twentieth century, some go back as far as 1837. Not only can social agencies be studied, but trends and attitudes can

be traced. Topics covered include prison reform, child abuse, chain gangs, poverty.

*State Reports on Corrections and Punishment, Poverty and Public Welfare, Prior to 1930.* In Special Collections. Consult Catalog for call numbers of individual reports. This is a collection of over 2,500 microfiche containing reports from state agencies in California, New York, Ohio, and seven other states. Subjects covered include prisons, orphanages, child abuse, rehabilitation, chain gangs, and insanity. Among the reports are: California Board of Charities and Corrections, 1903-22; California Prison Directors Report, 1851-1879; Colorado State Board of Pardons, 1893-1920; Georgia Prison Commission, 1897-1930; Indiana State Probation Department, 1923-30; Massachusetts Agent for Aiding Discharged Prisoners, 1846-1929; Massachusetts State Board of Lunacy and Charity, 1879-1898; New York State Commission to Examine Laws Relating to Child Welfare, 1921-1926; New York State State Prisons, 1848-1926; Pennsylvania Mother's Assistant Fund, 1917-1929.

*Theatre for the Forgotten.* Theatre for the Forgotten is a nonprofit drama group that uses the theatre as a rehabilitation tool in work with prison inmates and troubled youth. Since it was founded in 1967 to perform prison shows, it has grown to include prison acting workshops and inmate productions. In 1975 it initiated children's theatre workshops for youthful offenders and the emotionally disturbed. This collection contains videotapes and printed documentation of TFTF Alternative Educational Drama Program. A manual describes the contents of the tapes and provides suggestions for their use.

*United States Census Publications in Microform: Part I, 1820-1945: Section III. Dependent, Defective, and Delinquent Classes.* Microfiche Cabinet. Consult the reference librarian. Among the census publications in this collection are: Prisoners, 1904, 1910, 1922, etc.; Crime and Mental Disease, 1933; Juvenile Delinquency, 1933; Dependent and Delinquent Classes, 1933-45; Paupers in Almshouses, 1904, 1910; Insane and Feeble-Minded, 1904, 1910, 1923; Directory of Institutions, 1919; summary of State Laws, 1913.

*William H. Bell: Diary.* The diary of this New York City policeman and inspector of second-hand dealers and junk shops chronicles his activities during 1850-1851. From his undercover existence in the city's slum districts he acquired an intimate knowledge of crime and poverty. The text is a stream of impressions with an occasional aside, free of the moralizing which often clutters accounts of the poor. It is accompanied by Sean Wilentz's article from the History Workshop Journal which provides background to the daily "jottings."

## Indexes to Nineteenth-Century General Interest Popular Periodicals

Among the hundreds of popular general interest periodicals published in the nineteenth century, many were concerned with issues of crime, justice, and law and order. The keys to locating these articles, including most of those listed at the beginning of this chapter, are these two indexes:

*19th Century Readers' Guide to Periodical Literature.* 2 vols. Covering only the period from 1880 to 1900, this index was actually compiled in 1944 and is identical in format and indexing policies to the *Readers' Guide* with which you are familiar. (New York: H.W. Wilson, 1944.)

*Poole's Index to Periodical Literature, 1802-1906.* 6 vols. Rev. ed., reprinted. Mr. Poole began compiling his index in 1848. The third edition of the basic volume, covering 1802 to 1881, was published in 1882 and is the basis for the reprint edition. Although not difficult to use, the indexing does not have the consistency or uniformity which we have come to expect in periodical indexes; use with care and imagination. (Gloucester, MA: Peter Smith, 1958.)

## Nineteenth-Century Criminal Justice Periodicals

*Journal of Prison Discipline and Philanthropy. 1845-1920.* Microfilm. Printed in Pennsylvania, this was a substantial and long-lived publication, with close ties to organizations devoted to prison reform. Although a nineteenth-century tone of moral uplift is clearly evident, especially in the early period, the general orientation of this periodical reflects an increasingly professional outlook. It contains complete reprints of many official documents and summaries of others, original articles, and reprints of articles, sermons, and speeches, as well as news reports of interest to its readers. Items are from all over the Old World, as well as the New. (Wilmington, DE: Scholarly Resources, 1974).

*Moral Advocate: A Monthly Publication on War, Duelling, Capital Punishment, and Prison Discipline.* Vols. 1-3, March 1821-1824. Microfilm. A short-lived publication whose basic tone is reflected in its title, this was largely the work of one man and was published in Mt. Pleasant, Ohio. (Ann Arbor: University Microfilms International.)

*National Police Gazette.* 1845-1906. Microfilm. Originally, a gazette was a government journal reporting official news. The concept of a gazette as a way of officially reporting crimes goes back at least to eighteenth-century England; in the nineteenth century the term gazette was adopted by commercial publishers. For some years the *National Police Gazette* did contain official lists of army deserters, but it was part of the sensationalist crime press and never a government document. The value of this periodical for the researcher is as a picture of popular attitudes toward crime and sensationalism. In the first few years emphasis was placed on violent crime and criminal biographies, but there was a gradual movement toward greater concern with prostitution, and other salacious topics. Occasional appearance of a police blotter and some statistics could be useful in getting a picture of types and numbers of reported crimes. The journal is illustrated with woodcuts, some of which are exceedingly fine. Some sample headlines give the flavor of the Gazette: "A Brutal Assault; A Gang of Grain Laborers Attack One of Their Number; He is Beaten Unmercifully, and His Ear Bit Off; The Perpetrators of the Outrage Still at Large" (December 8, 1866, page 3); "A New York Pugilist Set Upon by Rowdies; He is Beaten and Almost Cut to Pieces in a Brothel; Not Expected to Survive" (September 21, 1867, page 3); "Audacity's Acme; A Wealthy Lady Assaulted, Garroted and Robbed of Her Diamond Earring [sic] on Fifth Avenue; In Broad Daylight; Amid a Throng of People, Who, with Her Companion are Paralyzed by the Bold Attack of the Thief" (March 1, 1879, page 11). (Ann Arbor: University Microfilms International.)

## Indexes to Nineteenth-Century Scholarly Periodicals

The development of scholarly disciplines in the nineteenth century and the related development of publications written exclusively by and for academics provide a rich history in the related fields of criminal justice. Many of these early academic periodical articles can be located through use of the sets described below. Articles written during the period you are researching can be considered primary sources if they document contemporary events. They are secondary sources if they describe events of earlier periods.

*CRIS: Combined Retrospective Index to Journals in History, 1838-1974.* 11 vols. (Washington, DC: Carrollton Press, 1977).

*CRIS: Combined Retrospective Index to Journals in Political Science, 1886-1974.* 8 vols. (Washington, DC: Carrollton Press, 1977).

*CRIS: Combined Retrospective Index to Journals in Sociology, 1895-1974*, 6 vols. (Washington, DC: Carrollton Press, 1978).

# 16

# Special Libraries

Several state and federally supported libraries maintain special or unique collections of criminal justice literature. The most famous of these is the Library of Congress—probably the largest library in the world—with comprehensive collections of literature and other materials in all fields of knowledge. The services of the Library of Congress are described below, followed by an alphabetical listing and brief summary of the holdings of other libraries having comprehensive, special, or unique collections of criminal justice materials.

## THE LIBRARY OF CONGRESS

The Library of Congress was established in 1800 as a reference library for members of Congress, and although its primary role is to serve Congress, it is available for public use as well. The Library's holdings include over 74 million items on virtually every subject, and new items come in at the rate of more than 7,000 per working day. This vast collection consists of 18 million books, 33 million manuscripts, 3.5 million maps and atlases, 4 million pieces of music, 9 million prints and photographs, a half-million sound recordings, 250,000 reels of motion pictures, and 3 million pieces of microform. Rare books, prints and maps, and Stradivarius violins are among the items on display.

For those who cannot visit the Library in person, a number of special, no-charge services are offered. The use of books and other academic materials are made available to public and academic libraries through interlibrary loan. A photo duplication service allows the public to purchase by mail, photographs, photostats, facsimile prints, and microfilms of research materials not subject to the copyright law. Written requests should be sent to: General Reading Room Division, Library of Congress, Washington, D.C. 20540.

Computer printouts of sources pertaining to a given subject, and searches for new titles and legislative histories can take only a few minutes when the computer terminals are used. Anyone can request a computer printout by writing to the Correspondence Section, General Reading Room Division, Library of Congress, Washington, D.C. 20540.

The Library can assist in locating literature or direct the request for information to an organization or agency that can provide the specific answers. The National Referral Center, sponsored by the Library of Congress, provides this type of service. The Center refers those who need answers to specific questions to resources or agencies that have the information and are willing to share it with others. A subject-indexed computerized file of 13,000 organizations is used by the referral service. Requests for this service should describe clearly and precisely the information needed. Inquiries should be directed to the Library of Congress, Science and Technology Division, Washington, D.C. 20540.

The Library of Congress has many divisions, including the copyright office, division for the blind and physically handicapped, general reference and bibliography division, geography and map division, law library, microfilm reading room, music division, prints and photographs division, plus several others.

## BOOKS AND DIRECTORIES OF LIBRARIES

*American Library Directory*, 43rd ed. Biennial. "A classified list of libraries in the United States and Canada, with personnel and statistical data, plus a selected list of libraries around the world." Lists 24,100 libraries in the United States, and 2,285 in Canada. (New York: R.R. Bowker, 1990/1991).

*The Bowker Annual of Library and Book Trade Information*, 35th ed. Annual. Statistical and directory information for United States and other countries; also covers library and book trade developments and trends during preceding year. Index. (New York: R.R. Bowker, 1990/1991).

*Directory of Special Libraries and Information Centers*, 13th ed. Brigitte T. Darnay (ed.). Lists more than 13,000 libraries and information centers. Semiannual supplements. (Detroit: Gale Research, 1989).

*Library and Information Science Abstracts*. Bimonthly. Supersedes *Library Science Abstracts*, 1950-68. International coverage; abstracts in English from about 200 journals in field of library science and technology. Classified arrangement; author-subject index cumulates annually. (London, UK:Library Association, 1969-date).

*Library Literature*. Bimonthly with annual and biennial cumulations. Subject index to domestic and foreign materials on library and information science. (New York: H.W. Wilson, 1934-date).

*World Guide to Libraries*, 9th ed. Gives addresses, indicates subject specialties and size for 36,000 public, academic, and special libraries in 158 countries. Subject index. (New York: R.R. Bowker, 1989).

## Catalogs of Other Libraries

Los Angeles Public Library. Municipal Reference Library. Catalog of the Police Library of the Los Angeles Public Library. (Boston: G.K. Hall, 1980).

The Information Resources Center. American Society for Industrial Security. Information Resources Coordinator, 1655 North Fort Myer Drive, Suite 1200, Arlington, VA 22209.

University of Cambridge. Institute of Criminology. The Library Catalogue of the Radzinowicz Library. (Boston: G.K. Hall, 1979). 6 Vols.

National Archive of Criminal Justice Data. Inter-University Consortium for Political and Social Research, P.O. Box 1248, Ann Arbor, MI 48106.

New York Public Library. Research Libraries. Dictionary Catalog of the Research Libraries. A cumulative list of authors, titles and subjects representing books and book-like materials added to the collections since January 1, 1971. New York, 1971 to date.

## CRIMINAL JUSTICE INFORMATION EXCHANGE

The National Institute of Justice/NCJRS is the sponsor of the Criminal Justice Information Exchange (CJIE) Group, an informal, cooperative association of libraries serving the criminal justice community. It aims to foster communication and cooperation among member libraries and enhance user services. Member libraries improve services in the criminal justice area through information exchange and interlibrary loan. In addition, group members furnish criminal justice patrons with information about CJIE collections, policies, and services.

The National Criminal Justice Reference Service (NCJRS), a CJIE member, coordinates the group and produces the CJIE Directory. NCJRS is an international clearinghouse of justice information sponsored by the National Institute of Justice (NIJ), a research arm of the Department of Justice. NCJRS also maintains or supports databases for other Department of Justice agencies and operates their clearinghouses. These include the Juvenile Justice Clearinghouse, the Justice Statistics Clearinghouse, the National Victims Resource Center, the NIJ AIDS Clearinghouse, and the Bureau of Justice Assistance Clearinghouse.

For more information about participation in the Criminal Justice Information Exchange Group, contact:

CJIE Coordinator
NCJRS
Box 6000
Rockville, MD 20850
(800) 851-3420
Web Site: ncjsr.com/

## Member Libraries

*Abt Associates, Inc. Library*
55 Wheeler Street
Cambridge, MA 02138-1168
(617) 492-7100
E-mail: webmaster@abtassoc.com

*American Bar Association Law Library*
740 15th St. NW
Washington, DC 20005
(202) 662-1010
Arizona State University
Hayden Library
Tempe, AZ 85287-1006
(602) 965-3417

*Armed Forces Institute of Pathology, Ash Library*
Bldg. 54, Room 4077
Washington, DC 20306-6000
(202) 782-1832

*Baltimore Police Department Library*
210 Guilford Ave.
Baltimore, MD 21202
(410) 396-2518

*Benedictine College Library*
1020 N Second St.
Atchison, KS 66002-1499
(913) 367-5340, ext. 2510

*Bowling Green State University Libraries*
Jerome Library
Bowling Green State University
Bowling Green, OH 43403-0170
(419) 372-2856

*California State University, Los Angeles*
*Government Publications Section, Library*
5151 State University Drive
Los Angeles, CA 90032-8300
(213) 736-3632

*Erie Bureau of Police*
City of Erie, Pennsylvania
626 State Street
Erie, PA 16501

*FBI Academy Library*
Quantico, VA 22135
(703) 640-1135

*Federal Judicial Center Information Services*
One Columbus Circle NE
Washington, DC 20002-8003
(202) 273-4153

*Federal Bureau of Prisons, Central Office Library*
320 First Street NW
Washington, DC 20534
(202) 307-3029
E-mail: dlomax@bop.gov

*George Mason University*
*Fenwick Library*
4400 University Drive
Fairfax, VA 22030-4444
(703) 993-2223

*Georgia Department of Corrections*
*Reference Resource Center*
Two Martin Luther King Drive SE
Atlanta, GA 30334-4900
(404) 656-4593

*Governors State University Library*
University Park, IL 60466-0975
(708) 534-4111
E-mail: r-bradbe@govst.edu

*Harvard University Library*
79 John F. Kennedy Street
Cambridge, MA 02138
(617) 495-3650

*Hennepin County Law Library*
C-2451 Government Center
Minneapolis, MN 55487
(612) 348-3022
E-mail: hclawlib@maroon.tc.edu

*Indiana Law Enforcement Academy*
David F. Allen Memorial Learning Resources Center
Plainfield, IN 46168-8478
(317) 272-4818
E-mail: wtpl@avonlibrary.org

*John Jay College of Criminal Justice, Library*
899 Tenth Avenue
New York, NY 10019
(212) 237-8265
E-mail: lesjj@cumyum.cuny.edu

*Kansas State Library*
State Capitol Bldg.
300 SW Tenth St.
Topeka, KS 66612-1593
(913) 296-3296
E-mail: duanj@ink.org

*Lamar University, Gray Library*
LU Station
Box 10021
Beaumont, TX 77710
(409) 880-8118

*Law Library of Louisiana*
Supreme Court Building
301 Loyola Avenue
New Orleans, LA 70112
(504) 568-5705

*Maryland State Law Library*
Courts of Appeal Building
First Floor
361 Rowe Boulevard
Annapolis, MD 21401-1697
(410) 260-1430
DC metro area: 858-8041 x3395
E-mail: mdlawstf@epflz.epflbato.org

*Maryland State Police Academy Library*
Department of Public Safety and Correctional Service
201 Reisterstown Road
Pikesville, MD 21208-3899
(410) 653-4357

*Mercyhurst College, Hammermill Library*
501 E. 38th St.
Erie, PA 16546
(814) 825-0234
E-mail: rstrausb@paradise.staff.mercy.edu

*Michigan Department of State Police*
Law Enforcement Resource Center
7426 North Canal Road
Lansing, MI 48913
(517) 322-1976
E-mail: lepiors@mlc.lib.mi.us

*Missouri State Library*
600 W Main
P.O. Box 387
Jefferson City, MO 65102
(573) 751-3615
E-mail: libref@mail.more.net

*Municipal Reference Library, Police Branch*
City Hall, Room 1004
Chicago, IL 60602-1276
(312) 744-4992
E-mail: jmalden@ci.chi.ilus.

*National Center for State Courts Library*
Box 8798
Williamsburg, VA 23187-8798
(757) 259-1819
E-mail: elow@ncsc.dni.us

*National Institute of Justice/NCJRS*
Box 6000
Rockville, MD 20849-6000
(800) 851-3420; (301)579-5500
E-mail: askncjrs@ncjrs.org

*Nebraska Legislative Reference Library*
*Legislative Research Division*
State Capitol
Box 94945
Lincoln, NE 68509-4945
(402) 471-2221

*Nebraska Library Commission*
1200 N Street
Suite 120
Lincoln, NE 68508-2023
(800) 307-2665

*North Carolina Justice Academy*
*Learning Resource Center*
P.O. Drawer 99
Salemburg, NC 28385
(910) 525-4154, Ext. 269
E-mail: dstacy@mail.jus.state.nc.us

*North East Multi-Regional Training*
Instructors' Library
1 Smoke Tree Plaza
Suite 111
North Aurora, IL 60542-1718
(630) 896-8860

*Northeast Louisiana University*
*Sandel Library*
Admin. Bldg. 2-104
700 University Ave.
Monroe, LA 71209-0101
(318) 342-1215
E-mail: brwall@alpha.nlu.edu

Northeastern University Library
400 Huntington Avenue
Boston, MA 02115
(617) 373-3332

Oklahoma State University Library
Stillwater, OK 74078
(405) 744-6540

Prison Fellowship Ministries
Information Center
P.O. Box 17500-0500
Washington, DC 20041
(703) 478-0100

Public Information Representatives
Oklahoma Department of Libraries
200 North East 18th Street
Oklahoma City, OK 73105-3298
(405) 521-2502

Rutgers University—NCCD Collection
S.I. Newhouse Center for Law & Justice
15 Washington Street
4th Floor
Newark, NJ 07102-3192
(973) 648-5964

St. Louis Police Library
315 South Tucker Boulevard
St. Louis, MO 63102
(314) 444-5581

Sam Houston State University
Newton Gresham Library
Sam Houston State University Library
Box 2281
Huntsville, TX 77341-2281
(409) 294-1613

State Library of Florida
R.A. Gray Building
Tallahassee, FL 32399-0250
(850) 487-2651

State Library of Louisiana
701 N. Street
Baton Rouge, LA 70821-5232
(800) 543-4702, (504) 342-4944

State Library of Ohio
65 South Front Street
Columbus, OH 43215-4163
(614) 644-7061
E-mail: sloinfo@mail.slonet.ohio.gov

State Library of Pennsylvania
Library Services Division
Main Capitol Bldg.
Room 157
Harrisburg, PA 17120-0030
(717) 787-6120
E-mail: eandrews@os.pasen.gov

Tiffin University, Pfeiffer Library
139 Miami Street
Tiffin, OH 44883-2162
(419) 448-3435
E-mail: ffleet@tiffin.edu

Troy State University Library
University Avenue
Troy, AL 36082
(334) 670-3266
E-mail: tsutxs@asntsu.asnnet.Dean

University at Albany, State University of New York
1400 Washington Avenue
Albany, NY 12222-0001
(518) 442-3568
E-mail: mb801@cnsvax.albany.edu

University of Central Texas Library
P.O. Box 1800
Killeen, TX 76540-1800
(254) 526-1237
E-mail: nschnitz@ctcd.cc.tx.us

University of Detroit Mercy Library
4001 West McNichols Rd.
Detroit, MI 48219-0900
(313) 993-1090

University of Iowa Library
College of Law
Iowa City, IA 52242-1420
(319) 335-5867
E-mail: lib-ref@uiowa.edu

University of Maryland
McKeldin Library
College Park, MD 20742
(301) 405-9128
E-mail: clowry@deans.umd.edu

The University of Mississippi, Law Library
University, MS 38677
(601) 232-6824

*University of Nebraska—Lincoln*
*Don L. Love Library*
Box 880410
Lincoln, NE 68588-0410
(402) 472-2526
E-mail: joang@unlib.unl.edu

*University of New Haven*
*Peterson Library*
300 Orange Avenue
West Haven, CT 06516
(203) 932-7190

*University of North Carolina at Charlotte*
*J. Murray Atkins Library*
9201 University City Blvd.
Charlotte, NC 28223-0001
(704) 547-2221

*University of Southern Mississippi*
*Cook Memorial Library*
Southern Station, Box 5053
Hattiesburg, MS 39406-5053
(601) 266-4241
E-mail: eddie.williams@usm.edu

*University of Tennessee at Chattanooga, Library*
615 McCallie Ave.
Chattanooga, TN 37403-2598
(423) 755-4506

*University of Washington*
*Marian Gould Gallagher Law Library*
1100 NE Campus Pkwy.
Seattle, WA 98195-6617
(206) 545-4089

*Virginia Commonwealth University*
*James Branch Cabell Library*
P.O. Box 842033
901 Park Avenue
Richmond, VA 23284-2033
(804) 828-1110

*Virginia Department of Criminal*
*Justice Services Library*
805 East Broad Street
Richmond, VA 23219
(804) 786-8478

*Virginia Department of Corrections*
*Academy for Staff Development*
1900 River Rd. W
Crozier, VA 23039
(800) 784-8641
E-mail: aellis@leo.usla.edu

*Washington State Library*
Box 42460
Olympia, WA 98504-2460
(360) 753-5590

*Westfield State College Library*
Westfield, MA 01086
(413) 572-5231

## DEPOSITORY LIBRARIES

Depository libraries are libraries that are designated to receive government publications. In return, the libraries must keep and care for the materials they receive. Each congressional district in the United States can have two depository libraries, most of which were designated as such years ago. Also, all land grant colleges are depository libraries, regardless of whether there are already two in that congressional district. Subject matter of the government documents available varies from library to library because each one is designated to receive materials from certain subject categories. However, there are also regional depository libraries in addition to those described above, and each regional depository library receives copies of all materials distributed. Thus, any regional depository library would have a wealth of government publications in criminal justice, or any other subject in which one might be interested. The following is a list of 50 regional depository libraries.

*Auburn University at Montgomery*
*Library, Documents Department*
Box 244023
Montgomery, AL 36193
(334) 244-3200

*University of Alabama Library*
*Documents Department*
Box 870266
Tuscaloosa, AL 35487-0266
(205) 348-7561

*Arizona State Library*
*Department of Library Archives and Public Records*
State Capitol Building, Rm 200
1700 W. Washington
Phoenix, AZ 85007
(602) 542-4035
Email: services@dlapr.lib.az.us

*University of Arizona Library*
*Government Document Department*
Rm A-349
Tucson, AZ 85721
(520) 621-2101

*Arkansas State Library*
*Documents Service Section*
One Capitol Mall
Little Rock, AR 72201
(501) 682-1527

*California State Library*
*Government Publications Section*
2000 State University Dr.
Sacramento, CA 95819-6039
(916) 278-5679

*University of Colorado Library*
*Government Publications Library*
Campus Box 184
Boulder, CO 80309-0184
(303) 492-0184
E-mail: james.williams@colorado.edu

*Connecticut State Library*
231 Capitol Avenue
Hartford, CT 06106
(860) 566-4777
E-mail: lnewell@csl.cstateu.edu

*Denver Public Library*
*Government Publications Division*
10 W. 14th Ave. Pkwy.
Denver, CO 80204-2749
(303) 640-6200

*University of Florida Libraries*
*Documents Department*
Library West
Box 117001
Gainesville, FL 32611
(352) 392-0342

*University of Georgia Libraries*
*Government Documents Department*
Athens, GA 30602
(706) 542-0621

*University of Hawaii*
*Hamilton Library*
*Government Documents Collection*
2550 The Mall
Honolulu, HI 96822
(808) 956-7203
E-mail: haak@hawaii,edu

*University of Iowa Libraries*
*Government Publications Department*
Iowa City, IA 52242-1420
(319) 335-5867
E-mail: lib-ref@uiowa.edu

*University of Idaho Library*
*Documents Section*
Moscow, ID 83844-2350
(208) 885-6534
E-mail: libadmin@idui.csru.uidaho.edu

*Illinois State Library*
3005 Second St.
Springfield, IL 62701-1976
(217) 782-7596, (800) 665-5596

*Indiana State Library*
*Serials Section*
140 North Senate Avenue
Indianapolis, IN 46204-2296
(317) 232-3684, (800) 622-4970

*University of Kansas, Watson Library*
*Spencer Research Library*
Documents Collection
Lawrence, KS 66045-2800
(913) 864-3956

*University of Kentucky Libraries*
*Government Publications Department*
Lexington, KY 40506-0456
(606) 257-0500

*Louisiana State University*
*Middleton Library*
*Government Documents Department*
Baton Rouge, LA 70803-3300
(504) 388-2217
E-mail: lbydir@lsuvm.sncc.lsu.edu

*Louisiana Technical University*
*Prescott Memorial Library*
*Documents Department*
Box 10408
Ruston, LA 71272-0046
(318) 257-3355
E-mail: stemzel@;atech.edu

*Boston Public Library*
*Documents Receipts*
700 Boylston St.
Boston, MA 02117-0286
(617) 536-5400

*University of Maryland*
*McKeldin Library*
*Documents Division*
College Park, MD 20742
(301) 405-9128
E-mail: clowry@deans.umd.edu

*University of Maine*
*Raymond H. Fogler Library*
*Tri-State Regional Documents Depository*
Box 5729
Orono, ME 04469
(207) 581-1661
E-mail: garwood@maine.maine.edu

*Detroit Public Library*
5201 Woodward Avenue
Detroit, MI 48202-4007
(313) 833-1000
E-mail: is@detroit.lib.mi.us

*Library of Michigan*
*Government Documents*
P.O. Box 30007
Lansing, MI 48909
(517) 373-1580

*University of Minnesota*
*Wilson Library*
*Government Publications*
309 19th Avenue South
Minneapolis, MN 55455-0414
(612) 624-4520

*University of Mississippi*
*J.D. Williams Library*
*Documents Department*
University, MS 38677
(601) 232-5857

*University of Montana*
*Maurene & Mike Mansfield Library*
*Documents Division*
Missoula, MT 59812
(406) 243-6860

*University of North Carolina at*
*Chapel Hill Library*
*BA/SS Documents Division*
CB3900
Chapel Hill, NC 27514-8890
(919) 962-1301

*North Dakota State University Library*
*Government Documents Department*
Box 5599
Fargo, ND 58105-5599
(701) 231-8886

*University of Nebraska*
*D.L. Love Memorial Library*
*Documents Department*
Box 880410
Lincoln, NE 68588-0410
(402) 472-2526
E-mail: joang@unlib.unl.edu

*Newark Public Library*
*U.S. Documents Division*
Five Washington Street
P.O. Box 630
Newark, NJ 07101-0630
(973)733-7800

*University of New Mexico General Library*
*Government Publications and Maps Department*
Albuquerque, NM 87131
(505) 277-4241
E-mail: cwatral@unm.edu

*New Mexico State Library*
325 Don Gaspar Avenue
Santa Fe, NM 87501-2777
(505) 827-3800

*University of Nevada—Reno Library*
*Government Publications Department*
Reno, NV 89557-0044
(702) 784-6500
E-mail: stevenz@admin.unr.edu

*New York State Library*
*Documents Control*
Sixth Floor
Cultural Education Center
Empire State Plaza
Albany, NY 12230
(518) 474-5930

*State Library of Ohio*
*Documents Section*
65 South Front Street
Columbus, OH 43215-4163
(614) 644-7061

*Oklahoma Department of Libraries*
*Government Documents*
200 Northeast 18th Street
Oklahoma City, OK 73105-3298
(405) 521-2502
E-mail: mhardin@aardvark.ucs.ucs.nor.edu

*Oklahoma State University Library*
*Documents Department*
Stillwater, OK 74078-1071
(405) 744-9729

*Portland State University Library*
P.O. Box 1151
Portland, OR 97207-1151
(503) 725-4617

*State Library of Pennsylvania*
*Government Publications Section*
Box 1601
Walnut Street & Commonwealth Ave.
Harrisburg, PA 17105-1601
(717) 787-4440

*Texas State Library & Archives Commission*
P.O. Box 12927
Austin, TX 78711-2927
(512) 463-5458

*Texas Tech University Library*
*Documents Department*
Lubbock, TX 79409-0002
(806) 742-2261
E-mail: liedc@ttacs.ttu.edu

*Utah State University*
Logan, UT 84322-3000
(435) 797-2631

*University of Virginia*
*Alderman Library*
Government Documents
Charlottesville, VA 22903-2498
(804) 924-3026

*Washington State Library*
*Documents Section*
Box 42460
Olympia, WA 98504-2460
(360) 753-5590

*State Historical Society of Wisconsin Library*
*Government Publications Section*
816 State Street
Madison, WI 53706
(608) 264-6534

*Milwaukee Public Library*
*Documents Division*
814 West Wisconsin Avenue
Milwaukee, WI 53233-2385
(414) 286-3000

*West Virginia University Library*
*Government Documents Section*
P.O. Box 6069
Morgantown, WV 26506-6069
(304) 293-4040

*Wyoming State Library*
*Supreme Court and Library Building*
2301 Capitol Ave.
Cheyenne, WY 82002-0060
(307) 777-7281
E-mail: wslref@wyld.state.wy.us

## SPECIALIZED CRIMINAL JUSTICE LIBRARIES IN CANADA

*Alberta Solicitor General Library Services*
10th Floor, John E. Brownlee Building
10365 97th Street
Edmonton, Alberta, Canada T5J 3W7
(403) 427-3421

*British Columbia Co-ordinated Law Enforcement*
*Unit Library*
2588 Cadboro Bay Road
Victoria, British Columbia, Canada V8R 5J2
(604) 598-4545

*Canadian Police College*
*Law Enforcement Reference Centre*
P.O. Box 8900
Ottawa, Ontario, Canada K1G 3J2
(613) 993-3225

*Centre of Criminology Library*
*University of Toronto*
*John P. Robarts Research Library*
Room 8001
130 St. George Street
Toronto, Ontario, Canada M5S 1A5
(416) 978-7068

*Justice Institute of British Columbia*
*Resource Centre*
4198 West 4th Avenue
Vancouver, British Columbia, Canada V6R 4K1
(604) 228-9771 X 200

*Ministry Library and Reference Centre*
*Ministry of the Solicitor General*
340 Laurier Avenue W.
11th Floor
Ottawa, Ontario, Canada K1A 0P8
Reference: (613) 991-2780
ILL: (613) 991-2787

*Ontario — Ministry of Correctional Services*
2001 Eglinton Avenue, E.
Toronto, Ontario, MIL 2M9

## Penology and Criminology Holdings

*Provincial Police Academy Library*
*Provincial Police Academy*
Queen St. West & McLaughlin Road
P.O. Box 266
Brampton, Ontario, Canada L6V 2L1
(416) 459-4193

*Royal Canadian Mounted Police*
*Law Enforcement Reference Center*
St. Laurent Blvd., N. and Sandridge Rd.
P.O. Box 8900
Ottawa, Ontario, Canada K1G 3J2
(613) 993-9500 X 233

*University of Alberta*
*Weir Memorial Library*
*Law Center*
Edmonton, Alberta, Canada T6G 2H5
(403) 432-5560

# 17

# Legal Research

Legal research is conducted for a variety of purposes. Research may be as simple as finding the language of a specific statute or as complex as determining the ramifications and impact of a landmark Supreme Court decision. The quality of legal research will depend upon many factors, including the legal holdings of the library used. A small junior college will usually at least have a copy of the state's general statutes and perhaps a copy of *Black's Law Dictionary*, while a major university with a law school may have a separate building containing only law books. Further, legal publishers have expanded their offerings to include online and CD-ROM legal research tools and publications. Many libraries are augmenting their legal holding with these electronic resources.

The student at the smaller school should not become discouraged. Nearly every county courthouse or district court will have a library of law books adequate to meet the needs of most criminal justice students. In addition, students near a federal courthouse may be able to use those excellent holdings, although it may be necessary to obtain permission from one of the judges or clerks.

A number of books, bibliographies, dictionaries, and legal encyclopedias are available to help students conduct legal research. Sources of assistance are provided below, but this description is not intended to be comprehensive in nature, for that would require an entire text in itself. It should, however, provide the basic foundation necessary to undertake legal research. In addition, students should not hesitate to request the assistance of the librarian, since legal research is sometimes intricate and time-consuming.

## FEDERAL STATUTES

*Session Laws*

Laws and amendments are published in chronological order for each session of Congress.

*U.S. Statutes at Large*. The official edition.

*U.S. Code Congressional and Administrative News*, 1944-date. This publication contains additional material, including full legislative histories.

*Codified Laws*

All laws and amendments currently in effect are codified into broad topics and published by three reporting services. The volumes are updated with bound annual supplements.

> *United States Code* (*U.S.C.*). The official edition.
>
> *United States Code Annotated* (*U.S.C.A.*). West Publishing Co.
>
> *United States Code Service* (*U.S.C.S.*). Lawyers Co-operative Publishing Co.

## STATE STATUTES

When researching the law of state crimes, or of a state judicial system or process, always begin your search with the state statutes or code. Ask your reference librarian for the volume on criminal laws or other topics. Always check the current status of state laws in the pocket-part supplement to each volume.

## COURT DECISIONS

### Reporters for the United States Supreme Court

The decisions of the United States Supreme Court are immediately published online by the Court. Weekly updates of recent Supreme Court decisions are found in *United States Law Week* (Bureau of National Affairs, Inc., Washington, D.C.). The decisions are ultimately published by three reporting services.

> *United States Reports* (U.S.). The official edition.
>
> *Supreme Court Reporter* (S.Ct.). West Publishing Co.
>
> *U.S. Supreme Court Reports, Lawyers' Edition* (L. Ed.). Lawyers Co-operative Publishing Co.

For example, the U.S. Supreme Court case *Miranda v. Arizona* can be found in the following volumes:

| Volume | Page Number | Year of Decision |
|--------|-------------|------------------|
| 384 U.S. | 436 | (1966) |
| 86 S. Ct. | 1602 | (1966) |
| 16 L. Ed. 2d | 694 | (1966) |

### Reporter for the United States Courts of Appeal

The United States is divided into 11 circuit United States Courts of Appeal. Selected decisions for all circuits are found in the *Federal Reporter* Series published by the West Publishing Company. These decisions are cited as follows: _____ F.2d _____ (circuit number and year).

### Reporter for the United States District Courts

United States District Courts are trial courts which are located in every state and U. S. territory. Selected decisions are found in the *Federal Supplement* Series published by the West Publishing Company. These decisions are cited as follows: _____ F. Supp. _____ (district and year).

## Reporters for State Courts Decisions

The decisions of the highest courts of each state appear in the National Reporter System according to the state's geographic location. The National Reporter System was developed to facilitate legal research. The system grew out of a successful attempt by the West Publishing Company to provide the legal profession of the state of Minnesota with reliable and quick sources of information in 1876. One geographic reporter after another was added until the entire country was eventually covered. The following seven Reporters now comprise the National Reporter System.

*Atlantic Reporter.* Contains select decisions of the appellate courts of Connecticut, Delaware, District of Columbia, Maine, Maryland, New Hampshire, New Jersey, Pennsylvania, Rhode Island, and Vermont.

*Northeastern Reporter.* Contains select decisions of the appellate courts of Illinois, Indiana, Massachusetts, New York, and Ohio.

*Northwestern Reporter.* Contains select appellate court decisions from Iowa, Michigan, Minnesota, Nebraska, North Dakota, South Dakota, and Wisconsin.

*Pacific Reporter.* Contains select appellate decisions of Alaska, Arizona, California, Colorado, Hawaii, Idaho, Kansas, Montana, Nevada, New Mexico, Oklahoma, Oregon, Utah, Washington, and Wyoming.

*Southern Reporter.* Contains select decisions of appellate courts of Alabama, Florida, Louisiana, and Mississippi.

*Southeastern Reporter.* Contains selected appellate decisions of Georgia, North Carolina, South Carolina, Virginia, and West Virginia.

*Southwestern Reporter.* Contains select decisions of the appellate courts of Arkansas, Kentucky, Missouri, Tennessee, and Texas.

## FEDERAL ADMINISTRATIVE AGENCIES

While the rulings of state and federal administrative agencies have had only limited application in researching the law of traditional crimes or criminal procedure, their regulations are becoming more important in today's world. When properly passed, the rules and regulations of administrative agencies have "the force and effect of law."

*United States Code of Federal Regulations (C.F.R.).* The *CFR* is an annual compilation of federal rules and regulations in force at the time of publication. The rules and regulations are arranged by broad subject areas into 50 titles, some of which correspond to the titles of the United States Code. The *CFR* includes a number of special volumes which aid in its use. These are:

(1) The General Index volume which provides access to the rules by both subject and issuing agency.

(2) The Finding Aids volume serves as a general guide to *CFR* by providing a number of specialized finding tools. It includes a detailed table of contents for the entire *CFR* set.

*Federal Register (Fed. Reg.).* The *Federal Register* serves as a daily supplement to the *CFR*, updating the *CFR* by publishing the texts of all new federal rules and regulations. To determine the current status of a particular *CFR* rule, consult the latest issue of the *CFR's Cumulative List of CFR*

*Sections Affected* and the "List of *CFR* Parts Affected" in the most recent daily issue of the *Federal Register*. These lists refer the researcher to the *Federal Register* citations which modify the *CFR* rules. In addition to new rules and regulations, the *Federal Register* includes the texts of proposed rules and regulations, presidential orders and proclamations, and notices concerning modifications in the structure and function of government agencies. Each issue of the *Federal Register* contains a subject/agency index. These indexes are then cumulated on a monthly, semiannual and annual basis.

*Federal Rules Decisions.* 1941 to date. (cite as: *F.R.D.*). Publishes opinions, decisions and rulings concerning only one field of federal administrative law: that relating to the Federal Rules of Civil and Criminal Procedure. These Rules, although generally thought of as part of administrative law, have actually been enacted and are therefore included in the U.S. Code. (References to *FRD* cases are included in the annotations to the U.S. Code Service.)

## ANNOTATED ARTICLES

The *American Law Reports* (*A.L.R.*, *A.L.R. Federal*) annotated series, published by Lawyers Co-operative Publishing Co., gives citations and commentary to many cases that have been decided on a particular point of law.

## LEGAL ENCYCLOPEDIAS

*American Jurisprudence 2d ed.* (Am. Jur. 2d) A standard encyclopedia of American law. It will be a helpful place to begin your legal research, particularly to gain a better understanding of your topic. It is the easiest to read of the legal encyclopedias. (Rochester, NY: Lawyer's Cooperative Publishing Co., 1997).

*Corpus Juris Secundum* (C.J.S.) A comprehensive legal encyclopedia which is frequently cited as authority by federal and state appellate courts. It is an exhaustive work which purports to restate all American law based upon all reported cases since 1658. (St. Paul, MN: West Publishing Co., 1995).

## LAW JOURNALS AND PERIODICALS

Courts often cite the articles contained in law journals and law reviews as persuasive authority for their decisions. For the student, these articles and case notes, written by legal scholars and law students, are helpful in building an understanding of the legal, social, economic, and public policy issues surrounding important court decisions. (Also see Chapter 5, titled "Journals.")

*American Judicial Proceedings First Printed Before 1801: An Analytical Bibliography.* Wilfred J. Ritz. Attempts to list "every law report, trial, or separate event of judicial significance occurring in or relating to what was the United States in 1801, and for which there was something printed prior to that date (other than a newspaper account.)"—p. xvii. Arranged by geographical area and subject. Citations include library locations and references in early American imprints bibliographies and microform projects. (Westport, CT: Greenwood Press, 1984).

*Bibliographic Guide to Law.* Successor to the *Law Book Guide* (1969-74). Includes all material cataloged by the Library of Congress within each year; full cataloging information. Annual. (Boston: G.K. Hall, 1975-date).

*Bowker's Law Books and Serials in Print.* Contains citations to about 130,000 books and 4,000 serials titles drawn from the American book publishing record database, National union catalog, and MARC tapes. Contents: v.1, Books—Subject index; v.2, Books—Author index; v.3, Books—Title index; Subject index to cataloged titles; Serials—Subject index, Title index; Publishers and distributors abbreviations. Annual. (New York: R.R. Bowker, 1984-date).

*Bowker's Law Books and Serials in Print Update.* Materials on law and related topics recently published and to be published. (New York: R.R. Bowker, 1984-date).

*Checklists of Basic American Legal Publications.* Meira G. Pimsleur. Sec. 1 covers State statutes, revisions, compilations. Sec. 2 covers the Session laws of the various states of the United States. Sec. 3 is a Checklist of reports and opinions of the attorneys-general. Sec. 4 (1974-date) lists reports of state judicial councils and conferences. Sec. 5 (1976-date) lists American Law Institute restatements of the law and codifications. (South Hackensack, NJ: Rothman).

*Current Law Index.* This has more comprehensive journal coverage than the *Index to Legal Periodicals*, more specific subject headings and is generally the preferred index to law review articles. There are subject, author/title, case, and statute indexes. It began in 1980. (Foster City, CA: Information Access Co.).

*Hein's Legal Periodical Check List.* William S. Hein, Kevin M. Marmion and Ilene N. Hein. (Buffalo, NY: W.S. Hein, 1977-date).

*Index to Foreign Legal Periodicals.* 1960 to date. (Quarterly, with annual and triennial cumulations.) Covers law reviews from all over the world, except those from English-speaking countries. It therefore excludes all countries with legal systems based on principles of common law. (Berkeley, CA: University of California Press).

*Index to Legal Periodicals* (*I.L.P.*) Index to Legal Periodicals provides thorough indexing of articles in 500 leading journals, yearbooks, institutes, bar association organs, university publications and law reviews, and government publications originating from the United States, Great Britain, Ireland, Canada, Australia, and New Zealand. Law schools, bar associations, legal aid societies, law firms, attorneys, judges and jurists at all levels, business people, librarians, and other researchers use *Index to Legal Periodicals* for access to information on developments in all areas of jurisprudence including recent court decisions, precedents, new legislation, and original scholarship. Also, such topics as International Law, Constitutional Law, Malpractice Suits, Securities and Antitrust Legislation, Labor Law, Criminal Law, Latest Developments in Takeovers, Multinational Corporations, Discrimination, and Environmental Law are covered. In addition to the single alphabetical subject-author index which forms the main body of *Index to Legal Periodicals*, it also offers: Table of Cases arranged alphabetically by name of plaintiff and defendant; Table of Statutes arranged by jurisdiction and listed alphabetically by name; Book Reviews of current books relevant to the legal profession, indexed by author's name. Updated monthly, 1981 to date. (Bronx, NY: H.W. Wilson).

*Index to Periodical Articles Related to Law*. This index covers selected journals which are not included in the *Index to Legal Periodicals*. Quarterly, 1958 to date. (Dobbs Ferry, NY: Glanville Publishers, Inc.).

*Law Books, 1876-1981: Books and Serials on Law and Its Related Subjects*. Contents: v.1-3, Books—Subject index; v.4, Books—Author and title indexes, Serials—Subject and title indexes, Publishers, Online database producers and vendors. (New York: R.R. Bowker, 1981).

*Law Books Published*. v.1-. A quarterly record of books published in English during the year. The fourth quarterly issue is an annual cumulation. Quarterly. (Dobbs Ferry, NY: Glanville, 1969-date).

*Legal & Law Enforcement Periodicals: A Directory*. Over 3,800 periodicals published in the United States and Canada are listed in 50 subject categories. (New York: Facts on File, 1981).

*Legal Looseleafs in Print*. Arlene L. Sterne. A title listing of legal looseleafs published in the United States which are currently in print. Each entry provides title, publisher, year of original publication, number of volumes, price, frequency and annual cost of supplements. Detailed subject index. Annual. (New York: Infosources, 1981-date).

*National Indian Law Library*. Catalogue; an index to Indian legal materials and resources. Cumulative editions issued at irregular intervals. Published with the Native American Rights Fund. The 1982 cumulative edition includes about 3,400 items relating to "tribal existence, protection of tribal resources, promotion of human rights, advancement of tribal self-determination; and to the accountability of the dominant society."—Introd. A subject section, plaintiff/defendant, defendant/plaintiff table, and author/title table refer user to the numerical listing where complete bibliographic and file contents information are given. (Boulder, CO: 1974-date).

*National Legal Bibliography*. Recent acquisitions of major legal libraries v.1, no.1-, Jan. 1984-. (Buffalo, NY: W.S. Hein, 1984-date. Monthly.) Includes books, serials, government and other documents, theses and dissertations cataloged by about 15 university and public libraries. Broad topical arrangement (U.S. and general; international; foreign jurisdiction by country). Monthly. (Buffalo, NY:W.S. Hein, 1984-date).

*Supreme Court of the United States, 1789-1980*; An Index to Opinions Arranged by Justice. Linda A. Blandford and Patricia Russell Evans. Sponsored by the Supreme Court Historical Society. (Listed chronologically), opinions are organized by category, indicating majority, plurality, concurring, separate, or dissenting opinions, statements, or opinions as circuit judges; each listing provides name of case and citation to its appearance in the United States reports. Appendixes provide some biographical data and a chronology of succession of Justices from 1789 to 1980. (Millwood, NY: Kraus International Publications, 1983).

## BOOKS AND DIRECTORIES

Books, like law journal articles, are not considered sources of law, but, they can be helpful in understanding the development of legal doctrines and in explaining leading court decisions. The following texts are commonly available and highly recommended for general reading.

*American Legal Systems: A Resource and Reference Guide*. Toni M. Fine. (Cincinnati, OH: Anderson Publishing Co., 1997).

*Basic Text on Administrative Law*, Third Edition. K. Davis. (St. Paul, MN:West Publishing, 1972).

*Bar Admission Rules and Student Practice Rules*. Fannie J. Klein, Steven H. Leleiko, and Jane H. Mavity. This book is the result of an ambitious project: to complete the only comprehensive source of state and federal bar admission and student practice rules . . . a convenient, ready reference tool—an excellent source for beginning research in practice rules. (Cambridge, MA: Ballinger Publishing Co., 1978).

*Barron's Guide to Law Schools*. Profiles of ABA approved schools, ratings, and samples of LSAT. Also includes practical advice on applications, funding and job search. Annual. (Woodbury, NY: Barron's Educational Series).

*Effective Legal Research*. Miles O. Price and H. Bitner. Includes chapters on legislation, statutes, law reports, digests, legal periodicals, dictionaries, encyclopedias, and also addresses citations and citation style. (Boston: Little, Brown, 1979).

*Effective Legal Writing: A Style Book for Law Students and Lawyers*, Third Edition. Gertrude Block. Offers a method to improve legal writing through coverage of basic grammatical rules, legal style and organization, and various other expository techniques. Samples of unclear writing are shown and corrected. Writing assignments and legal problems with model answers are included. Materials are the appropriate teaching solution to courses on legal writing and legal research and writing. (Mineola, NY: Foundation Press, 1986).

*Finding the Law: A Guide to Legal Research*. David Lloyd. Written in nontechnical language, designed to assist first year law students and others unfamiliar with legal research, in using the law library. Appendices on common legal citations and abbreviations are included. (Dobbs Ferry, NY: Oceana, 1974).

*Fundamentals of Legal Research and Legal Research Illustrated: Assignments*. J. Myron Jacobstein and Roy M. Mersky. An assignment workbook in which each chapter corresponds to a chapter in *Fundamentals of Legal Research* (or *Legal Research Illustrated*). The book is divided into three parts. Part I introduces the reader to legal bibliography problems which are used to demonstrate how research on the same set of facts is accomplished in different types of index and research books. Part II provides the opportunity for the reader to apply the knowledge gained from working the exercises in Part I. The final section, Part III, is concerned with descriptions of sources of federal tax law and methods for locating these sources. (Mineola, NY: Foundation Press, 1983).

*How to Find the Law*. Ninth Edition. Morris L. Cohen (ed.). (St. Paul, MN: West Publishing, 1989).

*International Law and Organization: General Sources of Information*. Jacob Roginson. Lists reference works and periodicals on an international basis. (Leiden, Netherlands: Sijthoff, 1967).

*An Introduction to the Legal System of the United States*. Second Edition. Farnsworth. Designed for the foreign student, this introductory text also serves the American student with chapters on the judiciary, legislature, state laws, statutes and sections on civil and criminal procedure, contracts, torts, and many types of law. (New York: Oceana, 1983).

*Law Books Published*. A quarterly publication since 1960 that includes English language law books published during the year. (Dobbs Ferry, NY: Glanville).

*The Law in the United States of America: A Selective Bibliographical Guide*. Andrews, et al. Describes basic sources that should be included in the holdings of any law library. (New York: New York University Press, 1965).

*Legal Problem Solving: Analysis, Research, and Writing*. Rombauer. A basic text on conducting legal research. Contains chapters on briefing a case, analyzing opinions, interpreting legislation, conducting computer-assisted research, writing memorandums, and arguing a case orally. (St. Paul, MN: West Publishing, 1983).

*Legal Research in a Nutshell*. Morris Cohen. An introductory manual to the main areas of legal literature (judicial reports, case finding, statutes, legislative histories, international law, etc.). (St. Paul, MN: West Publishing).

*Legal Research Illustrated*. J.M. Jacobstein and Roy M. Mersky. A beginner's text which takes the legal researcher step by step into the legal research process. Contents include information on the legal process, court reports, federal and state court decisions, the national reporter system, annotated law reports, constitutions, federal and state legislation, administrative law, Shepard's citations, legal encyclopedias and periodicals, and many other research aids. (Mineola, NY: Foundation Press, 1990).

*Legal Research and Education Abridgment: A Manual for Law Students, Paralegals and Researchers*. Edward Bander with the assistance of David F. Bander. (Cambridge, MA: Ballinger Publishing Co., 1978).

*Legal Research and Writing* (1986), and *Case Analysis and Fundamentals of Legal Writing* (1989). William P. Statsky. These books provide clear introductions on subjects such as using the law library, types of law materials, principles of legal research, reading administrative regulations, and case law. (St. Paul, MN: West Publishing).

*The Living Law: A Guide to Modern Legal Research*. Designed to assist the legal researcher achieve an organized, systematic approach to legal research. Various publications which are incorporated into a legal research system known as the Total Client Service Library (TCSL) are described. The TCSL was created by the Lawyer's Cooperative Publishing Company and the Bancroft-Whitney Company. (New York: The Lawyer's Cooperative Publishing Company, 1983).

*Report Writing for Criminal Justice Professionals*, Second Edition. Jerold G. Brown and Clarice R. Cox. (Cincinnati, OH: Anderson Publishing Co., 1998).

*Supreme Court of the United States 1789-1980: An Index to Opinions Arranged by Justice.* Linda A. Blandford and Patricia Russel Evens (eds.). Sponsored by the Supreme Court Historical Society. (Millwood, NY: Kraus International, 1984 with supplements in 1990 and 1994).

*Using a Law Library; A Guide for Students in the Common Law Provinces of Canada.* Margaret A. Banks. (London, ON: University of Western Ontario, School of Library and Information Science, 1971).

*Using American Law Books.* Third Edition. Alfred J. Lewis. (Dubuque, IA: Kendall/Hunt, 1990).

*West's Law Finder: A Research Manual for Lawyers.* Describes law finder aids which are published by West Publishing Company. Publications and services described include the National Reporter System, West Key Number Digests, Key Number System Law Chart, Corpus Juris Secundum, United States Code, methods of search for United States Code, Words and Phrases, Federal Practice Procedure, Westlaw (West's computer law retrieval system) and sources of legislative and session law services. (St. Paul, MN: West Publishing).

## LAW DICTIONARIES

Legal dictionaries will give the user a precise definition of law-related terms. The most widely used are *Black's Law Dictionary* and *Ballentine's Law Dictionary*.

*Ballentine's Law Dictionary With Pronunciations.* James A. Ballentine. (Rochester, NY: Lawyer's Cooperative).

*Bieber's Dictionary of Legal Abbreviations.* Doris M. Bieber. (Buffalo, NY: William S. Hein, 1993).

*Black's Law Dictionary: Definitions of Terms and Phrases of American and English Jurisprudence, Ancient and Modern.* Sixth Edition. Henry C. Black. (St. Paul, MN: West Publishing, 1997).

*The Law Dictionary*, Seventh Edition. (Cincinnati: Anderson Publishing Co., 1997).

*Law Dictionary for Laymen.* John C. Howell. (Leesburg, VA: Citizens Law Library, 1980).

*Law Dictionary for Non Lawyers.* Daniel Oran. (St. Paul, MN: West Publishing, 1991).

*The Oxford Companion to Law.* David M. Walker. (New York: Oxford University Press, 1980).

## COMPUTERIZED LEGAL RESEARCH

There are several computer databases in the field of legal research. The most widely used are:

*Westlaw.* This database, produced by West Publishing Co., is the largest database of its kind. Included in this legal database are summaries and citations for reported cases that were heard in state courts since 1965. The database also contains information on federal cases dating back to 1790. The Westlaw computer holds a vast store of information important to lawyers, a national full text case law library, a specialized Federal Tax Library, the text of the U.S. Code, and Shepard's Citations. Westlaw provides the entire text of the U.S. Code, giving the researcher electronic access to the federal statutes. Special search methods make it easier to find the exact section or subsection you need as well as to scan related sections whenever needed. Also included are Supreme Court Reporter, from 1932 to date; Federal Reporter 2d, from 1945 to date; Federal Supplement from 1950 to date. Westlaw has a 50-state database. It provides the text of the Code of Federal Regulations, giving the researcher access to current federal administrative regulations and offers the capability of addressing commands based on fundamental units of ordinary English: sentences and paragraphs.

*LEXIS* finds cases by name, citation, or both. LEXIS as a citator can prove invaluable when only the name of the case is known, as when an important case is to be relied upon before it has been given a citation. Thousands of recent slip opinions are available only through LEXIS. LEXIS also contains thousands of cases that never appear in the reporters. You will find it a considerable advantage to perform a citation search by name as well as by citation. You will also appreciate the fact that LEXIS can find citations in documents other than cases, such as statutes, regulations, or Supreme Court briefs. LEXIS can also be used for a variety of legal research tasks: Locating cases involving specific fact patterns. LEXIS permits searching for specific fact patterns independent of the legal concepts and principles involved. Fact pattern searches are particularly useful in areas of law in which principles are well defined and cases are decided on nuances of fact. Locating cases involving specific legal principles, such as res ipsa loquitur and mens rea. Identifying opinions written by a particular judge, or in which particular counsel appeared. Locating cases or statutes containing particular terms or phrases (e.g. de facto segregation, unconscionable, short swing profits). Retrieving cases that discuss the language contained in a standard contract. Finding cases that construe particular statutory provisions or contain definitions of statutory language or discuss several statutory provisions. Locating a case when only the name of a party, or docket number, or other limited information is known. Using LEXIS as a citator to locate the most recent cases citing an earlier decision, statute, treatise, or article. Obtaining the text of a recent opinion that is not yet available in the advance sheets or of U.S. district court decisions that was not included in any case law reporter. Determining how federal circuit or district courts have applied a U.S. Supreme Court decision in subsequent cases. Double checking other research. LEXIS can be used to examine the accuracy of previously prepared work or of a brief submitted by opposing counsel. Along with general federal and state law, LEXIS offers a comprehensive collection of specialized law libraries. Among these are Tax, Securities, Trade Regulation, Bankruptcy, Patent, Trade-

mark, and Copyright, Communications, Labor, Public Contracts Law, Delaware Corporation Law, United Kingdom Law, French Law. LEXIS, along with Westlaw, ranks as one of the top two legal data bases. Shepard's Citations. All Shepard's case law citators are included in LEXIS: federal, state, and regional reporter series. Shepard's provides parallel citations, case history, subsequent treatment of the case, and all cases that cite the cited case. Shepard's is a product of Shepard's/McGraw-Hill. Auto-Cite offers a virtually instantaneous verification of a citation. Auto-Cite provides the name of the case cited, the date and place of decision, official and parallel citations, and the citation to any case that directly affects the official status of the case as precedent. Auto-Cite is a service of the Lawyers Cooperative Publishing Company and its affiliate, Bancroft-Whitney.

*Index to Legal Periodicals.* This Index is now computerized. For a complete description see Chapter 4, "Indexing Services."

*Legal Resource Index.* This is the database of the *Current Law Index.* This database is searched by putting into the computer the same subject headings that would be used if you were using the printed version of the *Current Law Index.* This database can also be searched to find a particular court case, a statute or an article by an author. It also gives bibliographic information in the field of law.

Additional computer databases that will contain law related information can be found by consulting Chapter 9, "Database Literature Searches."

## STEPS TO LEGAL RESEARCH

1. **Always Check Federal and State Statutes as Primary Sources of Criminal Law First.**
   Most state codes are annotated, meaning that at the end of each section on the criminal laws or court procedures there will be a list of reported court decisions which might have interpreted, applied, or ruled on certain aspects of that particular law. Begin your research here and follow through by reading the cited cases in the reporter which pertain to the offense or topic you are researching.

2. **The Key Number System**
   West Publishing Co., has developed a system of researching court decisions that is unique. It is based on a system of "Key Numbers," whereby every legal topic is referenced according to certain key words, and is assigned a key number. Find the key words, and your search for the law begins. Common key words in the criminal field might include "criminal law," "criminal procedure," or "constitutional law." These are then broken down into more specific topics for reference. Each topic, or point of law, is then assigned a key number. Find your key words and numbers in the *Digest to the Supreme Court Reporter*, or to the reporter of the state whose law you are researching.

3. **The Digests**
   Every reporter, the *Supreme Court Reporter*, the *Federal Reporter*, and each of the regional state reporters (e.g., *Atlantic Reporter*) of the National Reporter System has a *Digest of Cases*. Open your digest to the appropriate Key Word and begin your search. You will find "digests," or short para-

graphs summarizing many case decisions. By reading these summaries you can determine if one of these is important enough, or relevant enough, to read in its entirety. If so, find the case in the bound reporter and read it carefully. Be certain to check the pocket-part supplement at the back of each Digest to be sure you have found the latest court decisions on that topic.

*West's General Digest*. This *Digest* contains all state and federal cases included in the National Reporter System. Series since 1977 have been published in five year intervals. Earlier series were published in ten year intervals, were called *Decennial Digests* and contained cases as far back as 1658. *Digests* are available for each of the *Federal Reporters*, the *Regional Reporters* and the *State Reporters*. *Digests* for state court cases may be found in either the *Regional Digest* or the *State Digest*.

4. **Advance Sheets**

These online computer and paperback supplements are published monthly as updates to the digests and to the reported decisions. In the front of the advance sheet you will see the Digest of Cases. Check this digest for recent cases (if any) on your key word and key number. Remember, once you have found the key word (your topic) and key number (your subtopic), you can go through the advance sheets quickly by looking only for your word and number. Then turn to the rear of the advance sheet to read the actual case in its entirety.

5. **Shepard's Citations**

These volumes allow a researcher to take a previously decided court case (or a federal statute), and look at the history of that case and to find every single case in which that earlier case has been cited. For example, in the federal system, U.S. District Court cases (*Federal Supplement*) may have been overruled or upheld on appeal to the U.S. Court of Appeals for that Circuit (*Federal Reporter*) or to the U.S. Supreme Court (*Supreme Court Reporter*). If so, this history will be shown in *Shepard's Citations*. Cases often remain "the law" for many years, until changed circumstances call for a court to reverse the precedent. If this happens to a case which you are reading, go to *Shepard's Citations* and look up the case by volume and page number, and it will give you the complete history of the case. It will indicate whether the case has been mentioned by courts and what action they took that might influence or alter the precedential value of the case.

# HOW TO BRIEF A CASE

Unlike a lawyer's brief, a student's brief is intended to be a concise summary of a decided case for use in classroom discussion and for study purposes. The brief should contain the following sections:

1. **Case Name and Citation**.

Criminal cases will contain the names of the governmental entity bring the charges and the name of the defendant. A proper case citation will also including the volume number, reporter name, page number and year of the decision.

2. **Summary of Facts.**

The summary should begin with a one-sentence statement on the type of case being briefed or the type of offense involved. It may also include how the case came before the present court. The facts of the case are usually given in the beginning of the reported case, although concurring and dissenting opinions often give very concise statements of facts. Only the facts pertinent to the resolution of legal issues in the case should be included in the summary. Extraneous details are used only if they have a bearing on how and why the court decided the case.

3.   **Legal Issues or Questions of Law.**

This is often considered the most important section of a brief, although it should rarely be longer than a few short sentences. It can often be phrased as a question that could be answered with "yes" or "no." The question should be a question of law and not a factual question. For example,"Under the laws of the state of Mississippi, did the defendant commit the crime of burglary, when the required intent to commit a felony was not formed until after the defendant had already gained lawful entrance to the dwelling?"

4.   **Court's Decision.**

This section answers the identified legal issues and questions of law. Many times the author of the court's opinion has identified the explicit holding of the court. The court may have developed a judicial doctrine in the case that could be used to resolve the legal issues.

5.   **Court's Reasoning.**

Many case decisions result from the historical development of the common law. Other decisions will turn to an interpretation of a particular statute (legislation) or of the United States or state Constitution. Furthermore, cases are often decided on the basis of the social, economic, or political issues underlying the case.

6.   **Concurring or Dissenting Opinions**.

In a concurring opinion, the judge votes with the majority of the court, but has different reasons and feels compelled to set out those reasons. In a dissenting opinion, the judge sets forth his or her reasons for disagreeing with the majority decision. While these opinions are not the law per se, they do serve to sharpen the legal or policy issues involved in the case. They illuminate different points of view and often give clues as to how the court might decide future cases.

# 18

# Internet Research

The World Wide Web is the new frontier of scholarly research. In most libraries, the archaic system of card catalogs has all but disappeared. Computer terminals provide access to more information at a much quicker pace. Literature searches can be conducted in seconds, and researchers can browse the stacks of other libraries throughout the cyber world. Journal articles, government documents, and statistical reports can be downloaded and printed out rather than ordered in print form as in the past.

Search engines are used to search the World Wide Web. The following examples are just a few of the more common search engines on the Web.

## COMMON SEARCH ENGINES

| | | | |
|---|---|---|---|
| Alta Vista | www.altavista.digital.com | Lycos | www.lycos.com |
| Excite | www.excite.com | Webcrawler | www.webcrawler.com |
| Hotbot | www.hotbot.com | Yahoo | www.yahoo.com |
| Infoseek | www.infoseek.com | | |

FirstSearch, provided by Online Computer Library Center, Inc. (OCLC), is another search tool for accessing books, articles, films and computer software. Searches may be conducted by title, author, publication place and date, subject, and several other options. Some libraries may provide FirstSearch free to faculty, staff, and students via the Internet. If not, a researcher will need an authorization code and password to gain access to FirstSearch. The code and password can be provided by the researcher's librarian or professor.

Online catalogs from other universities can be searched for books or journal articles unavailable in the researcher's own library. The items can be obtained through the interlibrary loan process or by downloading the particular document. A search of FirstSearch should indicate whether a located document is the most recently published edition. Global Books in Print on Disk, which is a search tool on CD-ROM (refer to "Database Literature Searches," Chapter 9) is another tool which can be used to determine whether any more recent editions have been published. Global Books in Print on Disk has an indexed listing of all books currently in print. Internet researchers may also browse the homepages of government agencies and some of the more popular personal homepages.

Below is a list of web sites that may assist the researcher in conducting criminal justice research.

## GOVERNMENT AGENCY WEB SITES

| | |
|---|---|
| Bureau of Justice Assistance | www.ojp.usdoj.gov/BJA |
| Bureau of Justice Statistics | www.ojp.usdoj.gov/bjs |
| Federal Bureau of Prisons | www.bop.gov |
| Justice Information Center | www.ncjrs.org |
| National Institute of Justice | www.ojp.usdoj.gov/nij/ |
| Office of Justice Programs | www.ojp.usdoj.gov/ |
| Office of Juvenile Justice and Delinquency Prevention | www.ojjdp.ncjrs.org/ |
| Office for Victims of Crime | www.ojp.usdoj.gov/ovc/ |
| U.S. Census | www.census.gov/ |
| U.S. Department of Justice | www.usdoj.gov/ |

### State Government Web Sites

| | |
|---|---|
| Kentucky State Homepage (national toll-free numbers for information and referrals on victims' rights and services) | www.law.state.ky.us/victims/tollfree.htm |
| New Mexico State Homepage (listing of state attorneys general in various jurisdictions under links) | www.ago.state.nm.us |
| Ohio State Homepage (listing of full addresses of state attorneys general) | www.ag.ohio.gov |

## OTHER WEB SITES

| | |
|---|---|
| American Civil Liberties Union | www.aclu.org/issues/criminal/hmcj.html |
| Bibliography on Women, Crime, and Justice | www.towson.edu/~vanfoss/sokbibad.htm |
| Bureau of Justice Assistance Clearinghouse | www.ojp.usdoj.gov/BJA/ |
| Center for Rational Correctional Policy | pierce.simplenet.com/prisonerresources.html |
| Drugs & Crime Clearinghouse (Drug Policy Information) | www.ncjrs.org/drgshome.htm |
| Federal Court Locator (Federal Courts of Appeal) | www.law.vill.edu/Fed-Ct/fedcourt.html |
| FindLaw Internet Legal Resources | www.findlaw.com/01topics/09criminal/index.html |
| The Library of Congress | lcweb.loc.gov/homepage/lchp.html |

Legal List                                          www.lcp.com/The-Legal-List/TLL-home.html

Loyola University Libraries                          www.luc.edu/libraries/lewis/handouts/cjindex.htm

National Archive of Criminal Justice Data           www.icpsr.umich.edu/NACJD/

The National Clearinghouse for
Criminal Justice Information Systems                 www.ch.search.org/

National Criminal Justice Association               www.sso.org/ncja/

New York Metropolitan Addictions
Training (links to many
organizations and clearinghouses)                   www.drugteach.org/clearing.htm

Organized Crime: A crime statistics site            www.crime.org/homepage.html

Peace and Justice Center                            www.igc.org/pjc/

Prison Law Page (The  Other Side of the Wall)        www.wco.com/~aerick/

Prisons.Com                                         www.prisons.com

Research Tools                                      www.multinomoh.lib.or.us/da/resctool.html

School of Criminal Justice at
University of Albany (one of the
most extensive listings of court sites,
restorative justice, criminal justice
education, national organizations,
national and state laws, policing
and crime prevention links)                         www.albany.edu/scj

Sourcebook of Criminal Justice Statistics (over
600 tables on a variety of criminaljustice
topics from 100 sources)                            www.albany.edu/sourcebook/

Statistics on the Web                               www.execpc.com/~helberg/statistics.html

U.S. Supreme Court (current and archived cases)     supct.law.cornell.edu/supct/

## INTERNATIONAL WEB SITES

Amnesty International USA                            www.amnesty-usa.org

The Arab Security Studies and
Training Center                                     www.ncjrs.org/unojust/asstc.htm

Department of Justice Canada                         canada.justice.gc.ca/index_en.html

Latin American Network
Information Center                                  lanic.utexas.edu/

Library of Congress Country Studies                 lcweb2.loc.gov/frd/cs/cshome.html

International Archives of Education Data             lion.icpsr.umich.edu/topical.html

| | |
|---|---|
| International Centre for Criminal Law Reform and Criminal Justice Policy | www.icclr.law.ubc.ca/ |
| International Crime Statistics Link Guide | www.crime.org/links intern.html |
| Office of International Criminal Justice | www.acsp.uic.edu/index.html |
| Statistics Canada | www.statcan.ca/start.html |
| United Nations | www.un.org/ |
| United Nations Crime and Justice Information Network | www.ifs.univie.ac.at/~uncjin/uncjin.html |

# Glossary

Although each concept is normally explained in every section, a brief glossary is offered for the following terms.

*Abstracting Services*. Publications that list books, articles, or other literature by subject while also providing summaries of their contents.

*Annotated*. Containing notes or short descriptions about a particular publication that are supplied so that a reader may have knowledge of the nature of that literature.

*BBS*. Bulletin board system.

*Bibliography*. Compilations of references pertinent to a given subject; used to give suggestions for further reading and also to acknowledge the contributions of other authors.

*Biennial*. A term used to describe works that are published every two years.

*Biography*. Written account of an individual's life.

*CD-ROM*. Compact disk read only memory.

*Computerized Literature Searches*. A method of gathering literature on a particular topic by searching a machine-readable file of references.

*Cumulative*. A term used to describe a work that has been combined with several other works. For example, a cumulative periodical index will contain subject and/or author listings for several issues of that periodical, as with quarterly or yearly cumulative indexes.

*Database*. A set of interrelated data records stored on a direct access storage device; attempts to provide all the data allocated to a subject and to allow programs to use only those items needed.

*GPO*. The official abbreviation for Government Printing Office; indicates the literature is a publication of the United States Government.

*GPO Stock Number (#)*. A number which appears with the bibliographical information (author, title, publisher, location of publisher and date) of government documents; indicates that copies of the literature can be purchased from the Government Printing Office.

*Index*. Publications that list books, articles, and other materials by subject and/or author, and provide other bibliographical information about the literature so that it can be found within the library quickly and easily.

*Journal*. A term generally reserved for periodicals whose content is solely scholarly.

*Magazine*. A periodical containing miscellaneous articles and stories.

*Microforms*. Greatly reduced photographic reproductions of printed matter on film, usually 4" x 6" microfiche cards, which contain the approximate equivalent of 98 book pages. Microforms may also be available as roll film. A special microform reader must be utilized to read microform material.

*NCJ Number (#)*. The unique identifying number assigned to books and other materials in the NCJRS collection of 65,000 items. Documents in the NCJRS collection are arranged by this accession number.

*NCJRS*. An abbreviation for the National Institute of Justice/NCJRS (National Criminal Justice Reference Service).

*Online*. Information is introduced into the data processing system as soon as it occurs, is directly in-line with the main flow of the transaction processing.

*Periodical*. Published with a fixed interval between issues or numbers.

*Selected Bibliography*. A collection of references that have been compiled on the basis of selected criteria, such as year of publication, form, etc., as opposed to a comprehensive bibliography on a given topic.

*Topical Bibliographies*. Refers to bibliographies arranged according to subject or topics of specialty.

## Abbreviations

| | |
|---|---|
| AFL-CIO | American Federation of Labor and Congress of Industrial Organizations |
| ATF | Bureau of Alcohol, Tobacco and Firearms |
| BBB | Better Business Bureau |
| BIBL | Bibliographic Citation File |
| BPD | Bureau of the Public Debt |
| CCH | Computerized criminal history |
| CFDA | Catalog of Federal Domestic Assistance |
| CG | Congressional Status Files |
| CID | Criminal Investigation Division |
| CMIR | Currency or Monetary Instruments Report |
| CPA | Certified Public Accountant |
| CTR | Currency Transaction Report |
| D&B | Dun & Bradstreet |
| DBA | Doing business as |
| DD | U.S. Department of Defense |
| DEA | Drug Enforcement Administration |
| DOC | U.S. Department of Commerce |
| DOD | U.S. Department of Defense |
| DOE | U.S. Department of Education |
| DOJ | U.S. Department of Justice |
| DOL | U.S. Department of Labor |
| DOS | U.S. Department of State |
| EPIC | El Paso Intelligence Center |
| FAA | Federal Aviation Administration |
| FBI | Federal Bureau of Investigation |
| FCA | Farm Credit Administration |
| FCC | Federal Communications Commission |
| FDA | Food and Drug Administration |
| FDIC | Federal Deposit Insurance Corporation |
| FERC | Federal Energy Regulatory Commission |
| FHA | Federal Housing Administration |
| FHLBB | Federal Home Loan Bank Board |
| FMC | Federal Maritime Commission |
| FRS | Federal Reserve System |
| F&S | Funk & Scott |
| FSLIC | Federal Savings and Loan Insurance Corporation |
| FTS | Federal Telecommunications System |
| GAO | U.S. General Accounting Office |
| GAODOCS | U.S. General Accounting Office, Documents Retrieval System |
| GPO | Government Printing Office |

| | |
|---|---|
| GSA | General Services Administration |
| HHS | U.S. Department of Health and Human Services |
| HUD | U.S. Department of Housing and Urban Development |
| ICC | Interstate Commerce Commission |
| INS | Immigration and Naturalization Service |
| INTERPOL | International Criminal Police Organization |
| IRS | Internal Revenue Service |
| JURIS | Justice Retrieval and Inquiry System |
| LCCC | Library of Congress Computerized Catalog |
| MIN | House Member Information Network |
| NACJD | National Archive of Criminal Justice Data |
| NADDIS | Narcotics and Dangerous Drugs Information System |
| NASA | National Aeronautics and Space Administration |
| NCB | National Central Bureau |
| NCIC | National Crime Information Center |
| NCJRS | National Criminal Justice Reference Service |
| NCUA | National Credit Union Administration |
| NLETS | National Law Enforcement Telecommunications System |
| NNBIS | National Narcotics Border Interdiction System |
| NTP | National Texts and Periodicals Data Base |
| OCC | Office of the Comptroller of the Currency |
| ORBIT | Online Retrieval of Bibliographic Information, Timeshared |
| OSI | Office of Special Investigations, U.S. General Accounting Office |
| PAIS | Public Affairs Information Service |
| R&A | Research & Analysis, Office of Special Investigations, U.S. General Accounting Office |
| SBA | Small Business Administration |
| SEC | Securities and Exchange Commission |
| SIC | Securities Information Center |
| S&P | Standard & Poor's |
| SSA | Social Security Administration |
| SSN | Social security number |

| | | | |
|---|---|---|---|
| TECS | Treasury Enforcement Communications System | USDA | U.S. Department of Agriculture |
| TFLEC | Treasury Financial Law Enforcement Center | USNCB | U.S. National Central Bureau |
| | | USPS | U.S. Postal Service |
| USCG | U.S. Coast Guard | USSS | U.S. Secret Service |
| USCS | U.S. Customs Service | VA | Veterans Administration |
| | | WALES | Washington Area Law Enforcement System |